SOUTH AFRICA AND THE UNITED STATES

STUDIES OF INFLUENCE IN INTERNATIONAL RELATIONS

Alvin Z. Rubinstein, General Editor

South Africa and the United States

THE EROSION OF AN INFLUENCE RELATIONSHIP

RICHARD E. BISSELL

PRAEGER

PRAEGER SPECIAL STUDIES • PRAEGER SCIENTIFIC

1982

Library of Congress Cataloging in Publication Data

Bissell, Richard E.
    South Africa and the United States.

    (Studies of influence in international relations)
    Bibliography: p.
    Includes index.
    1. United States—Foreign relations—South Africa.
2. South Africa—Foreign relations—United States.
I. Title. II. Series.
E183.8.S6B57   327.73068   81-22663
ISBN 0-03-047026-9   AACR2
ISBN 0-03-047021-8 (pbk.)

Published in 1982 by Praeger Publishers
CBS Educational and Professional Publishing
a Division of CBS Inc.
521 Fifth Avenue, New York, New York 10175 U.S.A.

© 1982 by Praeger Publishers

23456789   145   987654321

Printed in the United States of America

For my parents,
who taught me to
see the world
with an open mind

South Africa is the U.S. dilemma of the 1980s. It raises controversial issues that cut across the strategic, political, economic, cultural, and moral universe of U.S. politics. How they are treated and resolved in the years ahead will be of critical importance for the United States, its relations with the nations of black Africa, and the future of the Western alliance. The only beneficiary of failure stands to be the Soviet Union.

The United States and South Africa share a number of vital concerns, but their interaction was relatively modest until the early 1970s. In that decade, the collapse of the Portuguese empire in Africa (1) brought independence to Angola and Mozambique in 1975; (2) promoted the end to white rule in Zimbabwe (Rhodesia) by 1979; and (3) facilitated the spread of black African nationalist pressure to the borders of Namibia (formerly, South-West Africa) – in defiance of repeated U.N. resolutions, South Africa resists granting independence – and beyond that to the bastion of apartheid, South Africa itself. This decolonization and its aftermath brought the United States and South Africa into protracted, often conflictual, contact on a wide range of problems related to the issues of Namibia and apartheid.

South Africa is a richly endowed, diverse, and troubled land. The total population is about 26 million, of whom about 18 million are black Africans; 2.5 million are coloreds (mixed racial background); 900,000 are Asians (mostly of Indian origin); and 4.5 million are whites, 60 percent of whom are Afrikaners, the ruling group whose ancestors migrated from Holland three centuries ago. In addition to a developed industrial sector and a productive agriculture, South Africa is rich in minerals – gold, diamonds, platinum, chromite, and uranium oxide. Only oil is lacking to enable it to withstand the siege of outside pressures.

For the moment, Namibia is on center stage. The United States, fearful of Soviet inroads in mineral-rich southern Africa and of a political destabilization that could spawn permanently anti-Western regimes in the region, has (depending on the incumbent in the White House) become a sometimes eager, sometimes reluctant, participant in the process of trying to fashion an acceptable solution. A major issue is the demand of the United Nations that South Africa implement Security Council Resolution 435 of September 29, 1978, which would permit United Nations-supervised elections. This would almost certainly bring the South-West Africa People's Organization (SWAPO) – South Africa's nemesis – to power in Namibia. Another important issue is the procrastination of South Africa as it tries to create a dependent alternative political coalition beholden to it.

The longer-term problem plaguing United States-South African relations is the system of racial apartheid devised by the ruling Afrikaner elite to perpetuate white rule. Apartheid has made South Africa a pariah state. While the world, as George Bernard Shaw noted, is not a "moral gymnasium," no U.S. president could long disregard the domestic repugnance to the resistance of the Afrikaners, the dominant force since 1948, to the principle of "one man, one vote" and the dismantlement of their racially inspired laws and practices. Yet reality is complicated and demands differentiated responses. For example, despite a polarized political environment in southern Africa, South Africa and the neighboring black African states of Mozambique, Zambia, Botswana, and Zimbabwe have interlocking economic interests and enjoy an active economic relationship. Some changes in the system of apartheid have been made, but critics argue that these are too few, too superficial, and too late. How to nudge South Africa toward greater compromise and change without wreaking political and strategic havoc with Western interests is the challenge U.S. policy faces.

In an obvious change of approach from the activism and emphasis on human rights of Jimmy Carter, Ronald Reagan has opted for a seemingly neutral position between South Africa and the African countries that are gearing up for an intensification of the campaign against the Pretoria government. On August 29, 1981, in a major policy statement, Chester A. Crocker, assistant secretary of state for African Affairs, declared in a State Department press release:

> Our task, together with our key allies, is to maintain communication with all parties — something we in the West are uniquely able to do — and to pursue our growing interests throughout the region. . . .
> In South Africa, the region's dominant country, it is not our task to choose between black and white. In this rich land of talented and diverse peoples, important Western economic, strategic, moral and political interests are at stake.

He took a position that is unlikely to survive the growing polarization: "The Reagan Administration has no intention of destabilizing South Africa in order to curry favor elsewhere. Neither will we align ourselves with apartheid policies that are abhorrent to our own multiracial democracy."

Dr. Richard Bissell analyzes the various aspects of the United States-South African relationship with commendable dispassion and keen insight. In the process of discussing the substantive issues, he makes clear the importance of personality and political leadership (or lack thereof) and offers illuminating vignettes of the main political actors in the drama being played out in southern Africa, the United Nations, and Western capitals. A recognized scholar, Dr. Bissell has traveled widely and often in the region and is able to set the issues in their proper context. His realistic assessment goes directly to the heart of the domestic, regional, and international dimensions of the problems facing Washington and Pretoria. The result is a thorough and up-to-date analysis of a complex and politically difficult relationship. Dr. Bissell's volume is a timely addition to the series on *Studies of Influence in International Relations*.

Alvin Z. Rubinstein
University of Pennsylvania

ACKNOWLEDGMENTS

This book would not have been possible without the accumulated contacts with policymakers and observers in the United States and South Africa over a period of years. Their willingness to share their experiences and views was generous beyond my ability to acknowledge it, and since such dialogues were undertaken in many cases without this book in mind, it would be unfair to thank them specifically.

Financial support for portions of the research came from the Lyndon Baines Johnson Foundation and the Dr. Scholl Foundation; their aid is gratefully acknowledged.

Most importantly, the study would not have been completed without the intellectual support of the series editor, Alvin Z. Rubinstein, as well as the indulgence of my wife, Suzanne, and my children when I travelled to South Africa and various cities of the United States for research, and drafted chapters late at night. The conclusions were greatly strengthened by their insights and their common sense, both crucial in the examination of influence and communication between two very different societies.

INTRODUCTION

The popular perceptions of South Africa by U.S. citizens, and of the United States by South Africans, have undergone remarkable transformations in a mere decade. From a mutual sense of "being on the same side of the fence," the headlines of newspapers refer increasingly to perpetual confrontation. The issue eroding past trust changes from month to month. Sometimes the issue is the development of nuclear weapons by South Africa, and at other times the apartheid policies in South Africa; otherwise, the issue can be U.S. policy on Zimbabwe, Namibia, or Angola. Awareness of their intertwined fate by the general publics in South Africa and the United States has dramatically increased, with a consequent rise in the expressions of frustration on the part of policy-makers. In each country, contradictory pressures on the governments give rise largely to paralysis of policy. Attempts to influence each other drive the countries apart rather than yield an image of constructive cooperation. In each country, the public sentiment is similar: "Why doesn't our government restore the harmonious relationship of the past and do something to change the idiotic policies of South Africa (the United States)?"

To "do something" means to *influence* the policies of the other government and society. The apparent failure to influence each other to the extent expected by the elites and publics in each country constitutes a major quandary in the foreign policies of the 1970s and 1980s. So many ramifications appear to flow from the lack of harmony between South Africa and the United States: the possible increase in Soviet and Cuban influence in southern Africa; the instability of the price of gold and the global monetary system; the prospect of interruptions in the flow of raw materials vital to the economic health of the U.S. and its allies; and the exacerbation of racial tensions in all societies as a spillover from South Africa. Concern about the future is rife. Many speculate on the possible effects of a continued failure of dialogue between the United States and South Africa. The constant growth of the ramifications of such a failure makes the casting of blame on various parties all the more likely.

Observers are just beginning to step back and consider the sources of such tensions. Such efforts necessarily require examining the entire relationship. The disagreements over policy goals are clear enough, yet there exists, in addition, a substantial number of areas where the two governments agree. These areas do not appear to be a great source of satisfaction, since the areas of disagreement foster such bitterness as to outweigh and, indeed, to poison the realms of cooperation. To a certain extent, the messianic character of certain policy goals introduces an emotional commitment whose frustration would certainly engender bitterness. On the United States' side, the commitment to racial non-discrimination often colors the perception of the entire relationship. On the South African side, the commitment to nationalist autonomy (expressed in the South African designs for apartheid) and anticommunism causes a fundamental misunderstanding of the U.S. establishment of priorities on a global scale. The strength of such "ideological" commitments is consistently underestimated because normal dealings with elites in each country do not bring such concerns to the fore.

South Africa, for instance, has a nationalist revolution that has been in power only since 1948, and its control of key institutions (particularly industrial) has only spread slowly since then. U.S. citizens, however, generally deal with the English-speaking elite, normally more cosmopolitan than the Afrikaner Nationalist elite, and less preoccupied with autonomous South African policies, whether on defense, race, or economic issues. It is from among South African English speakers, too, that the Communist Party has recruited most of its members, so the tolerance for dissenting presumably is somewhat stronger. Such is the traditional image of South Africans gained by U.S. citizens, whether in South Africa or from travellers in the United States. The traditional contact from the United States side has also been with people from business, particularly the U.S. corporations with investments in South Africa. Their concern for ethical issues (such as racial discrimination) or the shape of South African national development has been strictly secondary to the generation of adequate profit margins. U.S. businessmen, too, tended to be adequately anticommunist, which suggested that a real community of spirit existed between the United States and South Africa. The two governments had little contact, and the separate political goals rarely had cause to clash.[1] Those elites that did have consistent contact were close enough (even if not identical) in their views of the world and their respective societies to generate truly warm relations between the two societies during the twentieth century.

The sources of current tensions, then, appear to lie in the involvement of dramatically expanded constituencies in formulating United States-South African relations. The underlying thrusts of the two societies, which provide the initiatives in international relationships, have been quite divergent over the last decade. The *need to influence* that has emerged in the 1970s is a stunning replacement for the unconscious cooperation that had heretofore existed. The United States appeared to be more firmly committed to the elimination of racial discrimination in South Africa, Rhodesia, and Namibia since 1977. The United States also became concerned about the possible proliferation of nuclear weapons by South Africa, with the South Africans committed to obscuring from the United States whatever progress they are making. The South Africans have attempted to organize coalitions to deal with the presence of large Cuban forces in southern Africa since Angolan independence in 1975, as well as the potential for introduction of more socialist-bloc troops. And generally, the

South Africans have attempted to obtain more Western respect for their role as an independent force in African politics and in the military defense of the Cape route. In each case, the existence of long-term goals, where the other partner in the relationship has reservations over the goals (or the means to attain them), has resulted in an exploration for necessary leverage. And, in general, the need for leverage has been a need for short-term influence.

In recent decades, it has been quite unfashionable for political scientists to analyze international relationships on the basis of influence. For most observers, the term has a vague connotation, as in the phrase, "American foreign policy in Africa is greatly influenced by British actions and views." In the past, the concept of influence has frequently been used by those who could not define the international process more clearly and wished to merely characterize the diplomatic atmosphere. If the notion of influence were considered in an instrumental sense, however, the term takes on much greater specificity, and for that reason, influence is used here in light of its short-term utility. A more extended explanation of its rationale can be seen in recent writings of Alvin Z. Rubinstein.[2] As he makes clear, influence for each country is a process, indeed "a short-lived phenomenon," and a search for the instrumentalities that serve the long-range goals set out above.

We are not considering influence building, in part because the concept is nowhere adequately defined, and in part because influence in the international arena is rarely a static entity. South Africa and the United States, by the 1960s, had a very close relationship, but when a disagreement over policy emerged, they found they could not influence each other very much. Indeed, this study will seek to explain, as much as possible, the extraordinary gap that policymakers have come to recognize between their expected influence and the degree to which they could actually influence the other government. The failure may have been a conceptual one, a mistaken belief that a cordial relationship will automatically provide the means to eliminate differences that emerge. Such a formulation confuses goodwill with influence. Certainly, in a host of relationships with other countries, particularly European, the United States possesses a reservoir of goodwill derived from the historical experiences of cooperation in war and peace. The bonds that cement the United States and Britain are partly historical/cultural, such that the two societies know they share certain values that allow them to speak a common political language when faced by a challenge. The depth of those shared values is unusual among relationships between nations, however; certainly, the extent of shared experiences between the South African society and the U.S. society is of an entirely different character. Indeed, it is in the conflict over interpretation of that shared experience that U.S. foreign policy has a fundamental split. The basic point here is that we shall consider the accumulation of goodwill as only one factor in exercising influence. It might be argued, but outside the parameters of this study, that historical factors are of decreasing importance in the twentieth century, as the principal political determinants (the public, elites, or leaders) become increasingly historical in their thinking. Some evidence concerning this issue will be examined in Chapter 2.

HOW INFLUENCE IS IMPLEMENTED

Because influence is defined here as a short-term phenomenon, implementation and tactics become essential to an understanding. To influence is to project foreign policy goals into the political elite (and perhaps the general public) of another society. Thus we are dealing with a behavioral question, and we shall use actual behavior to assess the exercise of influence. The nature of long-term foreign policy goals is important only insofar as it serves as a backdrop for one nation's actions, and insofar as it influences the perceptions of the other nation's political leaders. Over time, the core of any study of influence must deal primarily with *tools*; in a literal sense, what are the levers that foreign policy-makers use to influence another society?

In this study, the levers are identified in six categories. Clearly, some will overlap and some will be described at greater length than may seem to be justified by current events. Different methods of influence, however, have their historical moments; they may have been more important in the past, or are more likely to achieve importance in the future, and thus are certainly worthy of discussion.

(1) Accumulated goodwill and alienation. The history of a relationship between any two nations establishes a certain momentum, visible in governmental bureaucracies, in the private sector with institutionalized contacts, and in public image.

(2) Political influence. These are the ties between those most influential in each country's political structure (allowing for changes in administrations), both through governmental mechanisms and through private channels. Given the existence of extensive political opposition in both South Africa and the United States, much influence is exerted outside official links.

(3) Military/strategic influence. A key factor in any influence relationship, particularly between a stronger and a weaker nation, is the issue of elementary security: do they operate as allies, dominator/dominated, or as enemies? The active threats to the security of the United States and South Africa since World War II, in particular, cause this category to be an important one.

(4) Economic influence. The existence of large corporations and banks autonomous of government control lead to the independent exercise of influence. The impact of such institutions, too, is far more than economic, considering the important effect of economic prosperity on the political and social orders of nations. Some economic transactions may be more important to South Africa (for example, capital investment and the organization of trade unions) than to the United States (for example, trade in basic resources).

(5) Nuclear influence. The role of nuclear issues has achieved unparalleled importance in the 1970s, as it has affected economic, security, and political areas of life. Enormous pressure groups have emerged in recent decades within and outside governments to press for various policy changes over nuclear weapons and energy. It has had particular political importance in the case of South Africa and the United States.

(6) Sociocultural influence. In an era of growing government intervention, some realms of life remain largely untouched and in the control of the private sector. The role of the churches in international influence continues, to some degree, nineteenth century traditions of the missionaries. There are also secular influences that attempt to influence the intellectual environment, particularly as education has become increasingly universal and as professional associations have accelerated the growth of their international affiliations.

The extent of the influence in all six categories depends upon an understanding of each society. A level of influence is used in one country, with an effect on a domestic component (not necessarily governmental in either case) in the other country. For a study of influence to be successful, it is necessary to identify the initiator, the issue, the influence process, and the party affected.

There is no guarantee in international politics that an attempt to exercise influence will yield the desired result. Indeed, a constant theme of the United States-South African relationship is the failure of levers to achieve the intention of the initiator. Aside from the methodological purposes of this study, it should be able to identify the reasons for failure — the miscalculations and idiosyncratic factors that have caused the relationship between these two nations to degenerate steadily over the last decade. It will be presumed here that the notion of influencing another government means that a visible change of behavior or policy can be identified in the object society. In many cases, after all, the purpose of the initiator is that the other government *not* do something. To attribute such a nonaction to the influence exerted by another party requires the closest scrutiny of what would be "normal" behavior for the object party. If the latter departs from such normal activity in apparent response to the influence exerted, it is as significant as the undertaking of a specific action.

The problem of data in such a study could be the object of an indefinite debate. In this study, there is no attempt to measure influence by use of a total catalog of the two countries' behavior. Some studies have attempted to do so through quantitative examination of a few interactive factors, and most rely upon correlations to "prove" the influence of one country upon another. The causal relationships in such studies are usually vague, if only because so many events are lumped into large aggregate conclusions (in order to have a statistically significant sample). It may be that some relationships are rich and diverse enough to justify the use of quantitative data; such investigations would also have to be conducted in the closed files of the Department of State, the South African Foreign Ministry, and innumerable private organizations. In the case of

South Africa and the United States, case studies will have to suffice. In a sense, they will only be illustrative, rather than proof for any hypotheses. But the examination of the dynamics between two countries, based on concrete issues where various forms of influence were exerted, should provide a view of how foreign policy influence actually works. Hopefully, the issues will be sufficiently representative to convey accurately how South Africa and the United States influence each other, as well as suggesting modes of analyzing influence between other countries.

NOTES

1. Certainly, there had been U.S. policy dilemmas on South Africa before 1960. See, for instance, Thomas J. Noer, *Briton, Boer, and Yankee: The United States and South Africa 1870-1914* (Kent, Ohio: Kent State University Press, 1978) on the issue of U.S. policy toward the Boer War. But the involvement of substantial U.S. political elements, as well as the emergence of autonomous South African policies toward the United States, came only with more general United States-African interactions in the 1960s.

2. See, in particular, *Soviet and Chinese Influence in the Third World* (New York: Praeger, 1975), pp. 7-15.

CONTENTS

South Africa and the United States

HISTORICAL DIMENSIONS

Historical momentum can provide a certain degree of influence in a relationship between two nations, but the extent to which such a potential for influence can also be destroyed in rapid order is extraordinary. This aspect of the influence relationship between South Africa and the United States can be seen only in particular trends. History appears to serve as an active agent of influence when the trend is moving toward increasing cooperation; on the other hand, where the relationship appears to be unravelling, historical consciousness becomes very short term. Past cooperation is forgotten. In other words, the utility of the past in influencing another country also brings the future into the picture; a shared past is useful only when the future is shared as well. This time dimension reduces the elements in each society that are thus affected by a common history.

The most prominent characteristic of past ties between the United States and South Africa is that they had *common* experiences, but not necessarily *shared* experiences. The extent of active cooperation between the two nations in the past has been quite limited. Geographically, the two countries are far apart, and the historical development of each country did not lead them into contact. Africa was oriented toward Europe, particularly in the context of the nineteenth century colonial system, and the United States has only lately had any interest in Africa. The first overseas interests of the United States were in Europe and then later in Latin America and Asia. South Africa's traditional orientation was twofold: a land orientation northward toward Africa as black groups migrated southward, and later white-ruled South Africa colonized northward, as well as a sea orientation toward Europe and India. The key role of the Cape, as a way station for the early spice trade, and later for connecting the many points of the British Empire, dictated the principal ties of the South Africans in their early development and later quest for influence. The United

States and South Africa grew separately and have felt the need for cooperation only as a result of the U.S. emergence as a global power, in combination with the degree to which their separate experiences had much in common.

The parallels of historical development between South Africa and the United States have been sufficiently significant to create (in the minds of many) opportunities for leverage. In this context, one has to include the influx of white settlers, the nature of the indigenous populations, the development of race policies, the basis of economic development, reactions to geopolitical developments of the twentieth century, and primary international bonds in the English-speaking world. Each of these factors deserves greater analysis, but for the moment, it is sufficient to note that the strength of this common heritage is built upon 300 years of parallel experiences, but a careful evluation of that heritage has occurred only during the last few decades. Critical analysis has occurred because of the recognition that, in some aspects, the historical experiences were not parallel at all, and indeed embarked on divergent paths.

The historical divergences of South Africa and the United States can be discussed in two senses. On the one hand, there are clear-cut differences between the two societies, creating different historical imperatives: strikingly different racial proportions in the two societies; the continuing strength of ethnic divisions in South Africa at a time when the United States was committed to the "melting pot"; a greater commitment by South Africa to state intervention in the economy since World War II in order to hasten industrialization; the maintenance of the parliamentary political system in South Africa as opposed to the U.S. division of political power; and a growing sense of physical threat to South Africa from internal sources. At the same time, an even more important source of divergences exists in the pluralistic nature of each society. What is viewed as authentic historical experience is widely debated within each society, and the other country's history is viewed with individualistic blinders affecting each person's perceptions. Thus, a black citizen in the United States will view South African history quite differently than will a white U.S. business executive. Likewise, within South Africa, different portions of the population see different U.S. experiences as providing historical guidelines for their own development. For instance, John C. Calhoun's advocacy of states' rights, long considered an outdated issue in U.S. political development, is greatly appreciated in some South African circles. These contradictory perceptions of valid historical experience complicate the debate over the nature of the historical relationship, yet are rarely debated publicly and forthrightly for fear of highlighting the divisions within each country.

The strongest common experience to both societies, and one that continues to condition their responses to one another, was their association with, and their disassociation from, the British Empire. The eastern seaboard of North America, colonized by various nationalities during the seventeenth century, and welded into a loose political unit by the British Crown, took its independence during the reign of George III. South Africa was also settled by many different groups seized from the Dutch in 1795, immediately after U.S. independence. That colonization lasted until 1910, when the settlers of the several southern African republics and colonies negotiated self-government in the wake of the Boer War (1899-1902). In each case, while local political institutions reached the point of maturity where they were able to press successfully for self-government or independence, they were also incorporated for a sufficient time in the English cultural world to develop legal or political institutions from the British model. No model survives unaffected by local conditions, of course, and therein lies some of the divergences. But the strength of the British political, economic, and cultural traditions were such to ensure much harmony between its offshots, including South Africa and the United States. The many spheres of life in which the British would make their mark, including the role of missionaries in religious life, the role of merchants in economic life, and the special role of civil libertarian traditions, encouraged the development of institutions and habits of life in both societies. What may be most surprising is not the commonality, but the extent to which it survived into the twentieth century despite very different conditions.

Consider, for example, the nature of the white influx into the region now known as South Africa. The area at the Cape of Good Hope had been settled in the seventeenth century as a small trading post, in order to enable ships and passengers on the East Indian-European route to replenish their provisions, take fresh water on board, and rest. The whites first settling in the Cape came across a small indigenous population (the Hottentots) that was nomadic, much like the indigenous American Indian population. At that point, however, the experience of the two cultures divides. As U.S. pioneers pushed further inland with their settlements, the Indians continued to be spread out, disease decimated their ranks, and the land was largely open to settlement with only episodic armed struggles through the nineteenth century. In South Africa, on the other hand, the further whites pushed inland, the denser was the population of indigenous peoples (not Hottentots, but various Bantu-related tribes) and thus greater resistance was encountered. In South Africa, native African diseases seem to have decimated the white settlers more than imported diseases damaged the Bantus, and when the territorial expansion of South Africa had reached its limits, the whites found themselves to be in a numerical proportion with blacks that was significantly different from that found in the United States.

Although the composition of the white immigrants in South Africa and America were essentially the same, the ensuing societies evolved differently, which was partially due to the contrasting environments. White immigrants were the usual mix that appeared in colonial settlements in the seventeenth to nineteenth centuries: adventurers, criminals, sailors jumping ship, religious dissenters, and a few younger children of aristocrats seeking to regain a fortune. They were all people of a distinctly individualistic bent, all armed with different personality quirks that would cause them to abandon the environment in which they had grown up. In the South African and American environments, the hardy souls survived the initial period. But in the U.S. case, there was quickly established a significant area of "genteel civilization" along the eastern seaboard, where more liberal attitudes could flower in a tolerant environment. The South Africans found little such easy comfort, for as soon as they left the actual bridgehead at Capetown and Stellenbosch, the atmosphere was a hostile one, in which the descendants of the original settlers had to be as tough as or tougher than their forebears. As the area of settlement expanded, the sense of danger increased, causing those settlers who shirked a good fight to move on to calmer areas, such as Australia or America. This Darwinian process meant that the two colonies, beginning with much the same population, rapidly moved in different directions. Yet the sense of identifying with one another's origins remained.

On the other side of the color bar, a limited sense of identification existed. The fact that blacks in South Africa became an oppressed section of the population over time meant that U.S. blacks could identify with them. The fact that they had arrived at their similar condition through different processes made little difference; indeed, the U.S. blacks' sense of identification with South African blacks may have been aided by an increasing curiosity about their African origins. South African blacks were less likely to identify with the detribalized U.S. blacks (at least until recently), since forced transport of slaves from South Africa was not common. The involvement of either black community with the other, however, has come slowly and has accelerated in recent years only with the increase of education and political involvement on both sides. On the South African side, the expanding settlements of blacks in the urban areas, with consequent detribalization, has given them an outlook increasingly similar to U.S. black counterparts. Likewise, on the U.S. side, blacks have encountered in the 1970s the "Roots phenomenon," an increasingly active interest in their African origins, expressed in expanded travel in Africa and active encouragement of education about their African heritage. The fact that significant differences between the two populations exist is undeniable, but the present momentum is directed primarily toward identification of elements of commonality.

When one then examines the interworkings of the races in each society, the parallel tracks of their race relations policies become much clearer. The transition to the banning of slavery came earlier in South Africa, where the British lead in the antislavery movement had an impact early in the nineteenth century. The pervasive inequality of the races, both economically and socially, persisted in both societies after the banning of slavery, with the institutionalization of that inequality emerging as legislation for the separation (and in theory, equality) of the races. The social conditions giving rise to such "separate but equal" doctrines were substantially similar. The U.S. black population was concentrated in the southern states, with black/white ratios similar to many parts of South Africa. The result was similar: those parts of the country with relatively sparse nonwhite populations legislated integrationist codes of race relations, while those with the greatest concentrations of blacks attempted to ensure separation of the races in the work place, in the schools, and in residential patterns. The movement toward industrialization of each society in the twentieth century provoked widespread movements of the black population, as blacks sought jobs in the expanding industrial sectors. At that point, the two societies divided, the United States moving toward integration (after World War II), and at the same time, South Africa establishing a vision of a segregated future in the apartheid legislation of the Nationalist Governments after 1948. What is important to note here is the existence of underlying social thrusts in each direction in each society, with one sizable section of the white population pressing for separation and another for integration. Those underlying forces continue to exist to the present day, with implications we shall note later.

The economic development in both countries also gave rise to many similar patterns. The wealth and international standing of each society were based upon the exploitation of natural mineral and agricultural wealth. The situation of each country in temperate latitudes of different hemispheres endowed them with beautiful farmland, which was ready to yield a surplus harvest for export to the "old world." The creation of an economic surplus on the land was used to purchase the capital assets (railroads, machinery, and technology) for extended economic expansions in the twentieth century. The existence of easily available lodes of raw materials for the industrial sector made both societies natural candidates for the development we have witnessed. Energy was available in sufficient quantities to fuel the opening decades of industrialization: coal in South Africa, coal and oil in the United States. (By 1937, South Africa's per capita consumption of energy was already in the range of Switzerland's and Czechoslovakia's.) The requirements of heavy industry could be mined: iron ore, copper, and the alloys necessary for the development of a steel sector. Transportation networks were created for tying together internal markets as well as connecting the internal economy with global markets. The early push for industrialization also provided each country with the means to dominate their respective regions economically, with neighboring countries tied into the dominant economy through sheer size and activity. Curiously, both countries became intimately involved as well in the mechanisms of international monetary stability, as they represented the two new major steady sources of gold in the nineteenth and twentieth centuries. Many miners who had participated in the rush to the western United States in the nineteenth century moved on to the South African fields later in the century. An exact number cannot be determined but it was clearly significant, as can be seen in the establishment of U.S. consulates in Johannesburg in 1891, Pretoria in 1898, and Durban in 1906. (An earlier consulate had been established in Capetown in 1799 to care for U.S. sailors.) It turned out that the opportunities for wealth in South Africa were even more significant, with the sources of gold (and diamonds) showing few signs of being mined out to the present day. The opportunity for instant wealth, however, that came to the lowliest individual with the good fortune to find a sizable gold nugget or a rough diamond of several carats established a significant degree of social mobility in each society. It was paralleled by the opportunity for wealth and achievement through hard work in exploiting the natural riches of the land (mineral or agricultural). The direction of their economies provided similar opportunities to individuals willing to take entrepreneural risks and work hard; the attitudes of the people toward economic man thus shared many similar attributes.

As two societies with longstanding links to the British Empire, they also had to adjust to the diminishing role of Britain in the world politics of the twentieth century. The beneficient role of the British fleet in ruling the sea lanes of the nineteenth century had provided a useful screen behind which South Africa and the United States could develop. The military budgets of each country (aside from times of internal turmoil, such as the U.S. Civil War or the Boer War) remained negligible as their gross national products steadily rose. Their roles in World War I consisted primarily of armories and granaries for the Allies; they fulfilled such roles with honor, and such a role increased their economic development rather than causing the destruction experienced by several European countries. With the weakening of British global reach in World War II, both countries were forced to adapt to changing circumstances. They were bound together by their commitment to oppose Soviet expansion, with the South Africans contributing forces to the United States-organized effort to repel the North Korean invasion of South Korea. Close ties (of cooperation, but not alliance) emerged with regard to defense of the South Atlantic and the Indian Ocean. The importance of South Africa as a base and monitoring post for developments in the southern hemisphere was appreciated by the United States in its role as a global policeman, particularly in the days before the world could be monitored by nuclear-powered submarines and overhead satellites. The expansion of Soviet power since 1945 has thus resulted in both similar and shared policies in meeting that challenge. At the same time, South Africa and the United States have been driven apart by differing responses to the other major postwar development: decolonization. The advocacy of African independence by the United States and the clearly stated view of South Africa that decolonization was a regrettable tendency has created enormous tensions. What cannot be forgotten, however, is the agreement on a whole range of other issues that have achieved prominence in the geopolitics of the last several decades.

Although historical developments have tended to divide South Africa and the United States in a variety of areas, race relations are perhaps most prominent in the visions of the two societies. The commitment of the United States to integration has been facilitated by the raw numbers. In a sense, the role of blacks in U.S. society, roughly 10 percent of the population, was seen by some to be a continuation of previous ethnic meldings that have occurred in U.S. history: the Irish, the Italians, the Jews, and others. The national myth of the melting pot is a powerful one, and it facilitates the acceptance of one more ethnic group into the system. Such a myth is not universally accepted in U.S.

society, and those in opposition to the myth are most sympathetic to current South African policies. For it is in South Africa that the perpetuation of ethnic division is accepted by the vast majority of the white population and, in many cases, codified by the government. The tendency to divide ethnically existed among the white colonists, of course, as a reflection of the colonial wars to control the Cape; but this view was reinforced by the still tribally organized blacks that were encountered in South Africa. Where indigenous tribal organization was virtually stamped out in the United States, as the Indians were removed to politically irrelevant enclaves and imported blacks quickly lost their tribal identity, South Africa had no governing elements with a vested interest in reducing the sense of ethnic identity. As the English-speaking population went into opposition after the 1948 elections, they certainly stepped up their advocacy of interracial communication and the lowering of social barriers. Such a strident advocacy, however, could be a function of being in political opposition as much as a reflection of conviction. It may be that the conviction had existed from English tradition and could only flower in the nongoverning comfort across the parliamentary aisle. Somehow over the decades, the pressures of governing a country with such a sizable nonwhite majority (distribution being roughly 17 percent white, 9 percent colored, 3 percent Asian, and 71 percent black) had caused those convictions to emerge only rarely, since it was far easier to rule a population extensively divided into primary ethnic loyalties.

While much more could be said about different approaches to race relations, an important institutional point about the process of changing race relations is germane. Justly enshrined as a milestone in the history of U.S. desegregation is the Supreme Court decision in *Brown v. Topeka Board of Education*. What is often not appreciated, until one examines another society that attempted the same process, is the critical and uncommon role of an independent judiciary, with the ability to review the constitutionality of legislation. The South African parliamentary system does not allow similar latitude to its judiciary, with its role severely tested in cases involving electoral rights in the early 1950s. Just as Franklin D. Roosevelt had considered expanding the Supreme Court in the 1930s in order to overcome hostility to his New Deal legislation, so the South African Parliament in 1956 expanded the Supreme Court. In the process, the South African judiciary got the message that it would be futile to overrule the Parliament on issues of constitutionality.[1] The long-term social contract is thus decided in the South African Parliament, now that the concept of judicial review has been rendered irrelevant. The U.S. system, on the other hand, provides an alternative forum (other than the electorally influenced Congress) for consideration of basic rules of governance. The South African government thus provides new rules for race relations as a result of parliamentary sentiment changing rather than as a result of officials deliberating in judicial chambers.

For a wide range of reasons, therefore, the United States and South Africa moved on to different tracks in race relations, and when South African policies became a matter under international discussion in the post-World War II period, it was inevitable that there would thus be tension in the bilateral relationship.

RELATIONS IN THE 1960S

At the official level, relations between the two sides during the twentieth century were quite cooperative, but at a low level. A South African legation was opened in Washington in 1929, and a U.S. consulate had been in Pretoria since the nineteenth century. That consulate was upgraded to an embassy in 1949, and relations expanded in the following year when a South African Air Force squadron served in Korea with the U.S. units. But throughout this period, the governmental ties have never been as salient as those between private sectors, whether in science, business, or cultural spheres. There were simply very few matters to place on the official agenda, since the South Africans relied primarily upon the British government for external links, and the U.S. government saw little reason to intrude in the profitable activities of the private sector in South Africa. Thus U.S. energy was focused on developing new opportunities in black Africa.

To the extent that perceptions of influence matter a great deal, U.S. views have been relatively unchanged since the early 1960s. They were developed at the time of the 1960 Sharpeville riots and during the general African push for independence; among the U.S. foreign policy elite, most relegated South Africa to the category of a "colonial situation" that would eventually be solved by resort to black rule. Others with similar simplicity of logic decided that the white Anglo-Afrikaner elite of South Africa had a right to dispose of their territories as they chose, and that the United States had no business interfering. Those lines of perception were drawn and have budged very slightly in the intervening decades. Certain themes were established in the 1958-63 period that continue to recur as the accepted litany of the United States' proper role in South Africa's future.

Attitudes have changed rather more substantially in South Africa than in the United States. Groups and individuals in the South African political elite have shown major shifts in their views of the United States, the reasons for such a shift being a major theme of this study. In brief, the changes related not only to actions of the United States toward South Africa, but also to permanent movements in the power base of South Africa domestically: the collapse of the major English-speaking opposition party (the United Party), the gradual change in black political thought from integrationist toward black consciousness/ segregation, and the extraordinary growth of the power of the South African economy in the global system (whereby U.S. vulnerability to raw material imports became a new reality to integrate into perceptions). Both South African and U.S. perceptions are important to identify.

Given the relatively intermittent attention devoted to South Africa by U.S. foreign policymaking elites, the nature of U.S. attitudes is best determined by illustration rather than by comprehensive analysis of the last two decades. One of the first periods of profound reconsideration of South Africa's role in the world occurred in the wake of the Sharpeville riots in 1960 — the contrast between that bloodshed and the rapid independence of much of the rest of the continent was perceived throughout the world, and while many conclusions drawn at that time were dangerously oversimplified, they reflected an honest anguish over the dilemmas posed by a black-white problem in South Africa that could not be solved by simply running down the Union Jack from the flagpole. The atmosphere of confrontation with South Africa was heightened by the emergence of pan-African diplomacy in the 1960-63 period, culminating in the formation of the Organization of African Unity (OAU) and the request for mandatory sanctions against South Africa at the United Nations by the Africa bloc.[2] The U.S. response thus became crucial, and the South African issue could no longer be pushed aside as a British concern.

The voice of the U.S. foreign policy establishment, *Foreign Affairs*, published two articles in the 1963-64 period that summarized well the growing consensus on leverage toward South Africa.[3] Interestingly, neither author was from the United States — Patrick Duncan was a South African exile and Philip Mason was British — but that illustrates the extent to which in-depth knowledge of South Africa was rare in the United States, and people had to rely upon borrowed perceptions for decision making. The articles contained several themes. First, given the need for political and social justice for blacks in South Africa, one could not assume they would be able to obtain that justice on their own. Indeed, outside (U.S.) intervention was necessary to reverse the direction of South African society and to forcibly change its government. Duncan quoted Ambassador Adlai Stevenson disapprovingly: "We have utilized our diplomatic and consular establishments in South Africa to demonstrate by words and by deeds our official disapproval of apartheid." Duncan responded that "words have limited value," and the only deed made public was that nonwhites were invited to the Fourth of July celebration at the embassy for the first time.[4] What, then, is advocated for the introduction of a black-ruled, capitalist, democratic South Africa?

Duncan argued first for discouraging U.S. investment in South Africa: imported capital strengthened apartheid and "imperils the whole private-enterprise system tomorrow — for the African majority, when it votes, will vote against all who did business with apartheid."[5] In 1963, the argument that foreign capital was related to political stability of the South African system was quite persuasive, for in the wake of the 1960 Sharpeville riots, foreign capital investors had fled that country, and there were dire warnings about the perils of investing in a place as unsteady as South Africa. The South Africans were also uncertain about the meaning of the threats by the members of the Organization of African Unity to boycott South African goods, for black Africa was the principal market for South African manufacturers. The second part of Duncan's argument also found some willing audiences, and indeed that school of thought would grow: siding with the black revolution in South Africa would be portrayed as an investment in the future instead of the past. Curiously, those most willing to believe in investing in the future were not corporate leaders;

over the course of the 1960s and 1970s, their perceptions of investments in South Africa were converted to a large extent into short-term ventures rather than the long-term viewpoint of the 1950s.

The relationship between the plight of the South African black and foreign investment/prosperity was a controversy addressed by various anti-apartheid individuals in different ways. In the early 1960s, the withdrawal of investment was seen to be a tool to hurt the interests of white South Africans and, thereby, to coerce them into relinquishing control of the South African political system. U.S. citizens opposed to the withdrawal of foreign investment came to argue that such measures would hurt the black standard of living and, in the course of the 1960s, they even came to argue that the incorporation of the blacks into middle-class prosperity would then allow for their obtaining political rights. Mason had anticipated this argument and maintained that prosperity would not endow the regime with legitimacy, in the view of the black population, even if seen as a short-term transition to shared rule — a possibility not then conceded by the South African government. The important point, though, was that over the course of the 1960s and 1970s the focus of the argument had shifted: from the issue of damaging white economic interests through the withdrawal of foreign investment to the question of the effect of foreign investment on black prosperity and economic future. The black community in South Africa was enlisted in this argument and predictably came out on both sides of the issue.

An additional perception of continuing importance lay in the realm of operational sanctions, and here Duncan and Mason disagreed. Duncan argued for the imposition of United Nations sanctions, implemented by British/United States' leadership, with regard to one strategic commodity, oil. Mason, on the other hand, argued that only a total blockade of South Africa's trade could possibly be effective. In part, their disagreement reflected the several points of view expressed at a major international conference held in London in April 1964.[6] At this meeting, which combined aspects of an academic meeting and a political rally, there was only minimal U.S. participation, painfully juxtaposed with the recurring importance of the United States in the imposition of sanctions, whether general or selective, against South Africa. But the levers of influence within the United States that were important for sanctions were identified in the closing resolutions of the conference: "In the U.S.A. pressure by the Negro and Civil Rights Movements to influence State Department policy."[7]

The connection between the racial issue in South Africa and race relations elsewhere also became a part of the litany in the early 1960s. Both ideologically and tactically, blacks were seen as standing together in various separate political struggles. Duncan made this point the closing of his article: "But if apartheid were to continue much longer, or if the world were to stand aside from South Africa while the races mutilated each other and ruined the land's productive capacity, race relationships everywhere could be poisoned."[8] The argument was to be resurrected regularly in the following decades: that the ability of the United States to "solve" South Africa's problems was not only a barometer of U.S. racial attitudes, but also a determinant of racial peace in the United States and elsewhere. In this way, relations with South Africa became the most important foreign policy issue for U.S. blacks to include in their political platforms. Indeed, the issue was of far greater salience than relations with black-governed Africa for such groups in the United States, even though some U.S. blacks eventually became puzzled over the growing advocacy of violence by South African nationalist groups; after all, such had not been the theme for integration in the U.S. south.

PERCEPTUAL SHIFTS IN THE 1970S

The second stage in the education of U.S. policymakers about influencing South Africa came at the end of the 1960s. The evident failure of diplomatic efforts to alter the direction of South African domestic legislation caused blame to be passed from one group to another. The arrival of a Republican administration in Washington in 1969 was one natural target, particularly with the eventual leaking of National Security Study Memorandum (NSSM) 39, which was approved by Secretary of State Kissinger and called for "benign neglect" of South Africa's problems.[9] Henry Kissinger was the perfect focus for blame, representing the merging of "capitalist interests" in New York with the "imperial ambitions" of Washington, and until his departure from government in 1977, he was the *bête noire* for many U.S. activists on Africa. Another focus of blame was the nature of U.S. misunderstanding of South African society, in particular the laager mentality of the Afrikaner government. In a widely vilified column in the *New York Times* in late 1970, the distinguished former diplomat George Kennan argued that anti-apartheid initiatives were totally mistaken in choosing a confrontational tack and thereby strengthening the domestic political base of the beleaguered whites of South Africa. His view reflected, in part, the growing recognition that old white-white divisions in South Africa, between Brit and Boer, were disintegrating, with most ending up generally in the Nationalist Party camp. Kennan's view was attacked not only for his assumptions about Afrikaner motivation, but also for providing very few policy alternatives to those that appeared to have failed in the 1960s.[10]

The issue, however, was not to be easily settled. In several important academic contributions in the early 1970s, the question of the effectiveness of sanctions was reexamined.[11] The failures of sanctions implemented against Rhodesia and proposed against South Africa caused a major reevaluation. A number of new variables were established as contributing to the effectiveness of sanctions: for example, the expectations of the target state at the time of voting sanctions; the extent to which expectations can be shifted; the degree of homogeneity of the target society; the possibilities for blackmail in establishing positive sanctions; and whether sanctions are focussed on core values or secondary values in the target society. This work, indirectly at least, had the effect of cooling off some who were militantly in favor of sanctions. Those pressing for change in South Africa became rather more sophisticated in their terminology and in the combination of measures taken, mixing some rewards with sanctions — at least from a U.S. perspective. At the same time, South Africans began learning the vocabulary of change appreciated in the West: a "dialogue" was opened with black Africa, and cooperation was offered to the United States on issues of mutual concern, such as Rhodesia. South Africa established an information service to give the world their version of events in that country, including the gradual growth in black income, and the appearance of a conciliatory image on economic and political issues. Some observers felt that Kissinger's approach had proven its value, as indicated by the willingness of the South African government to change racial legislation (dismissed as tokenism by opponents), and to work with Kissinger on the Rhodesian issue. The generally unanimous sentiment against South Africa, then, began to be balanced by several schools of U.S. foreign policy or by serious questioning of the logic for sanctions.

With the crippling of the Nixon administration by Watergate and the subsequent resignation of the president, as well as the end of the Portuguese empire in southern Africa in 1974-75, old and new forces were unleashed in U.S. policy toward South Africa. The expectation of the Democrats that they would win the White House in 1976 hastened the evolution of ideas by individuals ready to implement a new policy. In southern Africa, with the front line moved to the South African border, apartheid was seen as inheriting a new vulnerability. Thus, in 1975, one saw the emergence of the new U.S. activism. Anthony Lake, who was to be named head of the Policy Planning Staff in the State Department in 1977, laid out some of the assumptions: (1) the policy approach of NSSM-39, as implemented by Henry Kissinger, was a failure; (2) South Africa was becoming more "enlightened," with promises of loosening the reins of apartheid; (3) but those promises had nothing to do with U.S. policy, rather "the threat of increased pressure on Rhodesia and South Africa from a black-ruled Mozambique has been the key to these changes in southern Africa"; (4) the United States cannot force change in South Africa and should simply "set clear limits on the scope of our relations with South Africa" until blacks obtain full rights; and (5) in the meantime, U.S. policy should "respond to the views of concerned blacks in America."[12] The extent of departure here from previous activist approaches was minimal: certainly Lake had no expectation that the United States would take the lead in a movement against South Africa, but he also made it clear that the government's policies would need to respond positively to initiatives by the U.S. black community or to choose between black and white Africa, in case the black African states decided to force the United States to make a decision.

This view was augmented in the same period by more extended, academic analyses, dwelling frequently upon the changed relative strength of Nigeria and South Africa.[13] The realities of the 1973-74 oil price rises were seen as important new factors: "to the degree that foreign policy is conditioned directly by the desire to maintain good relations with countries which are strong economic partners, South African needs and desires should have some influence over United States policy, but that influence should have declined substantially during the 1970s by comparison with that of Nigeria."[14] This perception became the focus of extensive argumentation in the remainder of the 1970s, as successive developments in Nigeria and South Africa would change the balance, including the dramatic rise in the price of oil and gold, the difficulties of the Nigerian economic development plan, the substitutability of Nigerian oil, and the perceived strategic minerals shortages at the end of the 1970s. The argument between competing schools of thought on African policy virtually boiled down to a quest for blackmail: an argument that the South Africans understood rather better than the Nigerians, and thereby used in their own information efforts more effectively than did the Nigerians by the beginning of the 1980s. The Nigerians never officially broached an oil boycott of the United States as a means of influencing U.S. policy in South Africa, whereas the South Africans were not reluctant to discuss the implications of a shut-off of strategic minerals for the U.S. economy.

What was being recognized on most parts of the political spectrum by the end of the 1970s was that there were remarkably few people in the United States able to make judgments on South African issues on their own merit. As Foltz argued (and was never contradicted), with evidence from a study by Bruce Russett and Elizabeth Hanson,[15] "Domestic ideology was clearly the most important factor."[16] More explicitly, he argued that "South Africa's lobbyists have long understood that the best practical way to affect the overall 'tilt' of American policy in southern Africa is to affect the balance in the American government between conservative racists and liberal integrationists, irrespective of their interests in southern African questions per se."[17] As we have shown above on the question of sanctions and in the revival of liberal activism in 1975, the other end of the spectrum attempted a similar approach by tying South African policy to the views of U.S. blacks, who were a force in presidential politics but often without great interest in South Africa itself.

During the 1970s, two rather more radical perspectives came to play a limited role in U.S. awareness of South Africa's future. One perspective was that of proponents of "genuine" socialist movement in the region, and the other called for a radical partition of South Africa into several countries, in effect, dividing the country between black and white. What the radical views shared was an assumption that the current complex of rules and traditions would not carry the South African polity into the twenty-first century as a peaceful, prosperous entity. Much of the discussion about radical alternatives escaped notice in the United States, only because the main U.S. political ideologies tend to be "mainstream" and reformist, rather than radical in character. The manifestations of this radicalism came either from the academic community or from journalists in touch with the developing realities in South Africa.[18]

The development of a socialist consciousness in South Africa was generally a slow and osmotic process. Such a movement, however, would have various implications: "The issue of what type of political economy has led to new and more complex regional and global associations, in which black-versus-white rule is replaced or juxtaposed with socialist versus non-socialist alternatives. Because of wider international concerns, this may introduce 'cold war' symbolism into southern Africa of a type which African leaders have strived to avoid."[19] Indeed, the hope held out by socialist intellectuals was for the creation of a socialist model for Africa in a postrevolutionary South Africa.[20] In this new constellation of ideological combatants, the South Africans were thrown into the same category as the United States, West European states, *and* the majority of the black-ruled states in Africa, which did not favor a violent confrontation with South Africa over its racial policies. The fact that racial and class conflicts did not coincide in their adherents made the struggle in the region rather more confused as the 1970s passed. As Shaw indicates, too, the appearance of Soviet and Cuban troops in the region as active combatants created an even more severe challenge for the socialist adherents. In the 1970s, when Western observers were beginning to be willing to live with the concept of "African socialism" and the African propensity for one-party states, the sudden appearance of communist-bloc forces oversimplified the ideological issues in the area to the disadvantage of the socialists in South Africa and their U.S. supporters. The unwillingness of most black nationalists in South Africa to be (or to appear to be) the instruments of an international socialist movement resulted in a setback for acceptance of socialist ideology when Cuban armies appeared in the region.

Sensitivity to the radical right among people in the United States came rather more slowly. An increasing number of journalists found that they were unable to fathom fully the decision making in South Africa without greater comprehension of the Afrikaner society and ideology; in this way, they eventually came to communicate the radical white ideology of South Africa.[21] Many who penetrated the mythology and traditions of Afrikanerdom were horrified, writing about the center of South African politics as though they had found a living dinosaur. Others approached the subject with some sensitivity, with an understanding that any effort to change South Africa's direction would involve reorienting this cultural monolith that had grown out of the South African *veld*.[22] For some, the conclusion to this racial and cultural conflict between Afrikanerdom and its neighbors would be the division of the land;[23] for others, it would inevitably be the destruction of the Afrikaner.[24] These nuances of class, color, and culture, however, were clearly not for the typical U.S. observer in the 1970s. One might say that U.S. views of South Africa were gradually changing from an image of a polarized, racial conflict involving two camps into that of a political spectrum. But even as that element of sophistication was appearing, it was not entirely clear what kind of spectrum was appropriate (racial, ideological, cultural) and continuing pressures from U.S. politics forced the debate in the direction of the racial dichotomy.

Top levels of the U.S. administration did little to help introduce sophisticated thinking. When Vice-President Walter Mondale met with the South African prime minister in Geneva in early 1977, Mondale was asked by reporters what kind of democracy was urged on South Africa: "One man-one vote, of course," he replied. In response, former Undersecretary of State George Ball argued for a return to the Kissinger policy of benign neglect and communication with the South Africans in order to induce change.[25] Whereupon, the Africanist establishment responded by enumerating 41 positive steps to take against South Africa in order to "bring the whites to their senses."[26] At the highest levels, the quality of the argument over South Africa did not appear to have advanced greatly, an ironic situation in view of the rapidly changing views of both white and black Africans. For the United States generally, however, the concerns about the future of South Africa remained largely as they were in the early 1960s: racial conflict leading to instability, the security of the South African contribution to Western economic strength, and continuing puzzlement over the real geostrategic value of South Africa in the East-West contest. Most U.S. observers took very clear-cut views on each of these concerns; normally, they were at odds with other vocal groups, since they rarely embraced the radical options of socialism or partition.

In terms of tactics, five broadly drawn approaches were prevalent in the U.S. literature: intensified economic development, communication, disengagement, gradual pressure, and comprehensive sanctions.[27] Each approach was identified with a particular public figure, either in or out of government in the 1970s, but they were not equally applied by the U.S. government. In terms of influencing the South Africans, however, each approach is important, since it can be argued that the actions of the U.S. government may not be as important as those actions taken by the private sector, whether business, church groups, labor unions, or others. The more balanced analyses have recognized the extended influence of nongovernmental organizations.[28] In this study, much time will be devoted to recognizing the pervasive influence of institutions outside government as much as those in political power.

SOUTH AFRICAN PERCEPTIONS

South African perceptions of U.S. policy changed substantially over the decades in question. Their estimations of their own power, of their political legitimacy relative to Western Europe and the United States, and of regional realities all combined to change a fairly passive foreign policy in 1960 into a very active, unilateral defense of South African interests in 1980. What has to be kept in perspective about the relationship between South Africa and the United States, however, is that the United States has never been the principal Western contact for South Africa. To the present day, the British enjoy closer contact with all levels of South African society — both the government and the black nationalists who are creating revolution. The contacts with British businessmen, the government, and anti-apartheid groups based in London combine to make Britain a focus of South African interest and concern to an extent not yet matched by the United States. To be sure, ties with the United States have greatly increased since 1960, and in terms of public visibility in South Africa, the United States sometimes looms larger than Britain. The preoccupation with Ambassador Andrew Young and President Carter between 1977 and 1980 in South African media was real, but it obscured the fact that the British ambassador saw Prime Minister Botha ten times as often as the U.S. ambassador did, according to a U.S. diplomat in Pretoria. British investment in South Africa remains many times larger than U.S. investment, and the most prestigious education for a South African, of whatever political persuasion, remains British.

The sense of independent direction in South African foreign policy, particularly toward the United States, is a relatively new development. Veteran observers of South Africa have found the traditional pattern to be one of passivity, and indeed, "the South African government has usually reacted to external pressures by a variety of withdrawal actions."[29] Even after the events of the 1960s, it was described as having a foreign policy that is "defensive, even inward-turning, and lacking in sustained insight, vigor, and competence."[30] That state of affairs has continued to change, particularly during the late 1970s, but at an uncertain pace.

South African perceptions of the United States were most profoundly affected by the realization that the South African image in the U.S. mind was generally quite negative (owing to the divergence in their racial policies), and a decision was made by South Africans to attempt to alter that image, *not* the policies that created the problem. The South African white power structure, whether in government or outside, has not been inclined to regard the direction of its racial policies as a mistake; to do so would mean to renounce the Afrikaner-based nationalist revolution of the twentieth century. The breakdown in cultural and social myths that would be implied by such a renunciation was unthinkable to the whites in South Africa. And they felt justified in this response, to the extent it was conscious, by the remarkable degree of the movement of non-Afrikaner whites to accept that tradition in the post-1948 period. The year 1948 marked the key point of divergence, when the Nationalist Party finally achieved political control for the long oppressed Boer majority in South Africa, and Hubert Humphrey galvanized the Democratic Party convention with a speech calling for racial equality and integration in the United States. The extent of those differences, however, was only recognized after 1961, when South Africa left the Commonwealth and President John F. Kennedy began to chart an African foreign policy somewhat independent of the British. Therefore, the growing task of South Africans was both to deal with an internal political drift that alienated the international community and to alter an image abroad that consisted primarily of the white racist. Some groups in South Africa attempted to accomplish both tasks at the same time; others focussed only on one.

Crucially, the South Africans began from a position of relative ignorance: "Most Afrikaners (and for somewhat different reasons, most English-speaking South Africans) found it increasingly difficult during the 1960s to comprehend the basis of international attacks on South African domestic policies."[31] They assumed that the political and cultural elements held in common with the United States would leave no room for controversy: both presumed to be anti-communist and members of the Judeo-Christian tradition. Economic allies were puzzled by the U.S. inclination to downplay the compatibility of the two economies – the consideration of economic sanctions made no sense in light of the close interconnections of trade and investment between South Africa and the United States. South African opinion was further confused by the multiplicity of voices coming out of the United States, as well as the inconsistency of policy: transitions between Democratic and Republican administrations contrasted sharply with the stolid, continuing rule of the Nationalist Party in South Africa.

South African concern centered on the U.S. move to detente with the Soviet Union. For decades, the Soviet Union and international communism had played crucial roles as negative symbols for South African alliances abroad. Events in the 1970s were not reassuring to South Africa on this score: the role of the communists in the Portuguese revolution of 1974; the U.S. failure in Vietnam against the communists; the negotiation of strategic arms limitation agreements with the Soviet Union; the role of Cubans in Africa both militarily and politically; and the apparent unwillingness of the Carter administration to combat communist influence in Africa. These various sources of concern were crystallized by the remark of Ambassador Andrew Young in 1977, when he characterized the Cuban troops in Angola as a stabilizing force. A key element of solidarity between South Africa and the United States was thus destroyed. Subsequent cordial discussions between Young and the South Africans, during which it became clear that they basically had different assessments of the nature of the Soviet threat and the means of combatting it, did little to change the public image. Young's version of anticommunism did not make sense to the South Africans, and this point made for very different approaches to regional problems. Young was arguing, in effect, that the Nationalist Party should abdicate political power to the black majority in order to save the economy from communism; the suggestion was not greeted with much enthusiasm. The South Africans attempted, instead, to go around the Carter administration and appeal to interest groups in the United States that might rally to the anticommunist banner; and the South African press lost none of its old enthusiasm for covering the Soviet threat.[32]

South Africa's conclusion that the United States and Britain would not be its bulwark against communist expansion was the main source of restlessness in South African foreign policy during the Carter administration. In large part, they began searching more actively for partners whose interests coincided, with the prime candidates being those countries that felt rejected by U.S. foreign policy and were also anxious about growing Soviet military power. This list came to include such diverse candidates as the governments of Argentina, Taiwan, Israel, Chile, Paraguay, Iran, and opposition conservative parties in a number of West European countries. From that list, it is well known that cooperation bloomed most profusely with Taiwan and Israel. In each case, there were ironies abounding: the Taiwanese officials had to be categorized as honorary whites for purposes of freedom of movement in South Africa, and the South Africans were reportedly making advances to the Peking government for trade and anti-Soviet cooperation while working with the Taiwanese.[33] The Israeli connection, involving wide-ranging joint enterprises in the military and energy sectors, was a drastic reversal of old nationalist attitudes, some of whose leaders had emulated national socialist doctrines in World War II. With the emerging entente between South Africa and Israel, the formerly apolitical Jewish population in South Africa suddenly found a degree of social and political respectability quite unprecedented. The Israeli government was even permitted to sell war bonds in South Africa.

One result of these unusual shifts in international alignments by South Africa was the appearance of numerous conspiracy theories. Some South Africans, for instance, took the view that the United States and the Soviet Union had secretly decided to overthrow the South African government.[34] Others thought that the United States was using the Israeli connection as a secret channel to the South Africans, presumably to keep some United States-source military supplies flowing to a "secret ally," the South Africans.[35] Finally, the rumored nuclear tests off the South African coast in 1980, consisting of "incidents" registered by a U.S. satellite passing nearby but never susceptible to confirmation by several scientific panels, gave rise to any combination of the French, Israelis, and South Africans testing neutron warheads in the atmosphere. It was even assumed that some parts of the governments involved might be working with the South Africans without informing other branches of government. More important than the veracity of such theories, however, is the fact that South Africans accepted the need for an "underground" foreign policy. The overwhelming vilification of South Africa in international forums — ejected from the United Nations General Assembly after 1974 — and the apparent acquiescence of the United States in this move led to the design of a foreign policy of secrecy: some agreements were open, but many more were undisclosed and never published.

In this environment, what was to be the official policy of the South African government? Such an issue periodically raised a great debate in South Africa. Some were quite openly "pro-West," and merged their concern about the inoperability of the apartheid system with a desire to be acceptable to Western public opinion.[36] Others argued for the feasibility of opting out of the Soviet-United States confrontation out of antipathy for communism and out of disappointment with the U.S. response.[37] Various terms were used, including nonalignment, to describe this disengagement. A basic assumption for this viewpoint was the presumed capability of South African forces to beat any combination of attackers, including the Soviet Union, in a pitched battle, and that the USSR was the principal threat to South African security. The United States, by implication, became a hazard to South African interests, by being a spark for greater Soviet and Cuban involvement in southern Africa. Many who would instinctively wish to cooperate with the United States were quite disillusioned by their experiences in Angola in 1975-76, when they believed that Secretary of State Kissinger had given them official encouragement to send forces into Angola. When the U.S. mission was aborted by the Clark Amendment of January 1976, Kissinger also dissociated himself from any support of the South African operation. To many South Africans, then, of what value was the United States' embrace? Such a view, however, was by no means permanent, and the Reagan victory in 1980 rekindled hopes of a major realignment of South Africa and the United States among those of persevering faith in Western ties.[38]

History thus plays two different roles in the influence relationship between the United States and South Africa. The centuries-old momentum created by parallel economic and social structures established a certain sense of shared interests, even if rarely put to the test of designing common policies. The experiences of South Africa and the United States as part of the British Empire did much to shape their outlooks, both internally and with regard to the world. Resulting close ties cannot be underestimated.

More recent history, however, suggests how quickly that momentum can be lost. The sundering of the relationship, whether over divergent racial policies, or over different assessments of the Soviet threat, has been dramatic and will have its own long-term influence on bilateral ties. An entire generation of U.S. and South African citizens is looking on the other side as a threat, in some way, to its own security and well-being. And as the number of issues on which the two countries can cooperate diminishes, the historical well of goodwill begins to go dry.

NOTES

1. See Albie Sachs, *Justice in South Africa* (Berkeley: University of California Press, 1973).

2. For an extensive history of this diplomatic effort, see Richard E. Bissell, *Apartheid and International Organizations* (Boulder, Colo.: Westview Press, 1977).

3. See Patrick Duncan, "Toward a World Policy for South Africa," *Foreign Affairs* 42 (October 1963): 38-48; and Philip Mason, "Some Maxims and Axioms," *Foreign Affairs* 43 (October 1964): 150-64.

4. Duncan, "Toward a World Policy," p. 43.

5. Duncan, "Toward a World Policy," p. 45.

6. The results were published by Ronald Segal, ed., *Sanctions against South Africa* (Harmondsworth, England: Penguin Books, 1964).

7. Ibid., p. 272.

8. Duncan, "Toward a World Policy," p. 48.

9. Text and analysis in Mohamed El-Khawas, ed., *The Kissinger Study of South Africa* (Westport, Conn.: Lawrence Hill, 1976).

10. See, for instance, Ernest A. Gross, "A Reply to George Kennan," *New York Times*, December 30, 1970.

11. See David A. Baldwin, "The Power of Positive Sanctions," *World Politics* 24 (October 1971): 19-38; and Margaret Doxey, "Sanctions Revisited," *International Journal* 31 (Winter 1975-76): 53-78.

12. Anthony Lake, "U.S. Policy on Africa," *New York Times*, February 26, 1975, p. 35.

13. See William J. Foltz, "United States Policy Toward Southern Africa: Economic and Strategic Constraints," *Political Science Quarterly* 92 (Spring 1977): 47-64.

14. Ibid., p. 49.

15. Bruce M. Russett and Elizabeth C. Hanson, *Interest and Ideology: The Foreign Policy Beliefs of American Businessmen* (San Francisco: W. H. Freman, 1975).

16. Foltz, "United States Policy," p. 53.

17. Foltz, "United States Policy," p. 64.

18. Even in the liberal mainstream, as exemplified by the dean of South African studies in the United States, Professor Gwendolyn Carter, the call was for U.S. communication with various black leaders in South Africa and leading the effort for a national convention in South Africa. See her chapter in Gwendolyn M. Carter and Patrick O'Meara, eds., *Southern Africa in Crisis* (Bloomington and London: Indiana University Press, 1977).

19. Timothy M. Shaw, "The International Politics of Southern Africa: Change or Continuity?" paper presented at the African Studies Association, Boston, November 1976, p. 14.

20. See Emmanual Arrighi and John Saul, *Essays on the Political Economy of Africa* (New York: Monthly Review Press, 1973).

21. See, for instance, Russell Warren Howe, "Downriver to Armageddon," *World*, July 17, 1973, pp. 18-23; and Jan Morris, *Rolling Stone*, June 2, 1977, pp. 47-53. In the world of fiction, see James Michener, *The Covenant* (New York: Random House, 1980).

22. See Edwin S. Munger, ed., *The Afrikaners* (Capetown: Tafelberg, 1979).

23. Howe, "Downriver to Armageddon," p. 23.

24. Morris, p. 53.

25. George Ball, "Asking for Trouble in South Africa," *Atlantic Monthly* (October 1977), pp. 43-51.

26. Clyde Ferguson and William R. Cotter, "South Africa: What Is to Be Done?" *Foreign Affairs* 56 (January 1978): 253-74.

27. These categories are widely accepted, although this particular wording is taken from James Barber and Michael Spicer, "Sanctions against South Africa – Options for the West," *International Affairs* 55 (July 1979): 390.

28. Ibid., pp. 385-86.

29. John Seiler, "Appraising South African Foreign Policy," paper presented at the International Studies Association, St. Louis, March 1977, p. 2.

30. Ibid.

31. Ibid., p. 3.

32. Note, for instance, the long interview with a recent Soviet defector, Igor Glagolev, that appeared in the *Sunday Tribune*, January 13, 1980.

33. Phil Kurata, "The Outcasts Forge New Bonds," *Far Eastern Economic Review*, November 7, 1980, pp. 40-41.

34. See, for instance, the articles published in *The Citizen* (Johannesburg) by the well-known political writer, Aida Parker, gathered together in Aida Parker, *Secret U.S. War against South Africa* (Johannesburg: S.A. Today, 1977).

35. This view was put forth in *The Economist*, November 5, 1977, p. 91.

36. Among the groups active in this regard was the South Africa Foundation. A speech by its director-general, Peter Sorour, in 1981 was given the headline, "West wants SA back in mainstream – but concrete legislative evidence of change sought abroad." See *The South Africa Foundation News*, March 1981, p. 1.

37. See Denis Venter, "South Africa: A Non-aligned Posture in Foreign Policy?" *South African Journal of African Affairs* 9 (1979): 178-90.

38. See John H. Chettle's report in "Foreign Reports," *South Africa International* 11 (January 1981): 167-69.

2

POLITICAL INFLUENCE:
THE PRINCIPAL FOCUS

Direct intervention in each other's political systems to change basic ideologies and major political positions became an increasing theme in United States-South African relations in the 1970s. To a remarkable extent — given the power disparities of the two countries in many economic and military aspects — they approached a relative balance of forces in the political realm by the end of the decade, even though that balance was still refused recognition by many key policymakers on both sides.

There were a number of prizes at stake in this contest, some ends in themselves and others simply tools to accumulate in the long-range battle over ideology. The best recognized prize was the direction of racial policies and, equally important, the international projection of those policies. There was little question of South Africa changing U.S. integrationist directions after the 1960s, for instance, but the extent to which U.S. policies were pursued abroad made all the difference to South Africa. The Europeans, after all, had a tradition of respecting local ethnically based race relations in Africa; it was the U.S. willingness to graft the African campaign against South Africa onto the traditionally intermittent U.S. projection of morality that made South Africa nervous. At best, South Africa hoped to eliminate the export of U.S. human rights standard. As a second-best solution, it was hoped the United States would place the South African situation in the context of either African ethnic problems in general or, even better, compare them to the systematic loss of life and human rights in totalitarian and communist-led states. For most U.S. citizens, the goal in South Africa was equally fundamental: ideally, a reversal of segregationist policies and the replacement of a constitution that excluded nonwhites from the political system. If that were not feasible (and most U.S. observers shied away from the revolutionary implications and related instability), the goal would be at least a change of direction, that is, to allow for an evolutionary inclusion of nonwhites in South African power sharing over the long term.

On the road to those major prizes, a number of lesser influences were prominent in South African and United States thinking:

1. Cooperation in the solution of southern African conflicts was eagerly sought throughout the 1970s. In the cases of the Portuguese colonies, Rhodesia/Zimbabwe, and Southwest Africa/Namibia, both the United States and South Africa had separate views of the process and the ideal end. Occasionally these views were tangential or overlapped, but much of the time they futilely attempted to persuade each other of their own views.

2. The symbolism of cooperation and conflict at the salient political level played a constant role. For the United States in its overall African policy, a great premium was placed on salient conflict, in order to maximize goodwill with the black-ruled states. Cooperation became a positive symbol only when certain U.S. domestic groups needed assurances, and when an image of potential progress on regional conflict issues needed to be projected. On the South African side, conflict was generally useful in the period before general elections, when the hard-line nationalists needed to be drawn back into the Nationalist Party fold. For South African internationalists (particularly the business community), the symbolism of cooperation was generally a top value, bespeaking the eventual reintegration of South Africa into Western councils.

3. The appearance of effectiveness in regional and global politics on both sides mattered a great deal in the 1970s. All normative issues aside, the United States and South Africa wanted to seek out the most useful diplomatic partners. Thus, South Africa used many subtle tools to build up its image as the *real* arbiter of the Rhodesian civil war. Likewise, Andrew Young, knowing the long-term need for South Africa to be reconciled with black Africa, constantly worked at being a bridge between the two camps through informal consultations. Each country sought to make itself so important to the other as to raise the opportunity cost of a failed political arrangement.

4. Given the relatively small number involved in policymaking on each side toward each other, major efforts were undertaken to reach the most influential groups: the Congress/Parliament, the media, special interest groups, and businessmen. The messages through these channels, however, confused rather than clarified the issues. The spectrum of views in both countries is equally broad, even if not equally distributed. The people outside the executive branches encompassed a wide range of political views. They played intermittent roles, but most important, did not harmonize their views, purposes, and means of achieving influence.

Several themes of historical importance need to be emphasized. The Portuguese revolution of 1974 and the subsequent devolution of the African colonies were catalytic in the United States-South African relationship. All assumptions built into Kissinger's NSSM-39 approach were destroyed, as well as many of the South Africans' assumptions about a 1,000-year buffer to the north. Given the ambiguity of United States-South African communications, however, much of the remainder of Kissinger's tenure was wasted for lack of coming to an understanding with South Africa's John Vorster. The second theme to be emphasized is the subsequent attempt by South Africa to have a major impact on U.S. thinking. As a regional power, South Africa set the agenda in the wake of the Portuguese coup very quickly and by various overt and covert methods attempted to involve the United States in that agenda, particularly in Rhodesia and Namibia. The third theme is the gradual evolution of a meaningful U.S. program for the area. Frequently, such a program has been expressed only in parts rather than a coherent whole, and frequently it has been implemented in ways apparently designed to offend. But by the early 1980s, the program restored some momentum to U.S. political activity toward South Africa.

SETTING POLICY FOUNDATIONS BY THE DEMOCRATS

The Democratic administrations of John F. Kennedy and Lyndon Johnson established the baseline of U.S. opposition to South African racial policies. Their commitments to racial justice in the United States made it inevitable that such priorities would be reflected in foreign policies as well. In large part, South Africa was not important enough in their international strategies for them to go out of their way to condemn South Africa; but when pressed, their administrations articulated clear opposition to South Africa. Most U.S. policy was made in the National Security Council staff of the White House, apparently owing to the preoccupation of the State Department's Bureau of African Affairs with building bridges to black Africa.

South Africa was increasingly on the White House agenda in 1964 due to a variety of issues. The arms embargo voted at the United Nations in late 1963 created countervailing pressures for exceptions. There were occasional indirect consultations with the South Africans over events in the Congo, as in conversations between Averell Harriman and South African Foreign Minister Hilgard Muller in late 1964. A judgment was also expected imminently from the International Court of Justice (ICJ) on the South-West Africa case; all expected the judgment to go against South Africa, and the Johnson administration expected to be in the position of supporting U.N. action against South Africa. In a memo to the president in July 1964, for instance, an aide warned that "we may be in serious crisis with South Africa next year."[1] In view of such expected tensions, the United States began developing alternate sites in Madagascar for its satellite-tracking stations, and freezing government guarantees for loans to South Africa.

A crisis did develop in 1965, but not the one they expected: the ICJ judgment did not emerge until 1966. Instead, the South Africans became very heated up about perceived hostility from the United States. Continued pressure from the United States for posting of black foreign service officers irritated the South African government, as did the ostentatiously integrated Fourth of July parties at the U.S. Embassy. The U.S.S. Independence incident occurred in May 1965, as described later. Then, in early summer, Prime Minister Verwoerd stated publicly that he would never allow integrated work forces at the joint United States-South African satellite-tracking facilities. When the United States submitted a protest over those remarks, the South Africans requested that three senior officials at the U.S. Embassy be withdrawn. With regard to the U.S.S. Independence incident, the South Africans were so keen to get their story out in public – the United States would have rather kept it quiet – that the South African Embassy gave the story to a UPI reporter for use without attribution. When ultimately splashed over newspapers in South Africa and the United States, the National Security Council staff felt obliged to find an answer for this "unprecedented" South African behavior. Three hypotheses were put forward: (1) the South African government wanted to blame the U.S. government for all the bad relations, in order to assuage the Capetown merchants deprived of business when the U.S.S. Independence did not call in port; (2) the South African government may have wanted to impress the "liberal" Cape province with its determination to press ahead on apartheid; or (3) the South African government mistakenly thought it could change U.S. government policies, perhaps because the South African Embassy talked regularly only with "Goldwater Republicans and other arch-conservatives sympathetic to their cause."[2] Given the general deterioration in relations – and questions of shipping uranium fuel rods were also poisoning the relationship – there was evidently a sense on both sides that political will was being tested.

Communication was minimal. At the time of South African Ambassador Naude's departure from Washington in January 1965, after six years of service, he expressed some bitterness about never having met Kennedy or Johnson outside polite exchanges at diplomatic receptions *en masse*.[3] Naude's hopes for a last-minute interview with Johnson, communicated through Charles Engelhard, were not to be satisfied. The closest thing to real presidential involvement came with an appeal through former President Eisenhower. In early 1965, Eisenhower was contacted by an old wartime friend, Sir Francis de Guingaud, who was chief of staff for Lord Montgomery in 1942-45 and had retired to South Africa in 1949. De Guingaud's viewpoint was perhaps best expressed in an article he wrote that spring: "What is totally incomprehensible to South Africans is the ostensible support given to these efforts [by the OAU and its Liberation Committee] by countries like Britain and the United States who have imposed arms embargoes against South Africa, which has never shown the slightest hostile intent or desire to acquire further territory."[4] Eisenhower was reportedly quite preoccupied with the need for de Guingaud to see Johnson, and put in a request to that effect.[5] A presidential decision was required, and Johnson decided that the messenger from South Africa should see Bundy instead.

The pressures within the administration on South Africa can be seen in the preliminary work for the U.N. General Assembly in 1965. The U.S. Mission to the United Nations, headed by Arthur Goldberg, was, as usual, looking for a way of taking the initiative on apartheid in the U.N. General Assembly, rather than just taking verbal beating from the African states for continuing ties to South Africa. As a result, the International Organization Bureau (IO) in the Department of State recommended to the secretary that the United States no longer guarantee U.S. investments in South Africa and discourage further private U.S. investments there. These policy changes would be saved for an opportune moment in the U.N. General Assembly debate, where Goldberg could announce them. The Commerce Department opposed the new policies, as it frequently found itself doing on South African issues in the 1960s. With Bundy's weight cast on the side of IO, however, Secretary Rusk went along with the recommendation.[6]

The remaining years of the Johnson administration could best be characterized as growing distrust between the two countries combined with impotence to affect the other. A crisis never really appeared: the South-West Africa case was dismissed by the International Court of Justice in 1966, increasing the level of black militancy in the United States over South Africa to compensate for the ICJ loss.[7] Inaccurate perceptions continued on both sides: on the occasion of the assassination of Prime Minister Verwoerd in September 1966, the National Security Council staffer in Washington quite mistakenly predicted that the successor, John Vorster, "will lead the white minority in a shrill, probably violent, witchhunt" with "mass arrests."[8] The U.S.S. Roosevelt incident, described in the chapter on military influence, testified to the bad judgment of the South African government. With the increasing amount of resources devoted to the Vietnam War, the United States was not about to take a dramatic course in South Africa: it would resolutely and publicly oppose apartheid but rule out any authoritative actions including a general trade embargo. The influence of the U.S. government could be deployed when instigated by domestic groups in the United States, but there was little strategic direction to such use of influence, and there was little evidence of coordination of influence with allies.

IN THE WAKE OF THE PORTUGUESE WITHDRAWAL

For both the United States' and South African governments, changes of government in Mozambique and Angola posed major challenges. For the South Africans, the buffer was gone and past opportunities to use the Portuguese as front-line elements of the South African defense were gone. And they were gone dramatically, with the introduction of the socialist FRELIMO (Frente de Libertacao de Mocambique) regime in Maputo and the emergence of the Marxist MPLA (Movimento Popular de Libertacao de Angola) in Luanda as the favorite of the communist-military coalition in Portugal.

The U.S. government could not have asked for a worse time to have an emerging crisis in southern Africa. The tortures of Watergate and the Nixon resignation were still fresh wounds in the body politic, and the Vietnamese negotiations were not yet completed. This was not a time to take a stand, with little in the way of resources behind U.S. diplomacy. But Henry Kissinger was not one to miss a possible solution; as a result, in early 1975 he replaced Donald Easums as assistant secretary of state for African Affairs with Nathaniel Davis, formerly ambassador to Chile and inspector-general of the Foreign Service. Kissinger had a wide range of reasons for doing so. The drift of thought in the Bureau of African Affairs for the previous ten years had been toward support of the black African view of South Africa, toward a tolerance of the emergence of African socialist governments, and for taking a "blind eye approach" to the growing involvement of Cubans and Soviets in Africa. Kissinger wanted these positions reversed and picked Davis, who was well acquainted with the covert operations of Soviet-bloc countries from his experience in Chile. Kissinger also needed somebody able to take an interventionist policy on Angola, where a civil war was rapidly developing; Mozambique was not a real concern, in that the U.S. government had informal contacts with FRELIMO for years. Finally, the Davis appointment was designed to send a message to South Africa that the need in southern Africa was for greater stability for the time being, and that the United States did not support the black African effort to keep the dominoes falling on through Rhodesia and South Africa.

The South Africans responded with understanding.[9] The OAU announced a formal resolution attacking "this deliberate affront."[10] The *New York Times* and Congressman Charles C. Diggs also attacked the nomination on various occasions.[11] Even Andrew Young, who was then a congressman from Atlanta, testified in committee hearings against Davis, even though Davis, as head of the pulpit committee of Washington's First Congregational churches, had once nominated Young as pastor.[12] Few vocal public voices came to Davis' support, although the *Washington Star* did so on February 25, 1975, just at a time when John McGoff, the Michigan publisher, was trying futilely to purchase the *Star*.[13] Much of the attack on Davis and Kissinger needs to be attributed to the fact that Kissinger's famous NSSM-39 had been widely leaked in late 1974, and this was the first visible policy development with which to express outrage over the general thrust of U.S. policy.[14]

The South African government began taking measures to shore up its new position after the Portuguese decolonization moves as well; some were predictable and some were quite innovative. The United States was to become involved in all aspects. On the domestic front, the Vorster government met pro-FRELIMO rallies held by the South African Students Organization and the Black Peoples Convention with a series of arrests and treason trials, in the fall of 1974 and spring of 1975.[15] The arrests did not have the intended deterrent effect, as evidenced by the Soweto riots in 1976. In South-West Africa/Namibia, the South Africans launched an internal constitution-drafting process that had several effects: it established the principle of South African approval for the independence of South-West Africa/Namibia; at the same time, it raised the possibility of South Africa disposing of that contested territory without consultation with the United Nations. On the Rhodesian front, Vorster decided to defuse the conflict, one whose fate seemed to be clear in light of the FRELIMO takeover of Mozambique. Thus in December 1974, the South Africans and Zambians negotiated an agreement to be accepted by Rhodesian Prime Minister Ian Smith for an early constitutional negotiation and arrival of black rule. For reasons exceedingly complex, the arrangement fell apart in early 1975, although Vorster made repeated attempts to put the deal back together.[16] On the African scene as a whole, Vorster pressed forward with his "dialogue" proposal, met positively only by a few countries, such as the Ivory Coast.[17] Toward the United States, there was still no great closeness, although much relief was expressed over the departure of Donald Easums. He was widely quoted as having said in Dar es Salaam shortly before losing his job as assistant secretary: "We are using our influence to foster change in South Africa — not to preserve the status quo."[18]

The United States allowed Vorster to pursue his initiatives on Rhodesia and toward the African states. Indeed, some credit was given to Vorster for having facilitated the December 1974 meetings in Lusaka on Rhodesia, and for Kissinger, the best way to exclude the Soviet Union appeared to be to build bridges between black and white Africa. On South-West Africa/Namibia, the United States was not about to let the United Nations do any serious damage to South Africa. Not only were sanctions opposed in Security Council meetings in mid-1975, but then Daniel Patrick Moynihan expressed an even harsher view of the United Nations for the Ford administration.[19] At the same time, Kissinger was not going to ignore key domestic U.S. constituencies. Distance from the South Africans was maintained by having Clarence Mitchell of the NAACP, serving in the U.S. delegation to the United Nations in the fall of 1975, rebuke the "barbaric" racial legislation in South Africa.[20] South Africa protested formally to the State Department over the speech. In general, Kissinger, who was almost solely responsible for U.S. foreign policy in 1975, was willing to let policy in southern Africa follow numerous different tracks, without worrying about the extent to which those with negative influences on South Africa were undercutting his efforts at influencing Vorster positively. The South African prime minister evidently could not tolerate Kissinger's maxim, "believe what I do, not what I say."

These problems of misinterpretation and multiple diplomatic tracks reached an apex during the culmination of the Angolan civil war. There are remarkably few "facts" available regarding this episode. Sometime in 1975, U.S. aid to two of the Angolan movements, the National Front for the Liberation of Angola (*FNLA*) and National Union for the Total Independence of Angola (UNITA), escalated in an effort to remove the Marxist MPLA and to counter the Cuban buildup in support of the MPLA. This covert supply to the combatants by the

CIA was accomplished via Zaire and did not involve South Africa. Jonas Savimbi's UNITA was getting aid not only from the United States; some additional help was arriving via Zambia, and at some undetermined point, additional help arrived via South Africa. When the South Africans decided to commit a small number of commando units to the Angolan war in late 1975 and early 1976, it was largely coordinated with UNITA. The extent of coordination between the United States and South Africa became a bone of historical contention. Few would care if UNITA and the FNLA had not lost, but passing out the blame is always painful. The United States also lost in the revelation of its CIA activities in late 1975 and the passage of the Clark Amendment on December 19, banning any support to parties in the Angolan civil war. And that amendment was passed just as the South African forces were within range of taking Luanda. When the South Africans immediately decided to withdraw, it was assumed by all observers that they had been in Angola in the first place at U.S. instigation. Within a few months, Vorster came out with statements to that effect, and he considered Kissinger's denials to be the last straw of double-dealing. After the Angolan episode, Kissinger became a figure of ridicule in the South African press. The South Africans were not alone in this view, for black Africans shared Vorster's view.[21]

By April 1976, Kissinger was ready to take control of U.S. policy in southern Africa, to attempt to restore U.S. influence in the area, to reverse the Cuban/Soviet momentum in the area, and to give as much attention to implementing his policies as to their design.[22] Developing a new policy after the Angola fiasco involved three steps: making peace with the black Africans angry about U.S. collusion with South Africa in Angola; getting the front-line black states to accept some general terms for a peace process in Rhodesia and South-West Africa/Namibia; and then selling the terms to South Africa, which would force a diplomatic settlement with Smith in Rhodesia and the South-West Africa/Namibia territory. Kissinger was even careful to cover his domestic tracks on this approach: Senator Charles Percy, of rising rank on the Foreign Relations Committee, took a fact-finding trip to southern Africa in April; key Democrats, such as Senator George McGovern, were sufficiently closely informed to give public support to Kissinger's early moves. Kissinger neglected only his right flank, and he rapidly became vulnerable to the galloping momentum of Ronald Reagan's 1976 presidential attempt.[23]

Kissinger's first major move was a speech in Lusaka, Zambia, in which he hoped to speak primarily to the black African states, concerning South Africa, his program of negotiations over Rhodesia, and a definite timetable for independence for South-West Africa/Namibia. With regard to South Africa, Kissinger remarked: "Our policy toward South Africa is based upon the premise that within a reasonable time we shall see a clear evolution toward equality of opportunity and basic human rights for all South Africans. The United States will exercise all its efforts in that direction. We urge the government of South Africa to make that premise a reality." He then went on to challenge South Africa to show its good faith "by using its influence in Salisbury to promote a rapid negotiated settlement for majority rule in Rhodesia."[24] His intended audience in black Africa was listening, but so were those who would not take his rhetoric seriously. Ronald Reagan began blasting Kissinger's foreign policy and winning presidential primaries in Texas, Indiana, Georgia, and Alabama. South African media followed both Kissinger and the Reagan reaction with great interest.[25] But when Kissinger returned to Washington, he reported to the Senate Foreign Relations Committee that he had a deal in his pocket with the black front-line states and by mid-May had begun negotiating with South Africa's ambassador in Washington, Pik Botha. Pretoria was greatly heartened by this opening of negotiations, even though the tradeoff was not entirely to its liking. Kissinger argued that primary responsibility for bringing Smith to a transfer of power in Rhodesia would be Vorster's, if only because Kissinger had to maintain his credibility with the black states already signed on to the Kissinger deal. At the same time, Kissinger offered soothing words on South-West Africa/Namibia, "that the U.S. could declare itself prepared officially to acknowledge the current efforts to attain a peaceful settlement there," referring to the South African-supported Turnhalle constitutional talks.[26] President Ford even got in his gesture of friendship for South Africa (as well as beating off the Reagan challenge) by suggesting a possible meeting with Vorster in response to a reporter's question.[27] As preliminary talks moved forward between Pik Botha and Kissinger, by June it was announced that Kissinger would meet with Vorster in West Germany in the later part of the month.

A frantic four months of meetings then ensued, with Kissinger flying to all parts of Africa and Europe to hold meetings and to hold together his fractious coalition necessary to bring peace to Rhodesia. Meetings were held with Vorster in West Germany, in Zurich, and then in South Africa itself. Vorster, however, was virtually crippled from the start by the outbreak of the Soweto riots just two days before the meetings in Germany. Kissinger had no intention of raising the South African problem in discussions with Vorster — but the riots were traumatic for Vorster. He responded very slowly and hesitantly to the riots and had little political energy left for pressuring Ian Smith. At the same time, the Soweto riots raised the price for the black front-line states to stay in the negotiations. At the end of negotiations, when Vorster and Smith had finally been pinned down to a deal during long meetings in South Africa during September, it was two key black states that withdrew from Kissinger's plan for regional peace.

Kissinger's effort amply illustrated the limited scope of U.S. influence in the region. One journalist noted in mid-1976 that "U.S. policy is still largely rhetoric, our diplomacy lacking both the will and the ability to take measures that would genuinely affect the current descent of the region into violence or truly change our position there."[28] For what purpose could the limited influence of the United States then be deployed? By and large, the United States was limited to education of the parties, not having the resources to force solutions to the deeply rooted conflicts of the region. Kissinger, too, had few long-term interests in Africa. Influence, then, was valued for short-term goals (for example, peace in Rhodesia by giving more time to South Africa on Namibia) and the deals struck evidently did not last long enough to be put into effect. Little emphasis, then, was placed on the use of influence for the long-term goals of racial justice in the region and in South Africa; more immediate goals of peace and order became the objects of influence.

When pressed by the need for a settlement in Rhodesia, even Kissinger was not able to influence each of the parties. In the wake of his failure in late 1976, he appeared to blame the black Africans and his failed influence over them; but in part, he missed the point. The black African states both thought they could get a better deal from a potential Carter administration, and disapproved of the extent of the dialogue between the South Africans and Kissinger. Kissinger also lacked the kind of back-up staff to maneuver among the multiple hazards of a negotiation on southern African issues. The Bureau of African Affairs of the State Department was said to have virtually no expertise on white Africa, owing to its "clientist" approach to black Africa.[29] The experience of the abortive 1976 negotiations highlighted the need for a more sophisticated approach to South Africa, but at a time when South Africa, badly wounded politically by the Soweto riots, turned inward, less interested in responding to initiatives from the outside world. Even though Kissinger had negotiated a package deal of reasonable satisfaction to the South Africans,[30] the departure of the Ford administration and the internal problems of South Africa ensured the cancelling of that deal.

THE BLOOMING CARTER ADMINISTRATION INITIATIVE

The election of Jimmy Carter was recognized by all sides as likely to occasion a departure from past practice in United States-South African relations. A wide range of factors were thought to play a role in his view of South Africa: his Southern background, the role of the black community in his election, his close advisor Andrew Young, his religious fundamentalism, his advocacy of human rights and open diplomacy during the campaign, his lack of overseas experience, and his condemnations of Soviet imperialism in Angola and elsewhere. Needless to say, all these characteristics added up to an inconsistent portrait; after Election Day, when asked if he were worried about Carter, Vorster replied that it was "more a question of wondering rather than worrying."[31] Carter's discussions of influence on southern African affairs were necessarily ambiguous, on occasion he referred to using "American clout."[32] Much of that clout appeared to consist of the capital and technology that the United States could supply for development of South Africa's industrial potential, as well as the opportunity for South Africa to rejoin the West "as a member of standing and repute."[33] He also tended to discount boycotts as ineffective.

h African observers even took miscalculated comfort in the relative ummportance of the region in U.S. policy.[34] But they did not realize that such priorities would result in African policy being farmed out to the U.S. mission to the United Nations, under Andrew Young, where South Africa received much harsher treatment than if it had been firmly under the wing of the White House. The most critical element, though, was recognized by many and expressed in public only by a few: that the heart of the Carter administration was profoundly anti-South African. It was the heart that would allow Andrew Young to call the South Africans "racist" and the South African government "illegitimate" and let him remain in office. The heart of the administration was reflected in the Democratic Party platform, which was read by few South Africans but the most perceptive. They saw the support for "unequivocal and concrete support of majority rule in Southern Africa" to be a denial of recognition to the independent homelands, a tightened arms embargo, and a denial of tax credits and advantages for U.S. businesses in South Africa. A few were willing to say, "It is as well to prepare for the worst."[35] Somewhat more elliptically, the prime minister was profoundly uncheerful in his New Year's message about the direction of the United States: "The West has not only lost the initiative, is not only on the defensive everywhere but what is saddest of all, it has lost the will to take a firm stand against the ever increasing menace."[36] The first measures of the Carter administration reinforced his beliefs.

The credibility of the South Africans was quickly strained by Andrew Young's position on southern Africa after he became the U.S. ambassador to the U.N. Not only did he describe the Cubans as a stablizing force in Angola, but he also said that the South Africans would simply have to lean on Salisbury for a settlement in that civil war and that the United States would bring "all the pressure in the world" on Vorster to do just that. South African opinion was spinning in circles: having just disposed of Kissinger's allegedly excessive conspiratorial approach to diplomacy, they now had to contend with Young's outspoken diplomatic style. More substantially, the South African interest in joining forces with U.S. diplomacy was rapidly withering. Fanie Botha, who was the minister of mines, gave a speech in February 1977 that was meant to be a warning to the United States (although widely ignored as well) when he offered a South African deal: "The West cannot depend on future supplies of minerals if South Africa cannot depend on future supplies of capital."[37] Additional segments of the Nationalist Party structure were getting restive about pursuing cooperation with the United States, and various forms of leverage were considered for the creation of a separate course for South Africa. What made this development most troublesome for Young was that his view was based on the premise that South Africa fundamentally needed and wanted respectability from the West, specifically the United States. The interest of the South African elite in such an acceptance, which was never universal, was to be sorely tested by the behavior of Young. In April, the putative successor to Vorster in the Nationalist Party, Connie Mulder, made a lengthy speech in Parliament with veiled allusions to finding new friends in the world; some listeners, such as Parliament member Helen Suzman, even interpreted his speech as an argument for a Chinese-South African alliance. Mulder insisted he was thinking only of various anti-Marxist and anti-United States countries.[38]

But before South Africa began any major moves, there were attempts to move the relationship away from harsh rhetoric. Denis Worrall, one of South Africa's most distinguished liberals, argued for ignoring the arguments and making concrete progress on a South African version of majority rule. U.S. friends of South Africa were even doubting the value of cooperation with an unstable South Africa, he noted, and that made a new political compact necessary in the very near future.[39] The U.S. State Department, in cooperation with Ambassador Donald McHenry of Young's staff, was working on a different approach to the Namibian problem. Gone was the Kissinger formula of using South-West Africa/Namibia as a bargaining chip. The problem was to be attacked in its own right, and the internal Turnhalle constitutional process initiated by the South Africans, which was scheduled to lead to independence by the end of 1978, was to be terminated. The format of the demarche to the South Africans was to become familiar: the U.S. ambassador in Pretoria, accompanied by his colleagues from France, Britain, Germany, and Canada, called on Vorster and urged both an end to the Turnhalle and new negotiations involving the United Nations. At the initial meeting, on April 7, 1977, the results were typically ambiguous.[40] But in this manner the five-country approach on the Namibian issue became standard operating procedure.

The Carter administration was not yet ready to let go of the public track, however, and the propaganda war escalated. In the Congress, Congressman Charles Diggs inspired a resolution of condemnation for the first homeland given "independence" by the South African government, the Transkei, but the resolution was beaten back with some help from South African lobbyists.[41] The executive branch decided to invoke some high-level pressure on South Africa and scheduled a meeting for Vice-President Walter Mondale with the South African prime minister in May. Nothing substantive was expected of the meeting, unless the Carter administration somehow thought that the South African would fly a white flag of surrender, but Mondale got in some verbal jabs at Vorster that would dog U.S. diplomacy in the region for the remainder of the 1970s. His famous "one man-one vote" definition of democracy in South Africa caused a drastic lurch rightward of white public opinion in South Africa. Perhaps more fundamentally, he carried a message from Carter that the fundamental view of southern Africa was "no deal": "There was a need for progress on all three issues: majority rule in Rhodesia and Namibia, and a progressive transformation of South African society to the same end." Vorster's response was predictable, given this abandonment of Kissinger's approach: if the United States had nothing to offer South America, then there would be no pressure on Smith.[42]

The emphasis of U.S. policy — and the focus of influence — thus became racial justice once again, which was in line with the policies of the earlier

Democratic administrations. The sacrifice of short-term goals in the late 1970s, however, had a much more dramatic effect; after all, very active guerrilla wars were ongoing in both Rhodesia and Namibia, and the costs of removing the United States from its role of arbiter of those wars could be considerable. The Carter administration was reluctant to recognize the tradeoffs between long-term and short-term goals. The focus on racial justice in all three countries simultaneously left little room for negotiation with the South Africans.

The resultant hardening of Afrikaner opinion was evident in all spheres. Secretary for Information Eschel Rhoodie, who would later achieve notoriety, took out an advertisement in the *Washington Post* to attack reporting on South Africa by that newspaper.[43] Foreign Minister Pik Botha was busy using whatever outlets were possible to decry the damage being done to the United States-South African dialogue, including interviews with C. L. Sulzberger of the *New York Times* and speeches to an investment seminar in New York.[44] Even the most forceful internal critics of Afrikanerdom, such as the author Alan Paton, commented that the United States had gone too far, for he believed that the Afrikaner Nationalist would rather choose the destruction of Afrikanerdom than accept majority rule. He urged that the United States consider a federal or confederal solution for South Africa.[45]

As on many other issues, the Carter administration pursued many tracks at the same time with South Africa. Some voices were quite shrill, unpredictable, and likely to have an adverse impact on South Africa; here one has to include Andrew Young and his approaches to the Rhodesian issue. His deputy, Donald McHenry, attempted to influence the South Africans in a very different way on South-West Africa/Namibia. McHenry, always having the appearance of the foreign service officer he once was, doggedly put together the Western Five approach in Namibia, kept it going, did his homework, and constantly leaned on the South Africans to take one more small step toward the independence of Namibia. The South Africans actually liked Young more than McHenry, who was too calculating for their taste, and over time they decided that he had made up his mind exactly what the final settlement in Namibia should be: a handover to SWAPO under U.N. auspices. The third track belonged to Secretary of State Cyrus Vance, who felt obliged repeatedly to venture into African policy with a major speech, justifying the policies of Young and McHenry by placing them in a traditional, historical context. His intention appeared to be to calm, and he was never part of the rhetorical wars between the United States and South Africa.

In July 1977, for instance, Vance made his first major address on Africa, to the NAACP Convention in St. Louis. He first lowered expectations: "We cannot impose solutions in southern Africa. We cannot dictate terms to any of the parties; our leverage is limited." At the same time, he returned to the bridge-building theme that enticed Henry Kissinger into the African fray in 1976: "But we are among the few governments in the world that can talk to both black and white Africans frankly and yet with a measure of trust." And then finally

Young and McHenry affirmed Vance's position:

> Some have argued that apartheid in South Africa should be ignored for the time being, in order to concentrate on achieving progress on Rhodesia and Namibia. Such a policy would be wrong and would not work. It would be blind to the reality that the beginning of progress must be made soon within South Africa, if there is to be a possibility of peaceful solutions in the long run. It could mislead the South Africans about our real concerns. It would prejudice our relations with our African friends. It would do a disservice to our own beliefs. And it would discourage those of all races who are working for peaceful progress within South Africa.[46]

Vance went on to elaborate the specific policies being undertaken on the three issues in southern Africa, and in each case pulled back from the most extreme rhetoric used by other administration officials such as Mondale or Young. In the Carter game plan, Vance was supposed to persuade, not threaten. But given Vance's rare involvement on African issues, South Africa was most conscious of and resented the frequent attacks by Young.

In its own curious way, South Africa was dealing with the issue of constitutional change. Professors from conservative Afrikaner universities were taking study trips to the United States to discuss constitutional structures, in particular, the implications of racial diversity for effective political structures. Those close to the government interested in the incorporation of nonwhites into political power sharing knew from experience that the best way to make progress was to *not* talk about it publicly. Afrikaner politics – and the issue here was the abdication of some power by the Afrikaners – had been secretive for centuries. And discussions were generally not conducted in English, putting them beyond the comprehension of U.S. journalists and policymakers. A few U.S. organizations such as the American-African Affairs Association, made attempts to communicate the subterranean political ferment in South Africa to people in the United States, but were largely unsuccessful. U.S. policymakers evinced no recognition of, nor interest in, such discussions, even when ideas surfaced from maverick Afrikaner politicians like Piet Koornhof, the minister of sport, who suggested in mid-1977 in a speech that South Africa consider a Swiss-style cantonal system.

In early August, Vance pressed for a more constrictive approach, in another of the quick up-and-down sequences that plagued United States-South African relations. He was just wrapping up the latest Rhodesian peace proposal with Britain's Foreign Minister David Owen. This was completed on August 12, with consultations in London involving the two of them and Pik Botha.[47] Vorster's cooperation in bringing Smith and Muzorewa to the settlement negotiations would have been very helpful. In the subsequent days, however, the Kalahari nuclear incident (described in a subsequent chapter) intervened, once again poisoning ties between the two countries. The U.S. officials, keeping their eyes on the Rhodesian problem, decided to put aside the nuclear issue in an effort to maintain Vorster's pressure on Smith. On August 26, for instance, none other than Young admonished a United Nations-sponsored conference on apartheid that "the United States would not be bludgeoned into accepting unenforceable sanctions against South Africa."[48] In the meantime, Vorster had made his decision not to cooperate with the United States, and called a general election for November 30 to reaffirm his mandate. In the election atmosphere, the rhetoric of the South African government naturally became more shrill in its attitude against the United States; major speeches by Vorster and Pik Botha were widely disseminated for domestic consumption, in appearances before the Cape National Party congress, University of The Free State in Bloemfontein, and the American Businessmen's Luncheon Club in Johannesburg. The last organization named gave him a standing ovation after his rebuke of the United States.[49] When Carter made a major peace overture to Vorster in a U.N. speech on October 5, thanking South Africa for its "cooperation" on Rhodesia, Vorster's response was to undertake the most important crackdown on black consciousness leaders (and associated whites) yet known in South Africa. Carter's low-keyed response was to recall the U.S. ambassador for consultations. Mondale, in the meantime, gave a very conciliatory interview to a Johannesburg reporter, transparently intended for South African consumption, which simply provoked more South African attacks on him as attempting to manipulate the South African general elections.

With the opening of a U.N. Security Council debate on the South African arrests, the Carter administration knew it would have to take measures.[50] Eventually these steps were decided on:

(1) Withdrawal of the U.S. naval attaché from Pretoria;
(2) Recall of the U.S. commercial officer in Johannesburg;
(3) Ban exports of spares and maintenance for past military shipments;
(4) Ban export of all "gray-area" military items, that is, civilian goods potentially for use by the military.
(5) However, any African-sponsored resolutions reaching beyond the above would be vetoed.[51]

The South Africans appeared to be largely unimpressed by these steps: the issues of representation were apparently just waiting for a trigger, having been written into the Democratic Party platform of 1976, and South Africa was getting virtually all useful military imports from Israel, France, or clandestine sources. The cutoff of U.S. supplies actually bolstered Vorster's reelection campaign. Young was pressed in subsequent public appearances about the purpose of the sanctions: "All we are trying to do in sanctions is say that we are prepared to try to help the more creative, conscientious, moderate leadership to develop immediately." Additionally, "an arms boycott is more effective than a total economic blockade because it makes it uncomfortable for South Africans without forcing them to become completely independent."[52]

In this manner, the flexibility of a new U.S. administration on foreign policy issues was used up. By late 1977, Vorster had taken his measure of the Carter administration and found it severely wanting. The senior U.S. officials, on the other hand, had finally evolved a division of responsibility and a set of policy priorities that naturally hardened like concrete. The U.S. rhetoric cooled down as the policy toward South Africa became harder. South Africa responded in the way adversity is dealt with: batten down the hatches, arrest the most dangerous opposition, rally the troops through a general election, and hope to ride through three more stormy years of Jimmy Carter.

THE TURBULENT YEARS

Given the fixed positions taken by the United States and South Africa by the end of 1977, the remaining three years of the Carter administration could have been quite boring for both sides. Many expected that it would be. But the uncontrollable elements in southern Africa and in the United States ensured that the time was turbulent, even if little visible progress was made on harmonizing their policies.

The black community in the United States began to split on the issue of influence. In early 1977, the Reverend Leon Sullivan of Philadelphia, also a member of the Board of Directors of General Motors, pioneered a plan for the integration of United States-owned plants in South Africa. Most of the Fortune 500 corporations signed up with the Sullivan Plan, since it provided some protection against assaults on corporate morality in the United States, as well as some protection against potential adverse reaction in South Africa to integrationist steps. The Sullivan manifesto is explored further in Chapter 4. In January 1978, however, much of the black community split with Sullivan, when the NAACP issued a policy statement calling for a total withdrawal of U.S. investment. In part, the NAACP was a response to the October 1977 crackdown in South Africa, and it was also an extension of negative preliminary evaluations of the effects of the Sullivan code.[53]

South Africa was not really interested in external advice and was taking its own path on southern African issues by cultivating influential people in the United States who might be helpful. Governor Meldrim Thompson of New Hampshire was given a red-carpet welcome and tour in January 1978. Dr. Ernest Lefever, director of the Ethics and Public Policy Center at Georgetown University (and later a controversial nominee of President Ronald Reagan to the human rights post in the State Department) made a visit given prominence in April. In the meantime, the new South African structure in the region was moving forward. The internal Rhodesian settlement between Smith and Muzorewa was negotiated in March to Pretoria's satisfaction. In South-West Africa/Namibia, the South African military pounded SWAPO bases in Angola; after the raid and the inevitable U.S. protest, Defense Minister P. W. Botha happily rejected the

United States: "South Africa would not be intimidated and would strike again if its security was threatened."[54]

In an effort to dislodge the South Africans, Carter and Vance offered several diplomatic openings. To the graduating cadets at Annapolis, Carter made an offer to the Soviet Union to join the United States in helping to solve the Rhodesian and South-West African/Namibian conflicts. Not only did this signal confuse the South Africans, but it alarmed them as much as the Vance-Gromyko statement on the Middle East startled the Israelis. The Carter move was perceived as a "radical shift in policy" and likely to end cooperation with the South African government.[55] After all, the principal value to the South Africans remaining in the U.S. tie was a shared anti-Soviet bias in foreign policy. If the United States abandoned that, the South Africans were likely to turn away even more substantially. Mr. Vance's moderating tone, on the other hand, was both badly designed and patronizing in tone; the South Africans were further alienated. Vance's basic message was: "Our policy towards South Africa should not be misunderstood. We have no wish to see the whites driven from the homes of their forebears." The South African Broadcasting Corporation was quick to take offense: "There is no power on earth (let alone Fidel Castro's mercenaries) that can drive the white man from the home of his forebears — established in an unsettled country more than three centuries ago at a time when Mr. Vance's forebears were establishing theirs in North America. The white man has every entitlement (in no way dependent on Washington's wishes) to remain here."[56] These statements by the top of the U.S. administration were not ignored by the new U.S. ambassador, William B. Edmondson, who arrived in the summer. His background was that of a career diplomat with ambassadorial appointments in various African countries, and he was given instructions to carry out the policy of deliberate pressure on Pretoria.[57]

The U.S. approach to South Africa in 1978 was doomed to failure, however, by several circumstances beyond the control of Jimmy Carter. On the one hand, there were already numerous people in the U.S. political system ready to undertake the 1980 presidential campaign, and the liability represented by Andrew Young made South African policy a ready target for emerging contenders. In August 1978, for instance, John Connally made a well-publicized journey to South Africa to denounce economic sanctions and Carter's policies in general, as well as to announce a new spirit coming: "We can't dictate to you. This view accords with most of the people back home. You are going to see the U.S. Congress reflecting this view and it will become more and more manifest as time goes by."[58]

Carter was also doomed by the unfolding drama of scandal in South Africa. With parallels to Watergate that frequently frightened spectators, the South African political system gradually revealed a set of scandals that reached to the highest levels, and that involved some people from the U.S. political scene as well. The problem began rather innocuously, involving a few thousand dollars, when it was revealed that South African sugar interests had been passing favors and money to a number of U.S. congressmen in charge of establishing import quotas for sugar into the United States. Among those named were W. R. Poage (Texas Democrat, then chairman of the House Agriculture Committee), John J. Flynt, Jr. (Georgia Democrat, then chairman of the House Ethics Committee), and William C. Wampler (Virginia Republican on the House Agriculture Committee). The Sugar Association was involved in the relatively low-level crime of giving away travel tickets and campaign contributions that were unreported, but it set the scene for the major drama that followed.[59] In September, the president of South Africa died, and there was some mild surprise when B. J. Vorster, the prime minister, indicated that he would like to be named to the largely ceremonial post of president. Some remarked, yes, the prime minister had not been in good health for some time and could use a less strenuous form of political involvement; but fundamentally, it was contrary to Nationalist tradition for an activist leader like Vorster to voluntarily relinquish such extensive powers. Vorster tried to clean shop as he left, notifying the United States that South Africa definitively rejected the U.N. plan for South-West Africa/Namibia. In Vorster's place, the Nationalist Party elected P. W. Botha, who was minister of defense and, most surprising, head of the relatively weak Cape Province branch of the Nationalist Party. Botha was marked as a liberal in South African politics — both for being from the Cape and for pioneering integration of the armed forces — although some people in the United States did not get the message. Andrew Young welcomed the appointment by saying that Botha would have to "be dragged kicking and screaming into the 20th century." Young appeared to be disappointed that the personable Pik Botha, foreign minister, was not successful in a briefly blooming campaign to be prime minister. P. W. Botha (called "peevee" [Afrikaans] for his initials) did not know what a time bomb he had inherited, but it began to emerge in the form of the "information scandal," the five-year plan by the secretary for information, Eschel Rhoodie, to subvert the English-language press in South Africa, Britain, and the United States.

The last U.S. effort to involve South Africa in a dialogue before the storm really broke came in October 1978 with a trip to South Africa by Vance. He was willing to introduce the hated concept of linkage, hated because Kissinger had used it in the 1976 shuttle diplomacy in Southern Africa, and because it implied a let-up of pressure on South Africa's internal change process in exchange for Pretoria's help in Rhodesia and South-West Africa/Namibia. There was clearly dissent within the State Department on this tactic: Donald McHenry was noticed by journalists to be visibly sulking, and lesser members of the delegations were heard to mutter complaints about Vance "giving away the store to the South Africans."[60] In a concrete sense, the linkage used was a handwritten letter from Carter to P. W. Botha, carried by Vance, and communicating a message that Botha was welcome to visit Washington (which carries some kind of intangible blessings) if progress could be made on Namibia. The South Africans leaked the invitation, and did nothing further on South-West Africa/Namibia, except to express willingness to discuss the matter further with the Western Five ambassadors' group.

The denouncement of United States-South African cooperation came in April-May 1979, with the resignation of President John Vorster due to the scandal and the expulsion of U.S. military attachés from South Africa. The escalation of the information scandal in the early months of 1979 gradually entrapped higher and higher ranking officials in the South African government. The relevance of this scandal to the United States was twofold: (1) the use of funds from the Information Department given to U.S. publisher John McGoff to try to buy the *Washington Star*; he failed, and bought the *Sacramento Union* instead; and (2) the secret passing of funds to nongovernmental South African organizations, which then attempted to influence U.S. opinion with the disclaimer of not representing the South African government. In this latter category would be included secret grants to the Institute for the Study of Plural Societies (University of Pretoria), the Southern African Freedom Foundation, and the Centre for International Politics (Potchefstroom University). Initially, the scandal unfolded because the secretary for information, Eschel Rhoodie, was clearly living at a standard far beyond his civil service salary. Internal government inquiries revealed major irregularities in his accounting, with funds siphoned off for personal use. Rhoodie was no sooner confronted with the facts than he implicated his boss, Connie Mulder, and fled the country for France.

With the implication of Mulder, the heir-apparent to leadership of the Nationalist Party, the scandal took on entirely new dimensions: above all, the political leadership of the Nationalist Party had been respected for personal honesty. The whole affair was promptly renamed "Muldergate," and he appeared willing to take the rap, even when he lost his ministry and resigned from the Parliament. A Parliamentary inquiry headed by Judge Rudolph Erasmus, however, refused to let the matter drop and ended up implicating both the head of the secret service, Hendrik van den Bergh, and the state president, J. B. Vorster. Vorster's resignation did not come until June 4, 1979.[61] The effect of the scandal was not only to paralyze South African diplomacy during its unfolding, but to cause the South African leadership to lose all sense of momentum in the wake of the scandal, given the elimination of several of its strongest personalities.

The implications of the information scandal were also interesting in terms of the exercise of influence. It represented an attempt to penetrate the internal political process of the United States in a relatively sophisticated fashion, and to force a change in U.S. policies toward South Africa through domestic channels. It was perhaps not a surprising development, in that the U.S. demands on South Africa amounted to an abdication of internal political authority — and the South Africans might be expected to respond in kind. In addition, since the normal channels of influence such as diplomatic bargaining had been closed down by the Carter administration, the South Africans naturally turned to more indirect forms of influence. In effect, the intertwined destinies of the two countries ensure that the governments will attempt to influence one another; developments on one side or the other, however, will deviate that quest for influence in various unusual directions.

In April, just before the culmination of the scandal, the prime minister instigated a fight with the United States for unknown reasons. The *cause célèbre* was the revelation of a spy camera underneath the seat of the pilot in the plane belonging to the U.S. ambassador. Three of the four U.S. military attachés stationed in Pretoria were expelled; in exchange, the United States ordered the removal of all but one military attaché in Washington. Specualtion naturally arose over the reasons for a highly public incident that would in normal times be treated circumspectly. A variety of reasons were put forward:

(1) The need to distract the South African general public from Muldergate, and a foreign enemy was the means to do that.[62]

(2) The need to break off the talks with the Western Five ambassadors (including Donald McHenry of the United States) over South-West Africa/ Namibia. In fact, in the previous two weeks, South Africa had tried to frighten off the United States on those negotiations on two occasions: by accusing the United States of deceit and double-dealing in the negotiations and by accusing the leader of the South African Parliamentary opposition, Colin Eglin, of indiscreet contacts with McHenry.[63]

(3) As a necessary preliminary step for realignment of South Africa to a truly "neutral" position. It was emerging during Botha's first six months as prime minister that he wanted a new overall strategy (political and economic) for South Africa's diplomacy; this was eventually to be enunciated as a "constellation of southern African states." For Botha, it is possible that it was felt necessary that the hopes of some South Africans to "return to the Western fold" be thoroughly shattered. By April's incidents, it had become standard to describe the United States as an "enemy."[64] The way that Botha was describing this policy by August was: "We will in the future adopt a policy of qualified neutrality. South Africa could avoid any firm commitment with the major powers and instead come to an arrangement with middle power countries, which showed the same philosophy with South Africa."[65]

For whatever reason the spy plane flap occurred, it sundered any real possibilities for continuing close negotiations on issues in southern Africa. U.S. diplomacy might have persevered except for two factors: the resignation of Andrew Young in August 1979, and the onset of the presidential race season, which relegated southern Africa to the private sector for any interest and activity. Control of the Rhodesian issue had been taken over by the strong-willed leaders in Britain, Margaret Thatcher and Lord Carrington. Despite all the Carter administration efforts to introduce new ideas and approaches for U.S. policy toward South Africa, a major survey of elite opinion at mid-1979 indicated that the majority was in favor of maintaining at least normal political and economic relations with South Africa. And the survey results emphasized the perpetuation of the old dilemma: the United States being in favor of pressuring South Africa to give blacks greater rights, but being unable to agree on how to do it.[66]

The U.S. private sector was more than willing to provide answers for South Africa's dilemmas, even if such answers were frequently quite one-sided. Senator Paul Tsongas was sent to the southern African region in January 1980 to generate some publicity for U.S. recognition of Angola and greater pressure on South Africa for change. In February, the Ciskei homeland in South Africa announced that it would *not* accept independence from Pretoria, in large part convinced to do so by two U.S. academics serving on a special Ciskei commission.[67] And the Study Commission on U.S. Policy Toward Southern Africa (funded by the Rockefeller Foundation for $2 million and headed by Ford Foundation President Franklin Thomas) struggled on toward a conclusion that was not to arrive until June 1981, but included several trips to South Africa in 1980. The South African government took little cognizance of their trips, although reformist South Africans apparently appreciated the interest thereby indicated by U.S. elite opinion.

At the official level, the diplomatic warfare so publicly noticed in April 1979 continued quietly in 1980 — for what purpose, nobody could say. The U.S. government accused the South Africans of spending $20 million annually in the United States on "propaganda." The South Africans regularly harrassed U.S. International Communications Agency (USICA) operations; USICA had a staff of 9 U.S. citizens and 30 South Africans in Pretoria alone, with additional staff in Johannesburg, Capetown, and Durban. The police, for instance, would visibly monitor attendees at a showing of the television program "Roots" in the Pretoria ICA Center. In retaliation, the U.S. government delayed the South African applications for honorary consulates in the United States in 1979 and 1980. The United States also dispatched State Department personnel as observers to "political trials" in South Africa, in order to build credibility with the black community.[68] All these measures, though, were apparently without strategic purpose. All eyes were basically focussed on the elections in Rhodesia, where Robert Mugabe received a solid mandate. Even the Namibian talks ground to a stop with South Africa effectively halting the talks in order to assess the outcome in Rhodesia and to hope for a more amenable administration in Washington as a result of the 1980 election.

THE CONFUSION OF EUPHORIA

The results of the elections in the United States in November 1980 exceeded the fondest hopes of South Africans of moderate and reformist stripe. The government took great heart from the evident drift in U.S. political thinking, expressed not only in Ronald Reagan's election but also in the control of the Senate by the Republicans (including the defeat of a *bête noire* for the South Africans, Senator Dick Clark of Iowa). The editorial of Radio South Africa opened with "We comment on a mighty victory." The government went on to express hope for a virtual alliance: "Mr. Reagan himself has said there should be an alignment between the United States and all countries which oppose Soviet expansionism and who have advocated military assistance to anti-Marxist forces whether in Afghanistan or Angola."[69] The mantle to be jointly worn by the United States and South Africa was soon described in even brighter terms: "The conservative intellectuals spoke first for the silent majority; now the silent majority, in resounding affirmation of America's true nature, has spoken for itself. It has called Mr. Reagan to problems which are immense almost beyond imagination but it is possible again now to imagine that the Western Christian culture will prevail over communism."[70] Such imagery had not been heard in South African media since the original victory of the Nationalist Party in 1948.

Early pronouncements of the Reagan administration during the transition period, to the extent that South Africa was a focus of position papers, put U.S. policy into another perspective. While the South Africans remained generally positive to the thrust of the views of Reagan, Secretary of State Haig, and Assistant Secretary of State for African Affairs Chester A. Crocker, they were also aware that the new order would not have any positive feelings about the continuation of apartheid.[71] What was certain was that all southern African policies of the Carter administration were up for review, and indeed all personnel were likely to lose their jobs (the influence of Senator Jesse Helms of North Carolina was visible here), which left the South Africans rather in the dark about likely future policies in early 1981.[72]

What emerged in the first six months of relations between a reform-oriented government in Pretoria and the new conservative establishment in Washington was a pattern of negotiations reflecting remarkably equal status between the parties. The opportunities for leverage on each other were evidently quite minimal after years of growing hostility, although there were frequent frank discussions of their ability to change views on opposite sides. The priority on the United States' side appeared to be to reestablish some basis for South African trust in U.S. diplomacy. Initially, this involved backing away from the U.N. plan for Namibia (and attempting to insert some constitutional guarantees for whites in imitation of Zimbabwe), inviting Foreign Minister Pik Botha to Washington for talks with Haig and Reagan, and normalizing the broken military attaché relationship. There was much dissent from this approach in the U.S. camp, with internal opposition in the Africa Bureau of the State Department taking the time-honored approach of leaking memos to the press.[73] A summation of the U.S. view was that even though the two governments "may continue to differ on apartheid, the U.S. can cooperate with a society undergoing constructive change."[74]

The South African government's view necessarily reflected both pleasure at the Reagan election and many years of perceived injustices at the hands of Washington. Those in control of the pace of change within South Africa argued that Reagan would have no more influence on race issues than had Carter. Others, particularly those outside the government in favor of speedier change in racial policies, argued that "the present reform measures wouldn't have happened if it weren't for international pressure." Such people did not like Carter's constant coercive approach but did express appreciation for approaches like the Sullivan code.[75] The effect of Reagan's initially friendly gestures, then, had different impacts on the South African audiences. Internationalists quickly saw the opening as useful in domestic battles. As the *Diamond Fields Advertiser* editorialized on March 6:

> South Africa must not delude itself that pressure for change away from apartheid will decrease. Apartheid remains abhorrent to Americans and the change of approach is obviously aimed at encouraging the elimination of racial discrimination in South Africa. The support the United States will give us is therefore conditional to what the government is prepared to do to provide a square deal for all South Africans. The ball is in our court.[76]

The South Africans thus became engaged in two simultaneous agendas in talks in Washington and Pretoria: (1) the redress of old grievances (military attachés, exchange of intelligence, nuclear fuel supplies, honorary consuls in the United States) and (2) the possibility of building a democratic order in southern Africa where the first litmus test would be on Namibia. Quite early in the administration, therefore, the United States began taking measures on the first agenda in order to keep the South Africans on the second track as well. In terms of persuading both moderate and conservative South Africans of U.S. goodwill, the Reagan administration did remarkably well in the first months; newspapers of all stripes were unusually gratified over Foreign Minister Pik Botha's trip to Washington in May 1981. Indeed, some of the English-speaking press worried over the undue cordiality, in possibly straining U.S. credibility with the black-ruled states:

> The best way to help the Americans get the plan [on Namibia] through is to enable them to show that they have leverage on this country. In the parlance of these negotiations the frontline states have long been in a position to "deliver" SWAPO, while the inability of the Western Five to "deliver" South Africa has led to their losing credibility as brokers who can actually achieve anything.[77]

In this case, U.S. leverage had diminished to the point where South Africans anxious for change actually wanted to increase U.S. influence, and said so publicly.[78]

A retrospective look at the political influence exercised by South Africa and the United States on each other in the course of 20 years provides some useful insights. Quite clearly, the size of a political system is not related to its ability to influence another country. The constantly growing disparity between the evident power in military and economic terms could not be translated into political influence. To a larger extent, it appears from the South African-United States relationship that political influence is determined more by opportunities than by intentions. That is to say, the weakness and openness of a particular political system will leave it vulnerable to the influence vectors constantly in the international environment. The U.S. government, for instance, has never changed its policy of active opposition to South African racial policies; thus the intent to influence has consistently been present over a period of several decades. Likewise, a clear and consistent policy of the South Africans (with very rare exceptions) has been to establish links with the United States that would endow political legitimacy despite the variance in race policies. In this mutual contest to avoid vulnerability, the South Africans have probably been marginally more successful than the United States. The South Africans have demonstrated remarkable adaptation mechanisms to shake off U.S. influence at times of domestic or regional turmoil for South Africa.

NOTES

1. Memo to President Johnson, July 29, 1964, from William Brubeck, LBJ Library.

2. Memo to McGeorge Bundy, May 13, 1965, from Rick Haynes, LBJ Library.

3. Charles W. Engelhard to Jack Valenti, January 13, 1965, LBJ Library.

4. Sir Francis de Guingaud, "South Africa: What It Means to the West," *NATO's Fifteen Nations*, April-May 1965, p. 8.

5. Robert Schulz, aide to Eisenhower, to C. V. Clifton, military aide to Johnson, March 16, 1965, LBJ Library.

6. Memo from Gordon Chase to McGeorge Bundy, November 3, 1965, LBJ Library.

7. See, for instance, the March 1966 Manifesto of Americans for Freedom in Southern Africa, coordinated by the American Committee on Africa.

8. Memo from Ed Hamilton to Walt W. Rostow, September 6, 1966, LBJ Library.

9. "South Africa Supports Davis for State Department Post," *New York Times*, February 22, 1975, p. 9.

10. See "Africans Drafting a Protest on Davis," *New York Times*, February 21, 1975, p. 5; and "OAU's Attack on Envoy Brings Kissinger's 'Dismay,'" *New York Times*, February 25, 1975, p. 20.

11. "The Davis Appointment," *New York Times*, March 1, 1975, p. 24; "Myopia on Africa," *New York Times*, January 31, 1975, p. 32; "Naming of Davis to Africa Post Should be Dropped, Diggs Says," *New York Times*, February 26, 1975, p. 12.

12. "Nomination of Nathaniel Davis to Be Assistant Secretary of State for Africa Affairs," hearing before the Committee on Foreign Relations, U.S. Senate, 94th Cong., 1st sess., February 19, 1975; see also Bruce Oudes, "Kissinger Confronts Africa," *Africa Report*, March-April 1975, p. 45.

13. Oudes, "Kissinger Confronts Africa," p. 46; it was later realized that McGoff was attempting to do this with South African money, as revealed in the Muldergate scandal.

14. A typical example would be by William Manning, "Tar Baby: Why the U.S. Backs S. Africa's White Regime," *African Development*, February 1975, pp. 21-23.

15. Some implications are explored in Walter Carrington, "Time of Trial," *Africa Report*, March-April 1975, pp. 7-11.

16. "Vorster to Move," *The Economist*, March 8, 1975, pp. 14-15; "Smith-Vorster Talks Begin," Johannesburg International Service, March 17, 1975, in *FBIS Sub-Saharan Africa*, March 18, 1975, p. E6.

17. "Ivory Coast Official to Make Visit," Paris AFP, July 15, 1975, in *FBIS Sub-Saharan Africa*, July 18, 1975, p. E5. This article comments on the minister of information's visit to Pretoria in August.

18. "A Key U.S. Appointment Angers Many Africans," *New York Times*, June 15, 1975, p. 2.

19. "Africa Sanctions Opposed by U.S.," *New York Times*, June 4, 1975, p. 6.

20. "Vorster Replies to U.S. Attack," *New York Times*, November 30, 1975, p. 4; "As Long as You Asked," *The Interdependent*, December 1975, p. 5.

21. Graham Hovey, "Bankruptcy in Africa," *New York Times*, March 2, 1976, p. A33.

22. Roger Morris once noted about NSSM-39, which was drafted in 1969-70: "Its premise was that historically the repression by the white minorities had only hardened with their ostracism, and that dialogue and contact with the outside world, including economic modernization, might work to expose, weaken and eventually destroy by peaceful evolution the evil absurdities of racism. But the subtle balance between influence and acquiescence in such a course proved too much for the Rogers State Department to which Nixon and Kissinger readily left African affairs" ("South African Unmentionables," *The New Republic*, June 26, 1976, p. 12).

23. Percy's report of his trip is a useful summary of U.S. dilemmas just prior to the Kissinger initiative: "The United States and Southern Africa," report by Senator Charles H. Percy to the Committee on Foreign Relations, United States Senate, June 1976.

24. Speech by Secretary of State Henry A. Kissinger in Lusaka, Zambia, April 27, 1976.

25. See *SA Digest*, May 14, 1976, pp. 11-12.

26. "Break-through in Washington," *Die Transvaler*, May 17, 1976.

27. We do not know if Ford's statement was just an accident. See "Ford Hints at Vorster Talks," *Washington Post*, May 21, 1976, p. 15. South African media were particularly enthusiastic over Ford references to "protection for white minorities in future constitutions."

28. Roger Morris, "South African Unmentionables," *The New Republic*, June 26, 1976, p. 11.

29. Ibid., p. 13.

30. With Kissingerian ambiguities, the deal apparently consisted of South Africa delivering Ian Smith to a Rhodesian settlement in exchange for the United States' slowing down U.N. pressure on South-West Africa/Namibia. See J. E. Spence, "Detente in Southern Africa: An Interim Judgment," *International Affairs* (London) 53 (January 1977): 9.

31. *SA Digest*, November 12, 1976, p. 1.

32. *The Argus*, November 4, 1976.

33. Ibid.

34. *Beeld*, November 4, 1976.

35. "Democrats Top in USA," *South African Foundation News*, December 1976, p. 1.

36. B. J. Vorster, "Our House Is Not Built on Sand," *South African Panorama*, February 1977, p. 30.

37. *SA Digest*, February 11, 1977, p. 21.

38. *SA Digest*, April 22, 1977, p. 4.

39. Denis Worrall, "Only Deeds Can Prove Our Point," *Rapport*, February 6, 1976.

40. Compare the headlines, which reflect the difference in the stories: "Vorster Seems to Resist Compromise Plan by U.S. on South-West Africa," *New York Times*, April 8, 1977, p. 2; and "Vorster Agrees to Namibia Talks," *Richmond Times-Dispatch*, April 8, 1977, p. A-4.

41. "Information Strategy," *SA Digest*, March 4, 1977, p. 1.

42. "Vorster Addresses Parliament on Talks with Mondale," Johannesburg International Service, in *FBIS Sub-Saharan Africa*, May 31, 1977, p. E12.

43. "A Case of Journalistic Racism," reprinted in *SA Digest*, May 6, 1977, p. 15.

44. "Pik in U.S. to Put SA Case," *SA Digest*, June 24, 1977, p. 3.

45. See *SA Digest*, June 3, 1977, p. 2.

46. "Excerpts from Vance's Speech on Southern Africa," *New York Times*, July 2, 1977, p. A4.

47. See Department of State, *News Conference*, August 12, 1977, press release no. 389.

48. "U.S. Warns Radicals on South Africa," *Washington Post*, August 26, 1977, p. 1.

49. *SA Digest*, September 30, 1977, p. 2.

50. See an exploration of alternatives by someone close to the Carter administration, Anthony Lewis, "Facing South Africa," *New York Times*, October 24, 1977, p. 24.

51. See Department of State, *Press Conference Secretary of State*, November 2, 1977, p. 6.

52. "Young Says S. African Premier Is Over the Hill Intellectually," *Washington Post*, November 8, 1977, p. A14.

53. See "NAACP Calls for Total Pullout by U.S. Businesses in South Africa," *New York Times*, January 20, 1978, p. A2.

54. *SA Digest*, May 19, 1978, p. 1.

55. *SA Digest*, June 16, 1978, p. 6.

56. SABC, June 22, 1978, in *SA Digest*, June 30, 1978, p. 21.

57. *Die Volksblad* welcomed his first public speech with a description that he "was not only guilty of presumptuousness and bad taste yesterday, but also of a remarkable lack of insight and judgment." August 9, 1978.

58. "Americans Do Not Understand Situation in SA: Connally," *SA Digest*, September 1, 1978, p. 5.

59. "S. African Sugar Interests Admit Secretly Paying for Trips, Favors for Congressmen," *Los Angeles Times*, August 21, 1978.

60. "U.S. Shows S. Africa Bigger Carrot, Smaller Stick," *Washington Post*, October 23, 1978, p. 20.

61. Numerous details are revealed in "Vorster Quits After New Report Accuses Him of Cover-up," *Financial Times* (London), June 5, 1979, p. 1; "Vorster Quits in Disgrace," *Daily Telegraph* (London), June 5, 1979, p. 1.

62. "Contrived Scandal," *New York News*, April 14, 1979, p. 16; "Bush Spy Plane," *Baltimore Sun*, April 14, 1979, p. 16.

63. "Pretoria Loses Its Cool," *Washington Post*, April 15, 1979, p. 16; "Derailing Peace in Southern Africa," *Christian Science Monitor*, April 16, 1979.

64. An insightful early analysis was by Caryle Murphy, "South Africa, in Major Shift, Seeks More Independent Policy," *Washington Post*, April 15, 1979, p. 15.

65. Information Service of South Africa, in *FBIS Sub-Saharan Africa*, August 20, 1979, p. E5.

66. William J. Foltz, *Elite Opinion on United States Policy toward Africa* (New York: Council on Foreign Relations, 1979), pp. 18-21.

67. Robert I. Rotberg, "South Africa's Latest Homeland: A New Approach," *Christian Science Monitor*, February 12, 1980, p. 23. The South African government attempted to embarrass Rotberg by revealing his close ties to the opposition Parliament member, Helen Suzman.

68. Patricia M. Derian, "Human Rights in South Africa," *Current Policy No. 181*, Department of State, May 13, 1980, p. 4.

69. Johannesburg International Service, November 5, 1980, in *FBIS Mideast and Africa*, November 6, 1980, p. U1.

70. Ibid.

71. "Johannesburg Expects Reliability in Reagan Policy," Johannesburg International Service, December 10, 1980, in *FBIS Mideast and Africa*, December 12, 1980, p. U4; and John Chettle, "US Alliance with SA Unlikely," *South African Foundation News*, December 1980, p. 2.

72. The policy review and related confusion is described by Richard Deutsch, "Reagan's Unruly Review," *Africa Report*, May-June 1981, pp. 23-26.

73. See "U.S. Offers Terms for Closer Ties to S. Africans," *Washington Post*, May 29, 1981, p. A1.

74. Ibid.

75. See "South Africa Sees a Friend in Reagan," *Wall Street Journal*, March 27, 1981, p. 33.

76. *SA Digest*, March 13, 1981, p. 22.

77. *Rand Daily Mail*, May 19, 1981.

78. Such sentiments have been expressed privately for some time. This author, after giving a lecture in South Africa in early 1980 on the limits of U.S. influence, was made to understand quite strongly how much the reform-oriented audience did not welcome the decline of U.S. influence, even if the influence came in the form of Andrew Young.

3

MILITARY/STRATEGIC INFLUENCE: LOST IN THE SHUFFLE

Influence between two countries in military affairs is frequently a straight-forward proposition: because military affairs are generally dominated by governments, the ties between two societies either exist in official terms or they do not exist at all. It is thus striking that the issue of influence in the military relationship between the United States and South Africa gives rise to as many gray areas of influence as any other category. By virtue of the strained political relations between the two governments, official military ties in recent years have been at most covert, and to varying degrees indirect or informal. The resulting vagueness of military ties makes the enumeration of "facts" difficult. Great disputes break out in the open literature over such normally unambiguous issues as the weapons inventories in the South African armed forces, as well as the extent and nature of contacts between United States' and South African officials.

A major source of confusion concerns the mixing of means and ends. Is influence on military issues exercised for military and strategic ends? Or is it meant to serve political ends? Insofar as military ends are the focus, problems are much more categorical: the capability of the United States to influence South Africa militarily is known; the United States is a superpower and South Africa is not. Where an examination of military ties becomes problematical, however, is in assessing the ultimate political impact. Given the importance of arms boycotts and discussions of naval quarantines of South Africa, the question of the political effect of military influence has to be very germane to this chapter. As a result, it is essential to differentiate between influence exercised on military issues for political ends, and influence exercised with primarily military ends.[1]

The traditional role of military discussions between the United States and South Africa was related largely to strategic issues. In the years after World War II, the South Africans attempted in various ways to maintain the integrated cooperation with United States' and British armed forces that had developed during the war. The rash of military security pacts signed by those two powers after 1949 gave hope to the South Africans that a southern equivalent to NATO would be created. Many of the signatories of the Brussels Treaty of 1949 (which created NATO), after all, were also colonial powers in Africa, and for the South Africans, it only made sense that NATO members would want to find an analogous form of security in Africa, particularly with regard to the sea lanes. The outbreak of tensions in Berlin and Korea in 1949-50 accelerated the pursuit of these arrangements, and it took several years for the South Africans to believe that such an arrangement would not be made.

In the meantime, the South Africans were more than eager to contribute. In 1949 the South Africans sent air crews to help in the Berlin airlift, and in 1950 the No. 2 Squadron of the South African Air Force was sent to Korea to work with the United States.[2] What was achieved for the South Africans from those gestures was the signing of an agreement in 1952 with the United States under the U.S. Mutual Defense Assistance Act of 1949, essentially providing for aid in purchasing U.S. arms. In terms of strategic cooperation, the South Africans found a stone wall with NATO opposing a formal treaty arrangement in the African region, and so the South Africans were thrown back into the arms of the British. The Simonstown Agreement of 1955 thus resulted.[3]

The importance of the Simonstown Agreement, signed in 1955 and implemented in 1957, should not be underestimated, for it represented the agreement in place of the creation of a "South Atlantic Treaty Organization." It also established a benchmark for U.S. perceptions of expected military cooperation with the South Africans; in that sense, the historical influence of that agreement, even though now terminated, continued to affect the drift of much thinking in the United States about military ties with South Africa. The provisions of the agreement were contained in three separate letters of agreement between the British and the South Africans. Most parts dealt with administrative and financial details of transferring control of the Simonstown Naval Base from the British to the South Africans. But more important, the agreement provided for continuing use by the "Royal Navy and ships serving with the Royal Navy and by navies of allies of the United Kingdom. . . ."[4] Even though the United States was not a signatory of the agreement, the provisions allowed for United States' use of the Simonstown on an agreed basis, and U.S. ships did make a practice after 1957 of stopping at that base. The agreement had a far-reaching effect, in addition, in laying out some of the political assumptions attached to the military relations:

1. Southern Africa and the sea routes round Southern Africa must be secured against aggression from without.
2. The internal security of the countries of Southern Africa must, however, remain a matter for each individual country concerned.

3. The defence of Southern Africa against external aggression lies not only in Africa but also in the gateways to Africa, namely in the Middle East. It is therefore the declared policy –
(a) of the United Kingdom to contribute forces for the defence of Africa, including Southern Africa, and the Middle East;
(b) of the Union Government to contribute forces in order to keep the potential enemy as far as possible from the borders of South Africa, in other words for the defence of Southern Africa, Africa and the Middle East gateways of Africa.[5]

The attempt to detach internal security from the strategic importance of South Africa is notable as an overall guideline to the agreements between Britain and South Africa. Subsequent disagreements between Britain and the United States frequently revolved around the feasibility of such a separation; neither took a consistent position, but rather their positions reflected the ideological complexions of the governments in power at a particular time. A second illustrative point derived from the agreements lies in the third clause: even Britain and South Africa could not agree on the same definition of security. Each insisted upon defining it separately, and hoped that their "parallel policies" would add up to reasonably cooperative defense ties. Such a difference of opinion indicates that the South Africans, while very interested in alliance links with the NATO states, also insisted upon separate strategic planning. They hoped to be able to find common ground with France, Britain, and the United States – in the end, they found only a reasonable arrangement with the British.

Attempts were made to approach the United States. Aside from the important symbolic gestures in Korea and Berlin, missions of South African military leaders were dispatched to Washington to explore broader ties. In August of 1949, the South African minister of defense and the chief of staff visited U.S. military installations and had talks with the administration.[6] In September 1950, the defense minister once again visited the United States, after talks in London and Paris, in order to explore the possibility of an alliance.[7] The only result was the agreement on arms sales already described. In subsequent talks on African defense, as well as on the subject of a British-organized Middle East Command, the South Africans took part, but the United States did nothing more than send an observer. With the advent of the Eisenhower administration in 1953, U.S. attention was thoroughly preoccupied with the rimland containment of the Soviet Union, and there was no evident threat to South Africa. Given the terms of the Simonstown Agreement, which included the purchase of about 20 warships for the South African Navy to be built in British yards, the Anglo-American view was that South Africa could probably defend its own interests in response to the level of Soviet threat, and the NATO resources were best deployed on the more important fronts.

An identity of interests was recognized in one area: the protection of the sea lanes around the Cape of Good Hope. One of the letters in the Simonstown

Agreement dealt with the "Sea Routes Agreement":

> Recognizing the importance of sea communications to the well-being
> of their respective countries in peace and to their common security
> in the event of aggression, the Governments of the Union of South
> Africa and of the United Kingdom enter into the following Agreement
> to ensure the safety, by the joint operations of their respective mari-
> time forces, of the sea routes round Southern Africa.[8]

The cooperation that developed between the British and the South Africans
as a result was to establish a pattern of interaction for NATO with the South
Africans. The gradual transfer of responsibility to the South Africans − by the
mid-1960s, the South Africans were doing essentially all patroling of the Cape
route − did not mean a slowdown in the flow of information to NATO. Indeed,
the principle of joint concern over the Cape route simply meant that implementation of measures to meet that concern increasingly fell to the South Africans.

A key change in the South African relationship with NATO occurred in
1956, through the failure of the Franco-British intervention in Suez. The
disarray of the NATO allies in the Middle East, combined with the evident loss
of influence by the British in Egypt, indicated that an essential precondition of
British activity in the Indian Ocean had been lost. The British defense of the
Middle East took an entirely different cast; with the slow withdrawal from East
of Suez (completed in 1971), the British also saw their defense interests in South
Africa increasingly detached from future needs. As was evident in the wording
of the Simonstown Agreement, British interest in South Africa was a function
in large part of its defense of the Middle East. The slow British withdrawal of
interest in the South African connection gave the United States one more difficult choice to make in the British abandonment of empire.

THE MOVE TOWARD CONFLICT

There were few predilections on the United States' side to pick up British
responsibilities in southern Africa, even though many of the assumptions of the
Simonstown Agreement were accepted in the U.S. military: the salience of the
sea lanes in times of war, the disinterest in South African domestic affairs, and
the utility of the Simonstown naval base. At the political level, the domestic
consensus in the United States was moving even more dramatically away from
South Africa. The desegregation movement gave a heightened role to blacks in
U.S. politics, the interest in black Africa after the arrival of independence in the
early 1960s, and the internal crises in South Africa persuaded the United States
to shy away from military ties. The commitment of Democratic administrations
between 1961 and 1969 to black opportunity could not possibly be reconciled
with defense ties to a nation suffering race riots on the scale of Sharpeville. Thus,
one saw the United States moving against South Africa even more dramatically

than the NATO allies, calling, for instance, for an arms embargo against South Africa at the United Nations in 1963. In part, the arms embargo measure was portrayed as a compromise, for it was a voluntary arms ban declared by the United States at a time when the African states were demanding that the U.N. Security Council pass a mandatory arms embargo against South Africa. In order to preempt that Security Council debate, the Kennedy administration announced on August 2, 1963, that the United States would not sell arms after the end of 1963 to South Africa. The British and French were not particularly happy with the Kennedy approach, for they sought to continue selling arms and were apparently prepared to veto a mandatory arms embargo resolution. In the end, they went along with the U.S. approach but applied the policy so loosely as to allow arms sales much as before.

This measure against South Africa in the military field has to be understood in the context of momentum moving drastically against South African interests. The Sharpeville riots of 1960 coincided with, and spurred onward, the African diplomatic offensive against white rule in South Africa. The formation of the Organization of African Unity in 1963 represented the emergence of an organized political force of independent black-ruled African states, prepared to confront South Africa as a first priority. The entire period from 1960 to 1966 was also generally a crisis for South African diplomacy and internal political stability, with profound questioning of the survivability of Nationalist rule in a world where all forces were becoming dramatically hostile.[9] The United States did not stand out to a great degree in this growth of opposition to the South African government, particularly after the election of the Wilson government in Britain in 1964. Repeated incidents arising from the arms embargo poisoned relations with South Africa during the Johnson administration. The first major test of the embargo, for instance, came over the approach made by South Africa to the Lockheed Corporation for export of several P3A reconnaissance aircraft. The preliminary refusal of the United States to grant an export license precipitated a formidable lobbying campaign aimed at the White House. The president of Lockheed, Courtlandt Gross, sent messages to and met with McGeorge Bundy. Senator Thomas Kuchel of California, where Lockheed was located, lobbied the president. Within the government, the departments divided on the issue: the Departments of Commerce and Treasury were strongly in favor of selling the planes, the State Department opposed the deal, and Department of Defense's McNamara refused to certify that approval of the deal would enhance U.S. national security. Such certification was the one reservation stated by the United States that would allow for a violation of the arms embargo against South Africa.[10] When the decision had to be made, Johnson opposed the deal. The decision turned entirely on political criteria. The pattern was thus set, and for the decade, U.S. officials not only attempted to further restrict U.S. arms exports to South Africa but tried to prevent the export of arms from European allies. The principal tool applied was the approval required by the United States for the use of United States-origin parts in European military goods exported to other countries. Thus, one saw not only the refusal to Cessna aircraft of light-plane exports to South Africa in 1965, but also the 1966 denial of permission to export three French Mystere 20 jets to South Africa, since those jets included General Electric engines.

If one could pinpoint any concrete limitations on the extent to which the United States was willing to sunder military ties with South Africa, it came over the issue of the tracking stations in South Africa. With the rapid expansion of the U.S. space program in the 1960s, the United States became increasingly dependent upon a network of stations in the right locations around the world to monitor both U.S. and Soviet satellites. In South Africa, the stations included a radio-tracking station built under a 1957 agreement, a satellite-tracking station built in 1958, a deep-space monitor operated by South Africans for the United States, and a military-tracking station built under a new agreement in 1962.[11] In 1964, with increasing tensions between the United States and South Africa, U.S. scientists and diplomats began exploring the feasibility of other sites in southern Africa outside South Africa. Alternative sites had to be in the same general area, since Australia and southern Africa provided the only southern hemisphere coverage of space launch activities. In July 1965, Prime Minister Verwoerd made some comments to the press regarding the inadmissibility of integrated work crews at the tracking stations. The White House was on the verge of shutting down the stations, until warned that they were irreplaceable for the time being: "It is critical for the South African station to remain operational for the final phase of the 'Mariner IV' Mars shot (July-August 1965) and the first 'Surveyor' attempts at a fall landing on the moon (fall 1965, spring 1966)."[12] As years passed, the rationale remained largely the same; language in Kissinger's NSSM-39 on South Africa was even stronger, arguing that "non-availability of the South African station would impose serious mission operational constraints and would degrade ground tracking support to a high risk condition."[13]

The purposes of the arms embargo were entirely political, based upon the assumption that such open expressions of disapproval would both cause the South Africans to change their racial policies as well as to cement good ties with the black independent states of Africa. One notable gesture of this policy approach came in the U.S.S. Roosevelt incident in 1967. The aircraft carrier was scheduled to stop in Capetown to give the crew shore leave, and when publicity was given to the segregated facilities ashore, congressmen demanded that the White House take measures. The Roosevelt was told at the last minute to cancel shore leave, and stay at Capetown as little as possible.[14] U.S. policy has since been to use South African ports for emergencies only. The net effect of the arms embargo appears to have been to contribute to the temporary demoralization of the South Africans. The multifaceted rejection of the South Africans by the United States caused them to pause politically and engage in protracted self-doubt. The longer-term result, however, was to direct South African energies in the direction of greater self-reliance and a renewed sense of confidence by the end of the 1960s.[15] Indeed, by 1967, one could see the turnabout of South African views.

At the beginning of 1967, South Africa renegotiated the Simonstown Agreement with Britain, reducing the role of the British and their allies in South African defense planning. Coincidentally, the Middle East war in 1967 and the related closing of the Suez Canal enhanced the importance of the Cape route for the rapidly increasing oil supplies to Western Europe and the United States. The response of European and U.S. strategic planners to these events was to give the South African facilities another look. Africa had generally suffered a downgrading in U.S. foreign policy in the confusion of the Vietnam War effort. Bilateral U.S. relations with a range of African states were suffering, as those states expressed opposition to the U.S. role in Southeast Asia. The enhanced East-West conflict was one in which the sympathies of South Africa were not doubted, and so Western military officials were quick to recognize the advantages of ties with South Africa. South Africa encouraged this, as reflected in a statement of its foreign minister in 1966: "We acknowledge and we honour the United States as the leader of the Free World today. . . . It is the policy of this Government to steer clear of points of friction with the United States as much as possible . . . but to concentrate on points of common interest."[16] The shadow foreign secretary in Britain took the lead in responding positively, as seen in Sir Alec Douglas-Home's public speeches:

> It so happens that Britain has a defence government with South Africa which concerns the Simonstown Naval Base not far from Cape Town. Under its terms, in the event of hostile action east of Suez, Britain has the use of all South African ports including Durban. I forecast that this facility will be of greater value in terms of the defence of Western Europe from interference with her oil supplies and that it will in effect become an informal extension of NATO defences, although it will remain a bilateral treaty.[17]

In 1969 he further argued the complete case:

> With the closing of the Suez Canal and the permanent routing of the oil of the Persian Gulf round the shores of Africa and the simultaneous appearance of a Soviet submarine fleet which is oceanic in its range, South Africa's .geographical position assumes a new strategic significance. The policing of the South Atlantic and of the West of the Indian Ocean becomes important both to Britain and to Western Europe. These areas are in effect (although they may not formally be made so) an extension of NATO's responsibility for the security of Europe.[18]

Within a year, Sir Alec had become British foreign minister in the Heath government. South Africans felt encouraged to seek broad NATO ties, and some observers optimistically felt that they could be negotiated.[19] They were encouraged further by the arrival of the Nixon administration in early 1969, but were to be largely disappointed in terms of a broader military relationship with the United States and NATO.

South Africa never obtained an improved place in U.S. military planning during the Nixon administration for several reasons. First, the preoccupation of Nixon and Kissinger for most of their time in office was with ending the Vietnam War advantageously; it was thus unlikely that political capital would be spent on publicly reversing the policy on South Africa. Second, the Nixon administration suffered from the same problems of style plaguing all U.S. foreign policy; as Prime Minister Vorster said about that policy, "If I only knew what it was. Candidly, we don't know what it is. However, the little we know about United States policy towards South Africa, we don't understand at all. We fail to understand why the State Department adopts this attitude towards us."[20] The top levels of the administration (Kissinger) did not impose any active concept of a southern Africa strategy until too late, in 1975-76. Third, fundamental strategic priorities of South Africa and the United States were no closer to each other than the British and South Africans had been in 1955. As a result, agreements might be reached on political and economic issues, but the existing military relationship was generally (with minor exceptions) satisfactory for U.S. purposes. Costs could have been cut by using the Simonstown base, although there were few U.S. military vessels rounding the Cape, and it was known that the bases could be used in time of war. Above all, U.S. policy may have been too subtle for the South Africans. Nixon and Kissinger liked to engage in hints of policy change and expected to find gratitude for it; at the same time that U.S. delegates at the United Nations continued to blast South Africa, for instance, the Nixon administration approved the use of General Electric engines in French jets for South Africa (and thus reversed a policy of the Johnson administration). Kissinger expected the South Africans to believe his deeds and not his words; even his broad hints that the position of the U.S. ambassador to the United Nations was irrelevant to policy did not persuade the South Africans. For them, the harsh words undercut whatever influence might have been gained by the arms sales.

Tensions between the several arms of the executive branch in the United States created major difficulties for the Nixon administration. U.S. attention was drawn to southern Africa in the wake of the Portuguese coup in 1974, and a group of top South African military leaders was dispatched to Washington to compare notes with U.S. counterparts. They entered "on a private visit" with tourist visas, and would have carried out their visit incognito, had not a watchful official at the Africa Bureau of the State Department leaked the information to the newspapers.[21] It was, in fact, the second trip of the year, since Connie Mulder, a top-level Nationalist cabinet minister, had been scouting out possible relaxations of the arms embargo in January 1974 on a similar trip to Washington. Blame was quickly placed on the South Africans by Washington sources for "insisting" on the trips.[22] As far as one can tell from looking at the public record, the initiative was rebuffed.

Several members of NATO objected strongly to further cooperation with South Africa. At a time when the United States-European alliance structure was facing strains over the Vietnam War, the managers of NATO could not afford the additional political strain that would inevitably result from closer ties with South Africa. In effect, the political implications of any military ties with South Africa at the overt level had more leverage on Western and U.S. policy than did the inclinations of the military services. At the level of intelligence sharing, cooperation did continue between NATO and South Africa. Much publicity was given by the anti-apartheid forces to the South African construction of Project Advokaat — otherwise known as Silvermine — which was essentially a data collation center, with sensor hookups, for monitoring traffic around the coasts of South Africa. In this way, the South Africans were able to keep track of Soviet ship movements into the Indian Ocean from the South Atlantic. With the Suez Canal closed, that meant essentially all Soviet Navy movements. There appears to have been little gain of leverage on either side in this operation, however, owing to the simple trade of information for technology. The South Africans obtained first the hardware, and later the computer software, for cataloguing ship movements into the categories used by NATO, and then provided them with the information. Later, it was also alleged that this communications complex was used to handle weapons inventories in South Africa, on the basis of NATO codification forms. Since the forms were actually unclassified material from NATO's point of view, the allegation is probably true.[23] In effect, the United States used two channels to allow military-related goods flows to increase to South Africa: European producers (primarily France and Italy) of hardware and some software transfers from NATO. By all reports, the United States gained no leverage over South Africa from such transfers. Military facilities in South Africa increasingly came under national control — with the exception of the residual presence of British liaison officers at Simonstown — and the South African military was becoming increasingly self-sufficient in weapons production throughout the 1970s.

Ultimately, the attempt of South Africa to gain leverage over the United States and its NATO partners in the early 1970s failed as well, and it failed by virtue of the collapse of the "Simonstown logic." As explained by one of the most acute observers of South African defense, J. E. Spence: "Security is, therefore, indivisible for the South African Government — not so much in terms of the use to which particular weapons systems may be put — but rather because of the likelihood that any serious threat to its security must of necessity have both an internal and external dimension."[24] In effect, the posture that NATO could have a military tie without expressing any involvement in the domestic problems of South Africa was proven to be a myth. By virtue of the direction of the conflict within South Africa, such a distinction became untenable. Thus, the United States and the West Europeans who did not become committed to the government's side in an internal battle were also constrained from providing significant, overt aid to its external defense.

All subsequent attempts by the South Africans to enlist the United States in an alliance thus had to take into account the new realities. The "threat" became not only the Soviet presence in the region; it also encompassed the perils of domestic South African disorder for the flow of strategic minerals and of the possible emergence of an anti-United States regime after a revolution. General Magnus Malan, chief of the South African Defense Force, communicated this message to the United States in a number of forums in the late 1970s, in emphasizing the geographic location of South Africa, coupled with its mineral resources:

> Incredible as it may seem, Western leaders have apparently taken it for granted that these vital elements of the present South African situation are indestructible and that they would survive a revolution or radical change in government. So they see the incumbent Government of the RSA only as being incidental to a favorable alignment, and not as its cornerstone.[25]

Malan, later named defense minister and clearly one of Prime Minister Botha's closest advisors, expanded his thesis, warning "that further attempts to isolate South Africa . . . could retard the process of internal change in the country." and that "it is time the US and its allies included southern Africa in their global strategic design, instead of drawing the line at the Tropic of Capricorn and trying to believe that what lies to the south of this line cannot possibly affect the security of the West."[26] General Malan knew his audience, for he was the last South African officer to be trained at the U.S. Army's Command General Staff College at Fort Leavenworth (in the early 1960s). He has taken steps to integrate the South African armed forces, and has been a leader in attempting to obtain U.S. backing for these changes.

MILITARY SELF-RELIANCE: A REJECTION OF INFLUENCE

Minister of Defense Malan has also described the arms embargo as a "mixed blessing": "We are at this stage basically self-sufficient as regards surface weapons."[27] The implementation of the arms embargo in 1963, while not enforced with great vigor by the Europeans, was a source of great despair in South African foreign policy. Most South African defense planning had been predicated upon continuing ties with key NATO states, at least to the point of purchasing weapons. With the arms embargo, at a time when the United States was selling arms to black-ruled independent African states, South Africa actually realized that in the case of a war in southern Africa, the United States might side with those states north of the Limpopo. Such a thought was profoundly discouraging.

The decision taken by South African leadership, however, was not to cave in to such pressure; the course chosen was self-reliance. The financial dimensions, as well as resource commitments, have been detailed elsewhere.[28] Many aspects of this military buildup in South Africa do reflect, however, on the quest for influence that animated the U.S. initiative in the first place.

The manpower needs of a self-reliance strategy were substantial, and to begin with, morale problems in the South African armed services were not to be overlooked. Ever since the accession of the Nationalist Party to power in 1948, there had been endemic tension in the armed forces over efforts of the government to replace the old Anglophilic officer corps with young Afrikaner officers: bilingualism was stressed, and recruitment was carried out largely in Afrikaner areas. The result was a powerful defense force with major divisive influences within it, generally along linguistic lines. The mobilization in the mid-1960s, in the face of the arms embargo, solved that problem. White males were required to serve at least one year, with nine years' training duty after that, and then to be enrolled in a reserve unit indefinitely. Tensions between the linguistic groups in the armed forces were wiped out, and the South African Defense Force (SADF) generally became good operational units, entirely removed from politics.[29] In the period since the late 1960s, then, the numbers of people availabe to defend the country grew substantially: on active duty in 1980 were 71,000 in the Army, 4,750 in the Navy, and 10,300 in the Air Force; more important, the Active Reserve numbered 155,000 plus about 110,000 in "commando" units that contained people retired from the Active Reserves.[30] These are tremendous numbers, even when keeping in mind the 20,000 Cuban troops in Angola and the far smaller African military establishments in the region.

Demographic problems impede any further growth at past rates, however, and the SADF has recognized this by taking nonwhite soldiers into its ranks. New ranks have been opened up in the Navy for advancement by colored sailors, and there are at latest count seven colored officers, in addition to 17 percent of the total force. In the Army, coloreds have been allowed to volunteer for infantry service since 1976 and have had their own combat units since 1980. They were also allowed to enlist as paratroopers in 1978, and their service on the border areas of northern Namibia has been greatly praised.[31] With regard to enlistment of blacks, the Army was the first branch of the armed forces to create operational black units, beginning in 1974 under the leadership of General Magnus Malan, who was then chief of the Army. He created the 21st Battalion, which has served both as a training unit for homeland forces, as well as an operational unit in northern Namibia. With that experience considered successful, Malan, who had become minister of defense, has commenced the creation of many new black batallions, including the 111th, 112th, 113th, and the 121st.[32] Most units of this kind are organized to be homogeneous in tribal terms; whether or not that is a permanent policy has not been indicated. Malan's leadership in undertaking these moves for inclusion of nonwhites in the Defense

Force may or may not reflect his past training in the United States. If it is also a by-product of U.S. arms sanctions against South Africa, U.S. policymakers can presumably congratulate themselves on having had this effect. The successful inclusion of nonwhites in the armed forces is being pointed to, by other sectors of South African society, as a precursor of future integration in South Africa. If they are able to integrate the Army and Air Force to any substantial degree, the potential for South Africa being a focus of U.S. pressure would be greatly diminished.

In building a self-reliant armed force, the key issue for the South Africans was weapons acquisition. The original symbol, after all, had been the U.S. arms embargo of 1963, and so the response to that form of pressure was critical. That embargo happened to coincide with the fulfillment of the arms sales provisions of the Simonstown Agreement, under which the British would deliver modern frigates to the South African Navy; South Africa had obtained some Daphne-class submarines at the same time from the French. With the arrival of the Labor Government in Britain in 1964, however, the South Africans had to look to the continent for weapons. The U.S. arms embargo meant little in terms of the technological level of interest to the South Africans, except that it spurred the South Africans to obtain their own production capacity, instead of relying on imports. By 1967 they were producing their own Panhard APCs on French license. In 1968 they created Armscor, the government-owned Armaments Development and Manufacturing Corporation, for the large-scale production planned for the following decades. In June 1971, it was announced that Armscor would obtain the license to build Mirage-III and F-1 aircraft in South Africa.[33] South Africa was also soon producing its own Cactus missiles and Impala jet trainers. It was thought that the passage of a mandatory arms embargo by the United Nations in 1977 (with substantial U.S. support and leadership) would alter the capability of the South Africans; after all, even France gave every indication of accepting the embargo and terminating all contracts. By then, the South Africans were not about to cave in. As was remarked with regard to those weapons (particularly jets) produced under license, "It's like a woman who acquires a recipe for baking appletart. If she has to give back the recipe it will make no difference. She has learnt how to bake the tarts herself, or has made a copy of the recipe anyway."[34] As indicated by the same source, the cutoff of actual sales was not a major blow:

> there are innumerable agents abroad anxious to sell weapons illegally to South Africa. Such black market offers are regularly received for every kind of military hardware, including Mirages, Starfighters, and Leopard tanks. On the night the embargo resolution was passed by the Security Council, a high government official was telephoned by a man in New York who said he would deliver as many of a sophisticated American aircraft as might be required.

In the post-1977 embargo era, Anthony Sampson investigated these aï ings extensively, and found a case of 11 Bell helicopters built in Ital American license: they were exported to Israel, sold to a United States-controlled company in Singapore, and then shipped on to South Africa and Rhodesia.[35] South African forces have not been starved by the arms embargo; indeed, they may have paid somewhat more (in some cases, twice the market price), but the diversification of sources has given them more confidence in future supplies. Embargoes of the future are likely to be even less successful, if only because of the rising value of South African goods – gold and diamonds – that are traditionally used to break arms blockades.[36]

South Africa has reached the stage in its military development where used (or secondary) weapons systems are frequently satisfactory for its purposes. The sophistication of heavy weapons on the international arms market has become quite extraordinary in recent years; for instance, South Africa was able to purchase (through a third party) 100 Centurion tanks from India in 1978. It already had 150 Centurions in its inventory, and it had the capacity to recondition the engines and replace the guns. In such an area, South Africa hardly had need of the new weapons market.[37] Indeed, given the relatively simple technology needed for the type of warfare likely to face the South Africans in the near future, it is reasonable to assume that there is more interest in South Africa in stockpiling weapons to weather some attrition than in moving up technologically. Such priorities diminish South African interest in the United States.

THE CARTER YEARS

The new administration entering office in 1977 brought along some rather different views about the influence to be gained on military issues. On the one hand, President Carter and his closest advisors were deeply committed to finding substitutes for the use of force in international affairs; thus one saw the repeated appeals to South African exile movements not to use terrorism and guerrilla tactics in their efforts to dislodge the South African government. On the other hand, the new U.S. administration was morally outraged by the apartheid system, and if one form of influence available to change Pretoria's policies concerned military issues, it would be escalated. Several issues thus became highly visible in Carter's approach to South Africa: (1) a tightening of the arms embargo by the U.N. Security Council in order to deny weapons to the defenders of apartheid; (2) the expression of great concern over the possibility of nuclear weapons in South Africa's hands with all the consequences possible for Carter's overall nonproliferation efforts; and (3) an avoidance at any cost of needing South African facilities (whether Simonstown naval base or the satellite-tracking stations) for the U.S. defense effort.

Much has been written about the leakiness of the arms embargo, confirming what people generally recognize about international arms markets — that they are largely uncontrollable. Investigative jounralism has taken much interest in the intricacies of corporate officials in the United States and elsewhere evading official controls on the movements of weapons.[38] The principal types of weaponry to evade the literal embargo by U.S. officials are rifles and ammunition of various types, including artillery shells. The amount of these sales in dollars is not large, and they have been attacked primarily as symbols of lax U.S. enforcement of sanctions.[39] Presumably such protest over leakages in the embargo caused manufacturers and the Department of Justice to be more sensitive to the issue. In no case, however, did any change in policy appear to result from such efforts.

The principal form of leakage, according to critics, is the distinction between civilian and military use of equipment. In what sense is a crop-duster plane only a civilian item, when it could be used as a spotter plane in case of a military emergency? What is the distinction between a Lockheed L-100 "Commercial Hercules" (sold to South Africa) and a Lockheed C-130 Hercules military transport (banned for sale to South Africa)? In 1977, the Carter administration rewrote the regulations of the embargo to extend the ban to equipment that *could* be used by the military in South Africa, such as the L-100. There may still be occasional exports of dual-use items, but only if accompanied by a certificate that they can be used only for civilian purposes; the leverage of that piece of paper has to be questioned. Thus, the arms embargo satisfies few people: the South Africans are antagonized, in having to use covert or third-party channels to obtain equipment expensively, and opponents of the apartheid regime simply insist on a general trade embargo for effectiveness. Finally, NATO relations are strained, given the extent to which various European countries are known to evade the application of the arms embargo to their export industries. Such was not the intended influence of the arms embargo, either when originally established, or when it was strengthened in 1977.

Self-reliance for the South African military also involved vastly increased defense expenditures. Whether measured in current rand, constant rand, or as a percentage of government expenditure and GNP, the South Africans have had to devote a greater amount as a result of their defense strategy as shown in Table 1. The budget shows several important phases. In the early 1960s, the increase in the budget reflected not the arms embargo of 1963, but rather the committed purchases of ships under the Simonstown Agreement. Thus the amount increased to above 200 million rand in spurts. The much smoother increase in the early 1970s represents the purchase of output from domestic arms industries and the increase in the size of the South African Defense Force. It had taken some years, particularly in the late 1960s and early 1970s, to construct the infrastructure of Armscor for domestic production, and once established, the defense expenditure has risen steadily higher. In the 1970s, too, before the 1977 mandatory arms embargo, the South Africans purchased a

TABLE 1
South African Defense Vote from 1960/61 to 1979/80

Financial Year	Defense Vote (in millions of current rand)	As Percent of Budget	As Percent of GNP	Percent Change from Previous Year
1960/61	44	6.6	0.9	—
1961/62	61	10.0	n.a.	+38
1962/63	120	15.0	n.a.	+96
1963/64	120	14.0	1.9	0
1964/65	230	21.0	3.5	+92
1965/66	219	19.0	3.0	−5
1966/67	248	19.0	3.1	+13
1967/68	256	18.3	2.8	+3
1968/69	252	16.1	2.5	−1
1969/70	272	16.8	2.4	+8
1970/71	257	13.0	n.a.	−7
1971/72	317	12.0	2.6	+23
1972/73	335	12.0	2.3	+6
1973/74	472	13.7	2.6	+41
1974/75	692	16.0	3.2	+47
1975/76	948	18.5	3.7	+37
1976/77	1,300	17.0	4.1	+48
1977/78	1,526	19.0	5.1	+9
1978/79	1,682	n.a.	n.a.	+10
1979/80	1,857	n.a.	n.a.	+10

Source: Adapted from Jaster, *South Africa's Narrowing Security Options*, p. 16, and South African government documents.

number of ships from the French and the Israelis in order to enhance their air and naval antisubmarine warfare patrol missions on the Cape route. While those sales terminated rather abruptly (and thus the 1977/78 figure is not as large as originally budgeted), the money has clearly been applied elsewhere. It might be added that, in the last four years, defense spending has barely kept even with inflation. South Africa is now recognized as the largest arms producer in the southern hemisphere, and the tenth largest in the world.[40] Given the merging of military and political interests at the top of the South African government (in Prime Minister P. W. Botha and Defense Minister General Malan), they are not entirely unhappy with the increased defense spending, particularly as it increasingly goes for domestically produced arms. Armscor now has 12 domestic subsidiaries and has become increasingly adept at copying foreign military technologies; the most recent being the Israeli Gabriel naval missiles, Rasheff-class patrol boats, and the Italian Oto Melara naval cannon.[41] Interestingly, the spinoff for local civilian industries is substantial. In 1979 negotiations for a complete diesel engine plant from the domestic Eaton Company, for instance, the government conceded that the plant would not be economical, compared with imported engines. But the importance of the plant lay in the flow of engines for the Defense Force and their use in Armored Personnel Carriers (APCs), tanks, and trucks.[42]

By increasing the cost of defense in the South African budget, the United States lost, in the view of most military observers, the most important strategic asset: any guarantee to protect the sea lanes. South Africa's growing defense budget could not handle all of the tasks that it considered important, and the reconstruction of its navy has been entirely toward coastal defense and harbor protection. Despite the extension of its territorial sea to 200 miles, the South Africans have moved toward the Resheff-class of small patrol boats that cannot effectively watch over the complete sea lane route. In making this shift of doctrine in the late 1970s, South Africa announced it only briefly, calling Western attention to the fact that South Africa could not guarantee the sea lanes.[43] The communications setup at Silvermine continues to monitor the lanes and does apparently exchange information with NATO. However, given the priorities of land defense, combined with inaccessibility to long-range air and naval craft for sea lane control, there is no extension of force beyond the coastal areas.

The United States has devolved the influence that accrues to an arms supplier to other states, most notably Israel and Taiwan. The links between South Africa and those states are not in the public domain, but there are consistent signals that allow for some piecing together of the relationships. The South Africans and Israelis consult on counterinsurgency tactics; indeed, a few Israeli observers were in Angola in 1975-76 with South African forces. When the South Africans bought Israeli patrol boats, the crews were trained at Israeli bases. The Israelis are also reliably said to have sold radar equipment to them, refurbished tanks, and supplied machine guns. In turn, South Africa provided special alloy steel for Israeli tank manufacture.[44] The Taiwanese connection, involving high governmental visits with pomp and circumstance in both directions, had included sales of small weapons and cooperation on atomic energy (publicly acknowledged to include provision of raw uranium by South Africa for Taiwan's nuclear energy generating plants). The relationships between the three countries gave rise to rumors in the fall of 1979, after a mysterious flash in the southern hemisphere, that they had jointly tested a nuclear device. One columnist went so far as to allege a nuclear warhead on a new cruise missile was tested.[45] The United States was fingered, as usual, as the original source of the cruise missile technology — allegedly smuggled to Israeli agents to be shared among the three countries. If influence exists on the basis of arms sales, in any case, it now accrues to the close friends of South Africa, and not to the United States.[46]

By 1979-80, military ties between the United States and South Africa had become sufficiently insignificant as to allow the sundering of what remained under pressure of the Carter administration. An incident blew up in April 1979 over the existence of a spy camera in the fuselage of the U.S. ambassador's plane. It turned out to have been there for some years, and had been utilized by U.S. intelligence to photograph South African defense installations, as well as installations in neighboring countries when the plane was used on diplomatic trips. The U.S. military attachés were expelled (only one post was allowed to remain filled), and in retribution the United States expelled all but one of the South African attachés in Washington.[47] Two different explanations for the event emerged. Some argued that the Botha government chose to reveal the spy camera at a time when it was under pressure from the information scandal (to be discussed later), and that this would pull political weight behind the government. Others blamed people in the U.S. government: they maintained that the spy camera was deliberately revealed through overuse in order to demonstrate an attitude of confrontation toward South Africa (and thereby curry favor with the black states), and to break the informal links between U.S. intelligence services and the South Africans. Some officials in the Carter administration remained unable to entirely terminate such informal ties, and may have felt that an expulsion of the personnel combined with a public incident would be necessary to break ties. Relations between the two countries then worsened: in January 1980, South African Air Force and Navy units "harrassed" a U.S. Navy battle group rounding the Cape, according to press releases from Washington. Similarly, N. J. Niewoud, the South African Defense Force surgeon-general, scheduled a visit to the United States in May 1980 to attend the annual congress of the International Aerospace Medical Association. He was told twice that a visa had been approved, only to have it withdrawn at the last minute; oddly, he had attended in 1979 without a problem.[48] The incidents were dismissed by the South Africans, but these events were indicative of the extent to which military questions were held hostage to the political atmosphere of United States-South African relations.

The subordination of military concerns could also be seen in internal U.S. debates. Any voice in the U.S. executive branch that defended the military value of South Africa to the United States was stilled during the Carter years. The professional officers corps realized that South Africa was off limits because of the operational code of peacetime forces in the United States. Studies were pursued by various parts of the Defense Department on strategically relevant aspects of South Africa, particularly issues relating to sea lanes of control (SLOC) and mineral supplies for the allied industrial base. Such studies, however, were filed away for another time. The pressure from Congress provided solid support for the administration's position. The relevant committees and subcommittees on foreign relations were tightly controlled by the liberal wing of the Democratic Party; the armed services committees, of a less-liberal persuasion, were pre-occupied with conditions on the central European front. As a result, the policies of Carter, Vance, and Young faced no dissent from that direction.

Throughout the changes of strategy by South Africa and the United States during the Carter administration, there was clearly little influence gained by the denial of arms. Each denial by the United States was matched by finding a new source of arms or the creation of a domestic capacity in South Africa. At the same time, there was some influence exercised on people by the expectation of increasing military ties. Such hopes motivated behavior on the part of South Africa and the United States, particularly as crises in Southwest Asia (the Soviet invasion of Afghanistan and the revolution in Iran) gave rise to calls in the United States for a greater defense effort. The principal regional focus for such a defense hike was initially the Indian Ocean, where the support facilities of South Africa could have played an important role.

THE PENDULUM SWINGS: REAGAN'S SEARCH FOR A POLICY

For the South Africans, some kind of defense guarantee from the United States, a loosening of the arms embargo, and in particular the supply of long-range weapons systems would all help to buttress the self-reliant structure of the South African military. The unseemly haste of the South Africans to express gratitude for Ronald Reagan's victory in the United States in 1980 betrayed the extent of their hopes. Some hopes sprung from people close to Reagan who had communicated an impending substantial shift in policy during the presidential campaign.[49] Thus it was quite embarrassing for both sides when, in the early days of March 1981, five South African top military officers showed up in Washington on tourist visas to explore changes in the administration's policies. Given the longstanding ban on official visits by South African military personnel, they were asked to leave the country when their real purposes were revealed. As pointed out, "Some officials were upset at the developments because the South Africans seemed to be trying to initiate contacts through military channels at a time when future policy toward South Africa is one of the most sensitive questions facing the Reagan Administration."[50] The damage was compounded when it developed that the head of the delegation was Lieutenant General P. W. van der Westerhuizen, head of South African military intelligence — thus giving the whole episode a cloak-and-dagger atmosphere — and that he had met with the U.S. ambassador to the United Nations, Jeanne Kirkpatrick.[51] The extent to which the new Reagan administration backed off when confronted with a South African sleight of hand communicated to all parties a qualified refusal of any renewal of military ties at that time. In terms of disappointing the hopes of the South African government and thereby losing influence once again, even though the fault lay with the South Africans and both official and unofficial U.S. friends, the United States was once again successful.

The hope on the United States side lies in the growing desire of some people, both in and out of government, to obtain access to the Simonstown base. Increased deployments to the Indian Ocean by the U.S. Navy make it necessary to find places for shore leave and repair of ships, and Simonstown remains a candidate. There was a small group of influential people in the United

States who had believed since the 1960s that the United States should pick up Britain's responsibility east of Suez and south of Gibraltar. Included in such thinking was access to the base at Simonstown. The base was a natural part of a global naval strategy for the United States, particularly in terms of an anti-Soviet deployment that would necessarily include the Indian Ocean. The deployment of Cubans into Angola heightened that view. Thus in the period since 1975, a regular stream of people who visited South Africa (as well as many who did not) called for United States' use of Simonstown. British denunciation of the Simonstown Agreement came in June 1975, with an immediate invitation issued by South Africa to France and the United States to use the facility.[52] The 1975-76 period was also a time of testing the tolerance of the U.S. foreign policy consensus for cooperation with the South Africans; in Angola, the fact that both the United States and South Africa were supplying UNITA with weapons put an intolerable strain on U.S. foreign policy when revealed. Such a reaction hardly augered well for the possibility of more overt military cooperation, such as United States' use of Simonstown.

Nevertheless, a campaign to obtain such access began in U.S. debates on foreign policy toward the region. The possibility was raised in the course of a longer list of remedial efforts required to renovate U.S. foreign policy.[53] The visits of U.S. representatives with connections to military and strategy organizations began to step up. At the 1978 national convention of the American Legion, a resolution was passed, stating that "It urges military cooperation. It recommends the US Navy reintroduce regular naval maneuvers with the South African Navy and fully utilize South African port facilities including the former British naval base at Simonstown."[54] In 1979 the American Legion sent a delegation to South Africa, calling once again for use of Simonstown.[55] In 1979 both Senator Harry Byrd (Va.) and the chairman of the House Armed Services Committee, Melvin Price, called for closer cooperation with South Africa; Byrd called for a "naval agreement" and Price urged the sale of long-range patrol craft for the coverage of the Cape route.[56]

With the invasion of Afghanistan, the South Africans believed that the United States would go after the bait. The South Africans stepped up their offers of Simonstown substantially, especially when the Carter administration began construction of the Rapid Deployment Force (RDF) and began searching for bases in the Indian Ocean region. The fact that they finally ended up with agreements for facilities in Oman, Somalia, Kenya, and Diego Garcia was disappointing to the South Africans, but the South Africans had tried. As one of their correspondents argued, "Now the Americans find themselves in the situation of beefing up their naval base at Diego Garcia in the Chagos Archipelago in the Indian Ocean while Simonstown, with readymade facilities and a strike capability in the Indian Ocean, is disregarded.[57] Afrikaner newspapers, in their editorials, insisted that the issue at stake was only a military one — the West would cooperate with South Africa, in using the facilities at Simonstown, in its own military self-interest. The English-medium newspapers argued that a political price would have to be paid in order to obtain such military influence on the West; in effect, the United States could take the bases only if racial policies were changed. As *The Star* argued, "The message is that this country is on its own. Vital though the Cape sea route is, the West still considers the racial cost of using Simonstown too high despite the gravity of the Russian threat. And it is up to the Government to change that by swiftly removing the taint."[58] The government line, however, resisted any connection between military and racial issues: the bases would be valuable to the West for their own sake.[59] As the prime minister commented at the opening of the expanded Simonstown base in March 1980, "These facilities are at the disposal of anyone who wishes to be on good terms with us, to their own great advantage."[60] From the South African perspective, the U.S. Navy would have been using Simonstown, on the advice of its naval leadership, had not the presidential election been held in the United States in 1980.[61] In other words, the black vote in the United States allegedly vetoed the use of Simonstown.

From the United States side, the plain message even from the new Reagan administration was that Simonstown would not be used by the U.S. Navy. As long as the State Department controls policy on such issues and South Africa continues to pursue its basic policies of racial separation with only marginal changes, military cooperation is not possible on such overt questions. At the same time, the multiplicity of contacts between the two countries ensures that military issues will arise. Reagan administration officials quickly indicated their intentions to increase military attachés and to provide training for the South African Coast Guard.[62] In the intelligence field, there is likely to be continuing, extensive sharing of data between the South African Silvermine complex and the United States/NATO satellite monitoring of the sea lanes. On occasion, South Africans wistfully indicate the desire for direct links between the two intelligence-gathering methods, but know that they have to settle for cumbersome exchange of information after processing.[63] In safeguarding against internal military threats, there is little scope for South Africans to involve the U.S. government in such efforts; on the other hand, the South African government has recently required many companies in South Africa, including foreign-owned companies, to organize all-white military reserve units for the Home Guard, which would be based in the factories and organized for factory protection.[64] Resistance on the part of companies to such moves is only temporary, and indeed, some companies would happily contribute to such defense efforts. The effect of such South African moves is to raise the visibility of U.S. investment in that country again.

Cooperation between the South African and U.S. militaries is not strictly a bilateral affair, and various episodes have illustrated the extent to which such relations are a function of pressure from other directions. As was already described, the original voluntary arms embargo by the United States in 1963 was implemented primarily to preempt a push by the African states for a mandatory embargo at the United Nations. Similarly, the expanded presence of the

Soviet Union and its allies in southern Africa has pushed the United States and South Africa closer together on military questions since 1975, with more and more officials on both sides indicating interest in finding a way to work together. In early 1981, perhaps to head off such cooperation by the new Reagan administration, the African states announced a new push for a total trade embargo against South Africa by the United Nations Security Council. The reason for that initiative lay in the apparent breakdown of the negotiating process for Namibian independence. The timing, however, was related to the arrival of the new U.S. administration, as well as the continuing existence of the Thatcher government in Britain. Conservative administrations had not coincided in the Britain-United States alliance since the early 1970s, and the Africans were worried about the possible community of interests they might find with the South African government.

CONCLUSION

The influence relationship between South Africa and the United States in the military sphere is not at all a reflection of capabilities. The psychological and political elements that infuse the perceptions on each side are much more important than purely military considerations. Even the potential for a military quarantine of South Africa by the United States and other countries is thoroughly discounted on both sides. The imbalance of military forces is less important than the South African determination to pursue its own strategy. There is a latent form of influence flowing from the symbolic role of the United States as the strongest Western state and the overwhelming technological superiority of U.S. arms; if a reasonable price (more political than economic) could be established for South African access to U.S. arms production and some granting of Western legitimacy to South Africa, the South Africans would be happy to bargain. Equally valuable to the South Africans would be some form of alliance guarantee, at the strategic level, that would pull them under the U.S. nuclear umbrella.

The South Africans have offered several items in such a hypothetical bargain. In a strictly military *quid pro quo*, the United States could have access to South African facilities, including Simonstown, as well as some voice in the allocation of South African resources in protecting the Cape route. There have also been discussions of guaranteeing supplies of basic mineral resources to U.S. consumers as part of such a bargain. Finally, some South Africans have discussed explicit tradeoffs between changes in South African race legislation and U.S. resumption of political-military cooperation with South Africa. All such bargains have never been formally undertaken. During the tenure of Henry Kissinger as secretary of state, the talks with Prime Minister John Vorster resulted in implicit bargains: for example, South African pressure on Rhodesia's Ian Smith to settle the Rhodesian civil war, in exchange for the United States giving South Africa more time in South-West Africa/Namibia. Such implicit bargains foundered, however, by being misunderstood or unfulfillable. Thus the United States-South African rift over Angolan policy not only created a local problem, it also persuaded the South Africans that any future deal with the United States would have to be much more explicit.

Thus the U.S. and South Africa have arrived at a stalemate over the years, owing in part to the political determination of the South Africans that they will pursue their own interests independent of, or in concert with (if the United States happens to be interested), the Western powers. This resistance to outside influence manifests itself at the microscopic level, for instance, observer/advisors from foreign countries who were attached to South African forces have commented on the bullheadedness of the South Africans in rejecting technical and tactical advice on military issues. At the broader, strategic level, the South Africans clearly reject the advice of the United States (as well as the rest of the world) with regard to more subtle ways of dealing with neighborly adversaries. The repeated bombing of SWAPO camps in Angola, the "hot pursuit" operations into Mozambique, and the seconding of South African forces to Rhodesia in the 1960s were all done with disregard for U.S. advice, which has argued for more sophisticated strategies in meeting "communist" threats. In the intelligence field, quite strict sharing of information, *quid pro quo*, has evidently developed, and any attempt to step over that tacit agreement, as in the case of the spy camera in the ambassador's plane, causes a major incident.

In terms of the operations of this relationship, there is an absence of symmetry. On the South African side, the principal institutions and operators are strongly centralized, with an apolitical Defense Force, a government-owned arms industry, and a political tradition (enforced by law) that defense matters do not enter public debate and the popular media. The openness of the U.S. system creates multiple opportunities for the South Africans to make contact. They can find new influence links inside or outside the government when they find old channels drying up. With regard to information, arms transfers at a fairly unsophisticated level, or the creation of domestic debate, the United States is far more permeable to the South Africans than the reverse. In the military field, this asymmetry is constantly visible.

NOTES

1. Also confusing in this context, but explored elsewhere, are the many meanings of the strategic value of South Africa: see Richard E. Bissell, "How Strategic Is South Africa?" in Richard E. Bissell and Chester A. Crocker, eds., *South Africa into the 1980s* (Boulder, Colo.: Westview Press, 1979), pp. 209-32.

2. Daan Prinsloo, *United States Foreign Policy and the Republic of South Africa* (Pretoria: Foreign Affairs Association, 1978), p. 58.

3. For these events, see the excellent summary in Agrippah B. Mugomba, *The Foreign Policy of Despair: Africa and the Sale of Arms to South Africa* (Nairobi: East African Literature Bureau, 1977), pp. 7-18.

4. Ibid., p. 254.

5. Ibid., p. 242.

6. Prinsloo, *United States Foreign Policy*, p. 58.

7. Mugomba, *Foreign Policy of Despair*, p. 8.

8. Cmnd. 9520 (1955), p. 4, quoted in Mugomba, *Foreign Policy of Despair*, p. 24.

9. For a lucid account of these movements, see James Barber, *South Africa's Foreign Policy, 1945-1970* (Oxford: Oxford University Press, 1973), chaps. 9-13.

10. Memorandum from Robert McNamara to President Johnson, November 20, 1964, LBJ Library.

11. Prinsloo, *United States Foreign Policy*, pp. 62-63.

12. White House Memorandum from Rick Haynes to Robert Komer, July 9, 1965, LBJ Library.

13. Mohamed El-Khawas and Barry Cohen, *NSSM-39: The Kissinger Study of Southern Africa* (Westport, Conn.: Lawrence Hill, 1976), p. 39. The stations, incidentally, were abandoned by the United States in 1975.

14. Prinsloo, *United States Foreign Policy*, p. 59.

15. See Barber, *South Africa's Foreign Policy*, chaps. 14-16.

16. Foreign Minister Hilgard Muller, to the House of Assembly, September 23, 1966, cols. 2804-5, quoted in Barber, *South Africa's Foreign Policy*, p. 290.

17. Ditchley Foundation Lecture, July 1968, quoted in Mugomba, *Foreign Policy of Despair*, p. 52.

18. Sir Alec Douglas-Home, "Why the Tories Will Sell Arms to South Africa," *The Daily Mail* (London), July 3, 1969, quoted in Mugomba, *Foreign Policy of Despair*, p. 62.

19. See G. R. Lawrie, "The Simonstown Agreement: South Africa, Britain, and the Commonwealth," *South African Law Journal* 85 (May 1968): 157-77.

20. Gail Cockram, *Vorster's Foreign Policy* (Pretoria and Capetown: Academica, 1970), p. 193.

21. Dana Adams Schmidt, "Military Chiefs of U.S., South Africa Confer Quietly," *Christian Science Monitor*, May 10, 1974, p. 1.

22. Ibid.

23. See Peter Niesewand, "NATO Supplies Go To Aid S. Africa," *Philadelphia Inquirer*, June 15, 1975, p. 6-C; "What Embassy Visitor Said He Saw," *The Times* (London), April 30, 1976; and "Magazine Reports on Government Communications Center," Paris AFP, in *FBIS Sub-Saharan Africa*, July 11, 1975, p. E7.

24. J. E. Spence, "South Africa and the Defence of the West," *The Round Table* (London), January 1971; reprinted in *Survival* 13 (March 1971): 78-84.

25. General M. A. Malan, "The Strategic Importance of the Republic of South Africa for the West," *SA Digest*, September 8, 1978, p. 5.

26. Gary Thatcher, "S. Africa Defense Head Bids West Oppose USSR in Africa," *Christian Science Monitor*, December 19, 1980, p. 4.

27. Ibid.

28. See Geoffrey Kemp, "South Africa's Defence Programme," *Survival* 14 (July/August 1972): 158-61; Chester A. Crocker, "Current and Projected Military Balances in Southern Africa," in Richard E. Bissell and Chester A. Crocker, eds., *South Africa into the 1980s* (Boulder, Colo.: Westview Press, 1979), pp. 71-106.

29. Douglas Brown, *Against the World: Attitudes of White South Africa* (Garden City, N.Y.: Doubleday, 1968), pp. 136-38.

30. International Institute of Strategic Studies, *The Military Balance, 1980-1981* (London, 1980), pp. 54-55.

31. Major C. J. Nothling, "Blacks, Coloureds, and Indians in the SA Defense Force," *South Africa International* 11 (July 1980): 21-28.

32. Ibid., p. 28.

33. South African Institute of Race Relations, *A Survey of Race Relations in South Africa 1971* (Johannesburg, 1971), p. 63.

34. An Armscor spokesman quoted in "The Tools," *RSA World* (Capetown) no. 2 (1978), p. 19.

35. See Anthony Sampson, "The Long Reach of the Arms Men," *The Observer*, February 4, 1979; and Robert S. Jaster, *South Africa's Narrowing Security Options*, Adelphi Paper no. 159 (London: International Institute of Strategic Studies (IISS), 1980), p. 16.

36. Jaster disagrees with this assessment, arguing that weapons technologies remain a key vulnerability: "But for a number of heavy and sophisticated weapons, including tanks, submarines, long-range maritime patrol aircraft, heavy artillery, radar and communications equipment, and certain types of ammunition, South Africa remains dependent on imports. A number of items, (for example, certain aircraft engines) are produced locally but they are dependent on foreign supplies of major components" (Jaster, *Security Options*, p. 40). Oddly, Jaster also argues that a South African confrontation with a major military power, such as the United States or the Soviet Union, is extremely unlikely in the next ten years — and those import items mentioned above are related primarily to defense against non-African threats to South Africa.

37. Chester A. Crocker, *South Africa's Defense Posture: Coping with Vulnerability*, Washington Paper no. 84 (Beverly Hills: Sage Publications, 1981), pp. 48-49.

38. Note, particularly, radical U.S. views in Western Massachusetts Association of Concerned American Scholars, *U.S. Military Involvement in Southern Africa* (Boston: South End Press, 1978); Michael T. Klare and Eric Prokosch, "Getting Arms to South Africa," *The Nation*, July 8-15, 1978, pp. 49-52; and other newspaper articles by the latter team. The African view is well represented by Mugomba, *Foreign Policy of Despair*.

39. See Michael Klare, "S. Africa Arms Sale: Gun's Still Loaded," *Boston Globe*, March 28, 1980, p. 17; Gilbert A. Lethwaite, "3 Nations Probe Reports of South Africa Arms Sales," *Baltimore Sun*, November 8, 1978, p. 2; UPI, "Vermont Firm Reported Subject of US Arms Case," *Journal of Commerce*, December 21, 1978, p. 9; "Olin is Charged with Arms Sales to South Africa," *Wall Street Journal*, March 15, 1978, p. 8; Michael T. Klare and Eric Prokosch, "How the United States Is Helping to Equip South Africa's Military," *Baltimore Sun*, February 19, 1978, p. 12; and Selwyn Rabb, "Inquiry in Smuggling Finds New York Role in Arms Trafficking," *New York Times*, July 21, 1981, p. A1.

40. Paul Ellman, "South Africa Is Gearing up Its Military," *Boston Globe*, September 28, 1980, p. 6.

41. See "A Nation at Battle Stations," *Newsweek*, September 29, 1980, p. 43; Noel Hughes, "South Africa's Navy Is Small, But Its Armaments Pack Wallop," *Philadelphia Inquirer*, October 19, 1980, p. 8-C; and Caryle Murphy, "Embargo Spurs S. Africa to Build Weapons Industry," *Washington Post*, July 7, 1981, p. 12.

42. *Business Week*, May 21, 1979, pp. 42-43.

43. Interview with P. W. Botha, reported in *FBIS Sub-Saharan Africa*, April 7, 1978.

44. Kenneth Adelman, "The Club of Pariahs," *Africa Report* (November-December 1980), p. 10.

45. Jack Anderson, "Nations to Begin Cruise Missile Project," *Washington Post*, December 8, 1980, p. B15, and 9, D8.

46. The extent to which the three nations may share a growing disregard for the United States, as a function of their individually disillusioning experiences with the United States, can be seen in a minor flap involving an Israeli official, Moshe Dayan; in late 1980, he was quoted on Israeli television as describing the U.S. Army as inferior; indeed, he maintained that, "Up to the rank of sergeants, most of the soldiers are blacks, who have a lower education and intelligence." For U.S. observers already sensitive to the Israeli-South

African ties, Dayan's remarks were worthy of indignant rebuttal. See Carl T. Rowan, "Dayan's Racist Remarks," *Washington Star*, December 5, 1980, p. 13.

47. One South African newspaper editorialized, "There is nought for anyone's comfort in the present acrimonious state of relations between the two countries. The US loses the ability to exercise any influence in this region." *Sunday Times*, April 15, 1979.

48. *The Star* (Johannesburg), May 17, 1980, p. 2.

49. See "Aide to Reagan, in South Africa, Says Arms Embargo Should End," *New York Times*, June 13, 1980. p. A11. The aide, Joseph Churba, was publicly rebuked by the Reagan campaign staff, was given no important post in the new administration, yet South Africans still indicated to the author that they thought Churba expressed the "real" views of the administration.

50. Bernard Gwertzman, "U.S. Challenges Visit by Top Military Men from South Africa," *New York Times*, March 15, 1981, p. 1.

51. "U.S. Says Mrs. Kirkpatrick Met South Africa Army Intelligence Chief," *New York Times*, March 24, 1981, p. A14; and Francis X. Clines, "White House Says Mrs. Kirkpatrick Didn't Know South African's Role," *New York Times*, March 25, 1981, p. A4.

52. "Washington was consulted by London on Simonstown, but according to American officials here [London], made no objection to ending the agreement" (Alvin Shuster, "Britain Cancels Pact Giving Her Use of South African Naval Base," *New York Times*, June 17, 1975, p. 11).

53. See, for instance, William P. Yarborough, *Trial in Africa: The Failure of U.S. Policy* (Washington, D.C.: The Heritage Foundation, 1976); and Walter F. Hahn and Alvin J. Cottrell, *Soviet Shadow Over Africa* (Miami: Center for Advanced International Studies, 1976).

54. Resolution 16, American Legional National Convention, New Orleans, August 22-24, 1978, in *The American Legion Magazine*, November 1978.

55. *SA Digest*, November 30, 1979, p. 6.

56. See *Defense/Space Daily*, December 5, 1979, p. 155; and *SA Digest*, February 2, 1979, p. 5. In the case of Senator Byrd, the South Africans misunderstood his position, describing him in their information publications as the majority leader of the Senate and "one of the most influential figures in the Senate." Such are the perils of analyzing influence in U.S. politics.

57. *The Star* (Johannesburg), January 11, 1980.

58. Ibid., January 10, 1980.

59. See "The Cape Route – Passageway to Survival," *Backgrounder* issued by the South African Embassy, Washington, D.C., no. 2, February 1980.

60. "Strategic Anchorages," *South African Panorama*, July 1980, p. 5.

61. See, for instance, George Young, "U.S. Navy Takes a Look at Simon's Town as a Depot," *Cape Times*, September 9, 1980.

62. "U.S. Seeks Closer Military Ties with South Africa," *Baltimore Sun*, June 18, 1981, p. 11.

63. See the comment by the Silvermine commander who argued in 1975 that the South African monitoring of the sea lanes "would profit greatly by a tie with United States satellite-monitoring facilities" (Michael T. Kaufman, "South Africa Develops Naval Base to Meet Soviet Threat and Hopes," *New York Times*, December 22, 1975, p. A13). The South Africans periodically remind the United States of the Silvermine complex by releasing their monitoring results publicly on movements of Soviet ships through the Cape area. These are publicized on Radio South Africa (Johannesburg International Service) or in South African newspapers and then picked up by the American *FBIS*.

64. "A Push from Pretoria for Company Militias," *Business Week*, March 2, 1981, p. 53.

4

ECONOMIC INFLUENCE: MOBILIZING THE PRIVATE SECTOR

The economic relationship between South Africa and the United States has become a virtual laboratory of nonmilitary coercion in the last two decades. But it has been only a laboratory, in that many forms of economic pressure have been proposed, discussed, occasionally applied by parts of the private sector on a pilot basis, but never fully implemented. In effect, the measures taken by both sides reflect the well-recognized consideration that a threat carried out is a diplomatic failure. This problem is particularly evident in the economic area, where economic coercion is quite distinct from economic sanctions; indeed, what we have witnessed in this area is overwhelmingly coercion. It is widely recognized, after all, that sanctions are unlikely to have the effect of changing South African policies. Economic sanctions might be adjuncts to military confrontation, but on their own, the sanctions cannot persuade the increasingly self-reliant South African society to change race legislation and the constitutional dispensation.

For most people on both sides, the goals of economic influence are only moderately coercive; few hope to precipitate a political (and certainly not an economic) cataclysm on the other side. Frequently, economic measures are urged only partially to have influence; they are also seen as a way to leave South Africa in isolation and to vindicate the United States with regard to an expected race war in southern Africa. For most U.S. policymakers, however, economic tools are the handiest and least militaristic means of changing South African race policies. For South Africans, economic coercion is meant both to dissuade the United States from carrying out threats and to focus U.S. attention on material threats to Western security.

Many different forms of coercion have been proposed recently: (1) trade embargoes against South Africa; (2) a ban on investment (or increased investment) in South Africa; (3) an end to U.S. multinational corporations' credits against U.S. income taxes for taxes paid by their subsidiaries to the South African government; (4) restrictions on raw material exports to the United States; (5) the use of U.S. corporations in South Africa as focuses of integration; (6) exchange controls on repatriation of profits from South Africa to the United States; (7) disruption of monetary stability by manipulation of gold prices; (8) the organization of black South African workers into activist, independent trade unions; and (9) a cutoff of oil flows to South Africa. These are simply the most prominent examples of a long list of attempts to force change in South Africa through its economy. Their success (or lack thereof) is widely debated, without conclusive result, and the reasons for the inconclusiveness explain much about the limits of economic influence.

The extent of economic ties between South Africa and the United States have provided an overwhelming political weight so far against the possible termination of the relationship as a form of leverage. Figures are frequently cited: over $2 billion in direct U.S. investment in South Africa, the United States now being the biggest trading partner overseas for South Africa, and the cooperation in technology that goes forward in a variety of fields. At the same time, there is not a single U.S. businessman working in some relationship with South Africa who is not aware of the pressures from anti-apartheid groups. The overwhelming majority of U.S. businesses have taken some steps to recognize a moral or political component in their ties with South Africa, and the holdouts against such pressure refuse to take measures conspicuously, as a matter of principle.

In each country, the economic elite has been seen as a special agent of influence in the other country. For those in the United States, the primarily English-speaking business elite has always been more attractive than the politically dominant Afrikaners. Those of English origin were generally more reform-oriented, prominent in opposition political parties, and had a greater stake in the maintenance of ties with the rest of the English-speaking world (including the United States). As a result, people in the United States tend to have a stronger affinity for them, attempt to overlook the fact that the English speakers have not been a meaningful political bloc in years, and attempt to put pressure on them to undertake changes in the South African political context. South Africans, on the other hand, see U.S. businessmen as a useful force for moderation or even reaction. The desire of U.S. businessmen to assure the security of capital and profits (their occupational mandate) tends to lead to a downgrading of the priority of human rights. This happens particularly frequently when the spectacle of mineral resource dependencies is raised. U.S. metal manufacturers have relied for many years upon the continuing flow of South African ores, and political instability arising from black discontent is a major threat to the viability of U.S. corporate planning. As a result, one has seen the group interests of U.S. corporations used as a balance when U.S. foreign policy would tend to swing toward confrontation.[1] Note also the formation of the American Chamber of Commerce in South Africa in November 1977, in Johannesburg, just when the pressure from the Carter administration on the South African government was reaching its apex. The obvious conflict was even addressed in press comments: "Officials of the chamber denied political motives and said they had been helped by the US Consulate in Johannesburg."[2] There were a variety of outlets in the United States for businessmen to spread the word that the United States could not afford to impose trade and investment sanctions, including conferences, magazines, trade publications, and even sources from the South African Embassy itself.[3]

In the meantime, throughout the course of the Carter administration, the position of the South African economy relative to that of the United States improved. In early 1979, the rand was freed from the dollar on the exchange markets. The price of gold in terms of dollars began to rise dramatically from the price fixed by the Bretton Woods system, reaching a high of $850 per ounce, with enormous implications for South Africa's balance of payments. And in 1978, South Africa's principal export market became the United States, with exports reaching $1.5 billion (19 percent of South Africa's exports) the United States was third in terms of South African imports, thus giving the South Africans a favorable balance of payments in the amount of $418 million.[4] Specific forms of technology were of interest on both sides, which fed further cooperation: the United States occasionally bought offshore oil rigs from South Africa.[5] South Africa bought agricultural technology from the United States,[6] and numerous U.S. companies attempted to buy South Africa's coal gasification technology.

Such cooperation would be crippled periodically, however, by reminders of the fundamental political unreliability of a country going through social change at too slow a pace. In the wake of the 1960 Sharpeville shootings, the 1976 Soweto riots, and again after the student and industrial unrest in 1980, U.S. investors had to reevaluate their position.[7] Inevitably, the effect on each occasion was to reduce the expected payback time on U.S. investments, and to lend a little more credence to those critics of U.S. economic involvement who argued for the primacy of politics. Even worse, U.S. multinational managers began to realize that their companies were emerging as the principal targets of activism both within and outside South Africa. Trade union growth among black workers grew most rapidly at the foreign-owned car assembly plants in South Africa, apparently with a sense that the multinationals were more likely to cave in to demands. All these political problems — described as the "hassle factor" by the president of the U.S. Chamber of Commerce in South Africa — did not prevent the United States from moving into first place in both exports and imports for South Africa in 1980.[8]

The importance of the question of economic influence between the two countries cannot be decided once and for all. The changes in the economies of the two countries over decades has been substantial in a structural sense. Even more important, the debate over changing South Africa's race policies inevitably returns time and again to the issue of economic pressure. In 1964, the journal

Foreign Affairs ran companion articles by two respected commentatoɪ South African affairs at that time, C. W. Manning and Philip Mason, and Maˌ argued for the use of economic sanctions against South Africa. Major inteˌ- national conferences were then held to debate that issue, yet, with the passage of two decades, more articles urging economic sanctions are still being published in *Foreign Affairs* and elsewhere, and far more conferences are being held.[9] After all this debate, the only generally shared conclusions are that the U.S. business community is inevitably ensnared in the issue of South African race policies, and that there is no simple solution. Beyond that, the nuances and disagreements over policies are numerous.

ROLE OF THE U.S. GOVERNMENT IN ECONOMIC SANCTIONS

The attempts of anti-apartheid forces in the United States to obtain eco- nomic sanctions against South Africa were a steady and growing movement throughout the 1960s and 1970s. At no time did the campaign reach the effec- tiveness or obtain the public posture of the analogous movement in Britain; in the latter country, closer ties with South Africa and a greater population of political refugees created higher visibility. As a result, the U.S. movement for sanctions received little attention until the 1970s, when the campaign began to focus its attention on multinational corporations. In the view of prosanction forces, it would be virtually impossible to sunder completely the United States- South African governmental ties (given the possibility of covert ties), so the avenue to significant raising of U.S. public consciousness was through demanding the withdrawal of U.S. corporations from South Africa.

For some U.S. corporate leaders, it was tempting to ignore the anti- apartheid forces. Those corporations with an autocratic leadership were better able to withstand the pressure, although the numbers dwindled over the course of the 1970s. The vast majority of corporations, however, began to develop counterarguments to sanction proposals. A representative set of objections would be: (1) Do the blacks in South Africa desire the withdrawal of U.S. investment? (2) What would be the effect of withdrawal? (3) Are the attitudes of those urging this action consistent?[10] For opponents of sanctions the answers were reasonably clear: few blacks did want sanctions, feeling that the principal impact would be a loss of black jobs; those urging disinvestment rarely apply the same logic to unpleasant governments in Uganda, the Soviet Union, or Uruguay.

The campaign for a ban on investment in South Africa occurred during the 1970s. In early 1971, the Episcopal Church of the United States demanded that General Motors close its manufacturing plants in South Africa.[11] A joint effort then gradually emerged involving the African-American Institute (AAI) in New York and combined church efforts, where the lead was taken by the Episcopal and the United Church of Christ. The AAI commissioned its Africa Policy

Information Center to focus on corporate involvement in southern Africa, even creating a periodic newsletter entitled *Update*. The center's action mandate focussed particularly on those African areas still under Portuguese rule, but it was rapidly becoming involved in South Africa itself. The churches were pressing shareholder resolutions of two types in the early 1970s: for withdrawal of investments and also for full disclosure of corporate activities in South Africa. As stated by one Episcopal Church official:

> The Church Project on Southern Africa has submitted disclosure resolutions in 1972 and 1973 asking companies to reveal (1) what they are doing within their plants and (2) what they are accomplishing in the country. The churches represented in the Project want information on which to base decisions, i.e., whether to urge that companies stay in South Africa or withdraw;
> Second, Mr. Francis observed asking for information produces movement.[12]

The principal targets in the early 1970s appeared to be Exxon, General Motors, American Metal Climax (AMAX), IBM, Mobil Oil, General Electric, First National City Bank (Citibank), Newmont Mining, and Phillips Petroleum, In IBM's annual meeting for 1975, for example, nearly an hour (or one-third of the time) was consumed by discussion of the resolutions submitted by 14 churches calling for withdrawal from South Africa.[13] The corporations began looking for a middle road by developing an institutional focus for comparing information about operating in South Africa without giving away trade secrets and losing a competitive edge. As a result, a small research group in Washington, the Investor Responsibility Research Center (IRRC), began to achieve prominence by its periodic assessments of corporate responsibility in South Africa. The reports were remarkably fair and frank, considering the fact that the IRRC was funded by annual membership subscriptions by the corporations under study.

An early test of the sanctions debate came in early 1976, when it became evident that the South Africans were about to let out the $2 billion contract for SASOL II, the new enormous coal liquification plant. The principal U.S. bidder for the project, Fluor Corporation, wanted to facilitate Ex-Im Bank loans to South Africa for the major components totalling about a billion dollars. The problem was that the Ex-Im Bank had been operating under tight restrictions since 1964: no direct loans to South Africans, and loans to U.S. concerns for South African operations up to only $2 million. It was apparent that Secretary of State Kissinger was more than willing to relax the restrictions.[14] After much pulling and hauling, including a public letter from 21 conservative congressmen, as well as letters from liberal forces on Capitol Hill, the president decided against changing the ban.[15] Fluor still became the principal contractor on the SASOL II project.

The increasing attention given South African issues by the Carter administration made it inevitable that pressure on corporations would step up. It was
not that the administration favored disinvestment — indeed, the policy of the
administration was to force change through maintaining investments — but the
change from Ford to Carter meant that the political center of gravity had shifted
leftward. One immediate casualty was the Polaroid operation in South Africa.
It was the first major target for disinvestment, dating back to the Polaroid
Revolutionary Workers' Movement of 1970. The company gave up its "Polaroid
experiment" in November 1977. South African medical authorities immediately
announced that they had already arranged to make a substitute x-ray film
locally in South Africa at less cost.[16] A very different voice was heard within
a matter of weeks, when Henry Ford II made a highly publicized inspection tour
of South African plants and announced, "we're here to stay." In a press conference, he said the U.S. government had exerted no pressure on Ford to pull out
and that U.S. managers were more enthusiastic than ever about operating in
South Africa.[17] The local reaction was positively euphoric; in a society where
business success is generally accorded the highest respect, the words of Ford
were received like Mosaic scripture: "At a time when negative statements about
South Africa are the order of the day, Mr. Ford's viewpoint is like a fresh wind
in an arid desert. One can only hope that the Carter Government will take note
of realists like Mr. Ford and revise the destructive policy they have adopted
towards South Africa."[18]

The prosanctions forces in the United States then went on to grander institutional forms. Much of the action shifted to the New York-based American
Committee on Africa (ACOA), which was critically important in unearthing the
evidence that forced Polaroid's withdrawal from South Africa. ACOA grew out
of the radical side of the civil rights movement, the founder being George
Houser, a white minister formerly active in CORE. It was able not only to obtain
endorsement of disinvestment by the NAACP in 1978 for the first time, but it
also established student recruiting efforts on numerous campuses, which helped
to spark protests against South African-related investments in 1977-79.[19]
Among the religious groups, the Interfaith Center on Corporate Responsibility
had rapidly become the coordinating center for the National Council of
Churches, both for shareholder resolutions and for liaison with "liberation
movements" in southern Africa.

The pressure on U.S. universities, which peaked in 1977 and 1978,
produced an interesting response. The sophistication of analysis applied to the
demands for disinvestment was probably higher than the campus crises over the
Vietnam War. The complications of the United States-South African relationship, combined with a genuine commitment on all sides to oppose racial
discrimination, led to the creation of innumerable committees of faculty, students, and boards of trustees. In many cases, the results were very carefully
crafted policies and extremely detailed reports on the relationship between
universities, investment practices, and the future of South Africa.[20] Most

committees of trustees eventually found refuge in a convenient formula, such as the Sullivan Principles; but there were major exceptions, as the president of the Stanford Board of Trustees indicated:

> The Trustees resisted student pressures for divestment, as well as the Commission on Investment Responsibility's insistence that we adopt an overall policy of corporate withdrawal from South Africa. Instead, the Trustees chose to consider each proxy issue by itself, and to place primary emphasis upon the corporation's own activities in South Africa, rather than the intangible benefits or injuries caused by their mere presence in that country.[21]

Examination of the issues had led most leaders of academic communities to reject divestment as a road to influence in South Africa, but careful withdrawal of investments from endowments was seen as potentially effective.

In the meantime, the Carter administration maintained its opposition to pending sanction legislation in Congress. The Black Caucus was pushing several bills, including a ban on Ex-Im Bank financing, a ban on government contracts to South African-based companies, a prohibition on all new investment, and a denial of tax credits to U.S. firms operating in South Africa. The Treasury Department strongly opposed any such financial measures; Assistant Secretary C. Fred Bergsten even argued that "the U.S. is more vulnerable to South African economic sanctions than South Africa is to U.S. action. The hard fact is that South Africa has more cards to play than we do in this area."[22]

The last area to come under attack by advocates of sanctions was the role played by private U.S. banks in making loans to South Africa. South African sources indicate that nondomestic capital imports accounted for one-third of the country's growth. By early 1977, South Africa's total foreign currency debt was approximately $7.6 billion, and U.S. banks held nearly one-third of that amount, or $2.2 billion.[23] In 1977 and 1978, South Africa's current account moved into surplus, just at a time when the United States-based Committee to Oppose Bank Loans to South Africa stepped up its efforts to end U.S. exports of bank credit to South Africa. The leading target of this strategy was Citicorp, reportedly holding over $1 billion of South African debts and generally the lead bank in syndicating loans from that country in the United States.[24] Citicorp had previously agreed to limit loans to South Africa "selectively, to constructive private sector activities that create jobs and which benefit all South Africans."[25] That policy was not a great sacrifice for Citicorp, since the government was heading into a period of trading surpluses, and it would be the private sector that was in need of loan money to weather the recessionary policies of the Pretoria government. As a result, it was hardly surprising that Citicorp received another public blast in early 1979 with the release of a United Nations/Corporate Data Exchange report; Citicorp's exposure in South Africa was said to have grown to $1.31 billion.[26] Some banks, including Chemical Bank, Mellon Bank,

Irving Trust, and Chase Manhattan, were reported to have ended all South African loans, while management at the Bank of America resolutely and successfully opposed a shareholder initiative to terminate about $200 million of loans in South Africa.[27]

The condition of the drive for disinvestment (and more generally for sanctions) by the end of the 1970s was thus quite strong. While the effort could not point to any real consensus, whether legislative or informal, an enormous number of U.S. institutions were either withdrawing from South Africa or making their involvement contingent upon further changes in racial policies. The only major group not yet actively involved was the U.S. trade union movement (with its enormous pension fund power), but some observers saw their involvement as being only a matter of time.[28] Legislation in the U.S. Congress was clearly going nowhere in the shadow of the Reagan administration, but that trend could not mask the impact the controversy had on a wide range of people in the 1970s. The challenge posed by the sanctions movement had caused a widespread reevaluation of the impact of U.S. corporations abroad. Interestingly, the challenge had not caused most corporate leaders to walk away from the problem; instead, they earnestly sought the most constructive avenue in terms of social progress for South African blacks as well as their own corporate investments.

U.S. ECONOMIC SANCTIONS

Even in its traditional role as a secondary element in Western economic ties with South Africa, the United States has been under particularly severe pressure to use trade ties to force a change in South African racial policies. Among the Western states, the United States has periodically been the most vociferous in championing human rights, and as a result, has encouraged domestic and foreign interest groups to increase pressure for sanctions. In addition, there is great diversity in the U.S. economic elite, and there have always been particular business leaders willing to accept the utility of sanctions against South Africa given a priority for social change in that country. For the most part, the campaign for economic sanctions has not been fought openly by U.S. corporate leaders; to oppose sanctions is to tempt opponents to make accusations of racist corporate leadership. As a result, much of the burden of fighting sanctions in the business world has fallen on those South African leaders and organizations from the English-speaking world with a particularly strong interest in not seeing old economic ties sundered.

The proponents of sanctions have been primarily church-related and political groups, whose argument for a total trade cutoff is ancillary to the need for radical political change. Their belief that it would precipitate a political crisis in South Africa is accompanied by a faith that it would bring forth a black-ruled state with significantly greater virtues than the present system in

South Africa (or any system likely to result from the present direction of reform in South Africa). To a degree, the proponents of sanctions have won part of the argument: increasing levels of military sanctions have been instituted since the 1960s in accord with United Nations resolutions, so that by the time of the Carter administration, a large number of civilian goods with possible military use were also being banned for export.[29] The effect of those military sanctions is problematical, as discussed in another chapter, and any move to extend them further into the civilian sector has been firmly opposed as being extremely costly with no guarantee of achieving the stated political goal.

South Africans have argued against extension of the sanctions on the basis of several points:

(1) Restrictions on trade and South African growth hurts primarily the black people in South Africa, since the prosperity of all people will depend upon export-led growth;[30]

(2) The sanctions will be largely ineffective in political terms as well as in economic terms: gold sales would be almost impossible to stop, and the Pretoria government has the legislation in hand for emergency mobilization of the economy.[31]

(3) Far greater damage would be done to the economies of the United States and the West, through the cutoff of mineral flows and the related unemployment (estimated at 75,000 in Britain, 80,000 in West Germany, and 250,000 in the European Community as a whole).[32]

(4) The damage done to the neighboring economies of Zimbabwe, Botswana, Lesotho, Swaziland, and Mozambique would be so large as to be unconscionable, given the likelihood that sanctions would probably have to be maintained for some time. The formation of the countervailing economic grouping of front-line states in 1980 — the Southern African Development and Coordination Conference — was created to meet this problem.

With the toughening of the respective political views on both sides in late 1979 and early 1980, the impetus for economic sanctions began to grow. Ironically, Ambassador Andrew Young had been a major force opposed to economic sanctions during much of the Carter administration, and his departure in mid-1979 led to a renewed effort at the United Nations and within the United States to force through mandatory economic sanctions against South Africa over the issue of South-West Africa/Namibia. The issue achieved greater salience with the Soviet invasion of Afghanistan, and the subsequent enactment of a U.S. grain embargo against the Soviet Union. For the sake of consistency, some argued, it was time for a trade embargo against South Africa. The South African government was led to issue a blast against the feasibility of an embargo.[33] Academic observers recounted the reasons for sanctions to fail.[34] Sanctions were seen, however, by their proponents as an active alternative to the Western Five Contact Group approaches to the South African government;

to the extent that the group's moves appeared to be fruitless, the movement for sanctions would revive. It was only with the passing of the Carter administration that the discussion became less shrill, with the growing unlikelihood that sanctions could be passed by any universal body. Even if passed by the U.N. General Assembly after a veto in the Security Council, the sanctions would not be universally enforced.[35]

The one area of the civilian economy where steady pressure for an embargo remained throughout the 1960s and 1970s was in the area of oil. The complete absence of oil and gas from the South African resource bank, even though complemented by tremendous coal reserves, has created an evident vulnerability in an age of widespread use of oil and gas in transport and space heating. A major South African challenge in the last several decades has been to reduce that area of vulnerability to outside pressure, and several major commitments were made to meet that need.

In the first place, the South Africans used a special relationship with the late Shah of Iran to assure themselves of oil flows to South African-owned refineries.[36] Thus any movement in OPEC to undertake an oil boycott of South Africa was largely doomed until 1979. With the arrival of the revolutionary regime in Teheran, in fact, the flow of oil to South Africa did in fact stop, and the equity share of the Iranian government in a major South African refinery had to be liquidated. The last effort to obtain Iranian sanctions against South Africa came in the summer of 1978, with the publication of a United Nations report on the feasibility of oil sanctions, the trip of Nigeria's chief of staff to Teheran, and pressure on the United States to place pressure on the Shah to go along.[37] Iran, then supplying 90 percent of South Africa's oil, still refused to agree to the idea.

The other, and well-publicized, measure taken by South Africa was to invest heavily in coal gasification methods, through a corporate instrument known as the South African Coal, Oil and Gas Corporation (SASOL). This government-owned company early adapted the German Fischer-Tropsch method of converting coal to liquid fuels, and although the first SASOL plant never supplied a great percentage of the liquid fuel needs in South Africa, it gave them great experience with the technology before the first oil crisis hit. Thus, in 1975, the South Africans decided to massively expand SASOL in order to provide as much of the liquid fuel needs as possible. The first contract, for over $1 billion, went to Fluor Corporation of the United States in early 1975 for construction of SASOL II.[38] Even though oil was meeting only 20 percent of South Africa's energy needs, it was in largely irreplaceable sectors. When SASOL II was planned, at a cost of $3 billion by a completion date of 1981, it was projected to meet about 15 percent of the country's oil needs.[39] The production costs projected for SASOL II were not terribly attractive ($12 per barrel), although it was a virtual bargain by the time of its completion. Several short-term responses to oil shortages were also developed: stringent limits on driving as well as stockpiling of about 2.5 years' worth of oil.

In 1979 South Africa's problems on the oil front multiplied. The cutoff of crude oil from Iran was complete, and it was forced onto the spot market to buy cargoes. Complaints were heard that the overall rise in oil prices during the "creeping oil crisis of 1978-79" was due in large part to the countries (particularly South Africa and Israel) forced onto the spot market by political changes in Iran.[40] The cost to the economy of rapidly rising prices in oil was also eating into the booming earnings of gold exports fueled by a price level of $300 per ounce. As a result, the South African government quickly announced a SASOL III, in order to double the capacity of SASOL II, which was still under construction.[41]

There was much less interest in the United States in oil boycotts of South Africa — although reports continued to urge its consideration[42] — than there was in utilizing the SASOL technology to solve U.S. energy problems. After all, the United States also had a great deal of coal and was suffering from rapidly rising oil prices. In past years, in fact, there had been test runs of U.S. coal in SASOL I to test the feasibility of the method given U.S. conditions.[43] Political problems emerged from time to time. In late 1979, "a senior SASOL executive said the State Department had already stopped the Department of Energy from having contact with SASOL."[44] But companies kept going to South Africa anyway, as SASOL made clear that it would be more than happy to license U.S. companies to use the SASOL process in constructing plants to meet President Carter's energy goals.[45]

Two events in March 1980 set the stage for the conflicts over oil supplies to South Africa. SASOL II began operating that month, with a consequent reduction in demand for oil from the global market. At the same time, a United Nations-sponsored seminar held in Amsterdam called for an international oil embargo against South Africa, with the creation of centralized planning for enforcement, all in the wake of a December 1979 General Assembly resolution on this subject. The United States was not represented at the seminar, but watched several of its allies, particularly Norway, attempt to tighten control over illicit flows of oil to South Africa.[46] A shipping bureau established in the wake of the conference began tracking all ships involved in any way in carrying oil to South Africa. The campaign had hardly begun, however, when the oil markets were decimated by the emerging glut of oil, a problem that afflicted particularly those African producers that were so loudly in favor of an oil embargo.[47] In effect, the period of real South African vulnerability had at least temporarily passed, and the implementation of the oil embargo weapon, if it would have even been effective, took so long that it came into being only when it was no longer relevant.

One can see both from the oil embargo question as well as from the larger trade embargo possibility that sanctions are closely tied to the issue of political will. The success of those implementing sanctions, as well as those resisting them, depends upon the mobilization of the nations that are required to sacrifice. It appears evident from the record of sanctions that South Africa is in rather better condition in this regard than the United States or African countries that are called upon to undertake such measures.

THE SULLIVAN PRINCIPLES

The United States quest for "racial change through engagement" is nowhere better illustrated than through the Sullivan Principles. At the same time, no theme of United States-South Africa relations represents better the slippery nature of social change in South Africa. And the use of U.S. multinational corporations to achieve that change proved to be both imprecise in impact and hazardous to measure, even assuming the best of intentions.

The history of pressure on U.S. corporations to change employment practices goes back many years, most notably to the actions begun against Polaroid Corporation in the early 1970s. The highly visible involvement of Polaroid in the apartheid structure — its cameras and film were reportedly used for preparation of the odious "passbooks" — made it a natural target, and Polaroid had reached a compromise with some protesters by promising to eliminate apartheid influence on its company operations. Very few employees were involved, and the South African made no apparent attempt to interfere. With the arrival of the Carter administration, pressures rose again for action by U.S. corporations. The human rights theme of the Carter foreign policy was understood by companies, and in a meeting in March 1977, 11 major U.S. companies met with Secretary of State Vance and black church leaders to issue six guidelines for U.S. operations in South Africa:

(1) nonsegregation of the races in all eating, work and comfort facilities;
(2) equal pay and fair employment practices for all employees;
(3) equal pay for comparable work;
(4) development training programs to prepare blacks for supervisory, administrative, clerical, and technical jobs;
(5) increasing the promotion of blacks to supervisory and management positions,
(6) improving the quality of employees' lives in nonwork environment (housing, transport, school, recreation, and health).

The leader of the black delegation to this meeting was the Reverend Leon Sullivan, a leader of the black community in Philadelphia and not incidentally the first black member of the Board of Directors of General Motors. He was personally close to Ambassador Andrew Young, and between them they arranged the meeting described above to announce to the world that it would no longer be "business as usual." The South Africans did not seem greatly impressed, arguing that South African business leaders were already ahead of the U.S. businessmen operating in South Africa in the area of desegregation.[48]

The South Africans could make a good case, given the founding of the Urban Foundation in Johannesburg in the fall of 1976. The South African business elite had decided that the social causes of the soiveto riots in the summer of 1976 would have to be addressed, and that the plight of the urban black could not be hidden. Within the next two years, 20 million rand were committed and a code of employment practices subscribed to by South Africa's major corporations. To avoid the appearance of just donating "conscience money" to Soweto, branches of the Urban Foundation were established in all large cities. The foundation did not spring solely from South African inspiration; indeed, the founders were proud to point to the precedents of the Urban Coalition and the National Alliance of Businessmen in the United States, both founded in response to ghetto riots of the late 1960s. David Rockefeller's speeches on the social responsibility of business were avidly distributed by the Urban Foundation.[49] Indeed, by late 1979, the U.S. contribution became more tangible than ideas; General Motors made the first direct U.S. gift by giving 500,000 rand to the Foundation.

The impetus for the Sullivan Principles came from another direction too: the European Economic Community (EEC) Code of Conduct. Modelled upon the British Code of Practice in operation since 1974, the EEC governments finally agreed to the code in September 1977. It was notable in being a governmental code, in contrast to the efforts in both South Africa and in the United States.[50] The British initiated the EEC movement for a code, and picked up West German support; both evidently wanted some institutional EEC protection for maintaining their investments in South Africa. The ultimate impact of the EEC Code is questionable, however, since compliance is voluntary by companies. The impact on the South African political scene was assessed in one set of hearings in West Germany in June 1980: "Asked to what extent the South African Government intervened in the practice of the code, company representatives replied that the government in fact encouraged West German companies to apply the code in order to diminish racial barriers as well as to encourage investment in South Africa."[51] With the aid of the code, South Africa was able to continue to raise funds in Eurocurrency markets, for example, $250 million credit in September 1980.[52]

With the broadening campaign for "corporate responsibility," Leon Sullivan published an expanded version of the original six principles in July 1978. They are enumerated below:

Principle I: Non-segregation of the races in all eating, comfort and work facilities.

Each signator of the Statement of Principles will proceed immediately to:
- Eliminate all vestiges of racial discrimination.
- Remove all race designation signs.
- Desegregate all eating, comfort and work facilities.

Principle II: Equal and fair employment practices for all employees.

Each signator of the Statement of Principles will proceed immediately to:

- Implement equal and fair terms and conditions of employment.

- Provide non-discriminatory eligibility for benefit plans.

- Establish an appropriate comprehensive procedure for handling and resolving individual employee complaints.

- Support the elimination of all industrial racial discriminatory laws which impede the implementation of equal and fair terms and conditions of employment, such as abolition of job reservations, job fragmentation and apprenticeship restrictions for blacks and other non-whites.

- Support the elimination of discrimination against the rights of blacks to form or belong to government registered unions, and acknowledge generally the right of black workers to form their own union or be represented by trade unions where unions already exist.

Principle III: Equal pay for all employees doing equal or comparable work for the same period of time.

Each signator of the Statement of Principles will proceed immediately to:

- Design and implement a wage and salary administration plan which is applied equally to all employees regardless of race who are performing equal or comparable work.

- Ensure an equitable system of job classifications, including a review of the distinction between hourly and salaried classifications.

- Determine whether upgrading of personnel and/or jobs in the lower echelons is needed, and if so, implement programs to accomplish this objective expeditiously.

- Assign equitable wage and salary ranges, the minimum of these to be well above the appropriate local minimum economic living level.

Principle IV: Initiation of and development of training programs that will prepare, in substantial numbers, blacks and other non-whites for supervisory, administrative, clerical and technical jobs.

Each signator of the Statement of Principles will proceed immediately to:

- Determine employee training needs and capabilities, and identify employees with potential for further advancement.

- Take advantage of existing outside training resources and activities, such as exchange programs, technical colleges, vocational schools, continuation classes, supervisory courses and similar institutions or programs.

- Support the development of outside training facilities individually or collectively, including technical centers, professional training exposure, correspondence and extension courses, as appropriate, for extensive training outreach.

- Initiate and expand inside training programs and facilities.

Principle V: Increasing the number of blacks and other non-whites in management and supervisory positions.

Each signator of the Statement of Principles will proceed immediately to:

• Identify, actively recruit, train and develop a sufficient and significant number of blacks and other non-whites to assure that as quickly as possible there will be appropriate representation of blacks and other non-whites in the management group of each company.

• Establish management development programs for blacks and other non-whites, as appropriate, and improve existing programs and facilities for developing management skills of blacks and other non-whites.

• Identify and channel high management potential blacks and other non-white employees into management development programs.

Principle VI: Improving the quality of employees' lives outside the work environment in such areas as housing, transportation, schooling, recreation and health facilities.

• Evaluate existing and/or develop programs, as appropriate, to address the specific needs of black and other non-white employees in the areas of housing, health care, transportation and recreation.

• Evaluate methods of utilizing existing, expanded or newly established in-house medical facilities or other medical programs to improve medical care of all non-whites and their dependents.

• Participate in the development of programs that address the educational needs of employees, their dependents and the local community. Both individual and collective programs should be considered, including such activities as literary education, business training, direct assistance to local schools, contributions and scholarships.

• With all the foregoing in mind, it is the objective of the companies to involve and assist in the education and training of large and telling numbers of blacks and other non-whites as quickly as possible. The ultimate impact of this effort is intended to be of massive proportion, reaching millions.

Periodic Reporting

The signator companies of the Statement of Principles will proceed immediately to:

• Utilize a standard format to report their progress to Dr. Sullivan through the independent administrative unit he is establishing on a six-month basis, which will include a clear definition of each item to be reported.

• Ensure periodic reports on the progress that has been accomplished on the implementation of these principles.

At that point in time, Sullivan had 103 companies formally committed to his principles, and he publicly articulated the view that the rules could be tightened periodically to ensure progress. In addition, he instituted a reporting program to monitor progress by companies.[53] Various universities responded by rejecting divestiture of stocks of companies operating in South Africa; in 1978, examples included Yale and Stanford.

Like the operation of arms control treaties, the verification process of the Sullivan Principles became and remained a highly contentious issue. In mid-1978, Sullivan selected Arthur D. Little, Inc. (ADL), a major consulting company, to help in the evaluation of responses to his questionnaire sent out in July. When the results came in and were summarized by ADL, much criticism was heaped on the cursory nature of the findings, and for the second report (December 30, 1978), ADL designed a 17-page questionnaire with much greater precision.

Controversy over the Sullivan process did not die down. On the campuses, groups continued to press for disinvestment. In a thoughtful rejection of the divestment position, Harvard President Derek Bok stated a view widely shared by the leaders of universities:

> Most persons who urge the sale of stock probably do so, not for the reasons just discussed, but because they believe that divestment will help to end injustice. . . . Those who take this position must know that universities cannot actually exert much direct economic pressure against American corporations by selling their stock, because such action will scarcely depress the value of the shares, let alone force management to change its policies.

Bok went on to reject divestment in terms of Harvard's mandate: "The Corporation has a legal and moral responsibility to administer Harvard's resources to further the normal academic purposes of the University and not to support causes or combat injustices for which we are not directly responsible."[54] The pressures on the universities then began to ebb, and Sullivan began to shift pressure to the Congress.

Sullivan found that he had carved out a position in the anti-apartheid war that was extremely exposed: he was the bridge between the proponents of divestment and the companies attempting a profitable bottom line on their South African investments. By early 1980, he appeared to weary of the war he was attempting to referee. Arthur D. Little, Inc. ceased processing reports because it had not been paid throughout 1979 and early 1980; Sullivan said that many corporations were not paying their dues to him, because he was getting too "radical." At hearings of the House of Representatives Africa subcommittee chaired by Stephen Solarz, Sullivan called for government enactment of a code, not only to move beyond voluntarism in principle, but also to rid himself of the verification headaches.[55] The outbreak of riots and strikes in mid-1980 intensified demands for mandatory code enactment. The decision about whether to introduce such a bill in Congress was left to Solarz, who evaded the issue by transferring to the East Asia Subcommittee with the new Congress in early 1981.

Without any support from Congressional or Executive leadership, Congressman William H. Gray III did introduce such a bill late in 1980, but it was not taken seriously.

The Sullivan codes were remarkable in being noncontroversial for so long. They coincided with a period in South Africa when management of all companies were labor-starved, and when they would have been undertaking the Sullivan recommendations anyway — just to fill the open slots. With good reason, then, the South African government had no public reaction to Sullivan's initiatives. His style was not appreciated, however, and his highly publicized trip to South Africa in September 1980 resulted in much bad press for his manner of scolding corporate executives in public.[56] Sullivan was lucky, too, in his initiative coinciding with the existence of the Carter administration. Andrew Young gave much help behind the scenes for Sullivan's initiative, increasing its impact, and ensuring Vance's endorsement at the inception of the campaign. In that sense, this effort was not entirely nongovernmental (as it is usually differentiated from the EEC Code of Conduct), and the effort was sure to weaken with the appearance of the Reagan administration.

LABOR: FROM CONFRONTATION TO SUBVERSION

The political instincts of U.S. labor were badly divided over the South Africa issue. At the apex of the AFL-CIO, the leadership had placed sufficient emphasis on national security and anticommunism as to justify a not unfriendly attitude toward South Africa. The conservatism of the legal white unions in South Africa was so extreme as to cause the AFL-CIO to throw in its lot with the largely disenfranchised black industrial work force in South Africa. The United States also found that it simply could not afford to give any impression of working with the South African government if it wished to have any credibility in black Africa. As a result, there were effectively no AFL-CIO programs in South Africa through the mid-1970s. The principal notice taken of South Africa was an occasional allegation of low-wage labor competing with U.S. industries; in 1974, for instance, the United Mine Workers attempted to avert plans of southern utilities to buy large quantities of South African coal.[57]

Changes began to occur in 1975, when South African regulations effectively banning black organization of trade unions were gradually not enforced. Membership in the unions expanded, recruitment of leadership cadres picked up, and occasionally genuine bargaining would occur with management.[58] Observers in the U.S. labor market saw some potential for working within the South African system for economic and political change.[59] The second element to give hope to labor reformers was the enactment of the Sullivan Principles by the major U.S. corporations operating in South Africa. While there were no provisions in the Sullivan Principles requiring the recognition of black labor unions, the principles represented a commitment by U.S. enterprise to working within the South African system. When it was recognized that the South African government was going to bend its laws significantly to allow the application of the Sullivan Principles, labor reformers saw an opportunity to test the South African system for a similar willingness to bend. To a large extent, they have found that ability to bend on a large range of issues.

Black labor was entering an enviable bargaining situation in the late 1970s. The need for skilled black labor was causing the rapid abandonment of job reservation in field after field, and the booming South African economy had to be deliberately cooled down by the South African central bank in order to keep pressures on labor and financial markets from going out of sight. The need for white immigrants was briefly aided by the Portuguese inflow in 1975-76, and by Rhodesians in the later years of that civil war. But such immigration could not conceivably satisfy the need for the rapid growth of job opportunities in South Africa. The boom in gold prices in 1978-80 only made things worse, with mines being opened rapidly, without any possibility of training sufficient labor in the immediate future. Foreign trade union organizers saw this as a fertile ground in which to organize additional unions among black workers, particularly among the 50,000 black workers employed by United States-owned businesses in South Africa.[60]

The South African government had also come to the reluctant conclusion that the most efficient path to labor discipline would be through the registration of black unions. As a vehicle for swinging public sentiment and laying the foundation for new legislation, the Wiehahn Commission was established and reported major suggestions for changes in labor legislation. The 1.2 million blacks permanently residing in "white areas" were given full rights to organize unions. The four million other blacks with temporary status were not given equal rights, although the Minister of Labor was allowed to make exceptions, and he has done so repeatedly since the 1979 government response to the Wiehahn Commission. American corporations were under particular pressure to sign an agreement with the newly registering unions in South Africa, in order to avoid condemnation from U.S. unions. In a large number of cases, in fact, the government was very slow in registering trade unions, and the companies negotiated with them anyway. By late 1979, there were 85,000 legal trade union members, with the largest being the National Union of Clothing Workers, led by Lucy Mvubelo, and having over 20,000 members.[61] Mvubelo became so prominent as a trade unionist that she made tours to the United States to argue against disinvestment, in both 1979 and 1980.

Movement was clearly coming at a pace somewhat too rapid for the South African government, and the growing infiltration of the AFL-CIO into South African training programs was not received by the government with continuous benevolence. Several years of experimental ties with South African black trade unionists had convinced the AFL-CIO that they were a worthy cause.[62] And just as major training programs were getting underway — for example, a seminar sponsored by the AFL-CIO given at Cornell University in the fall of 1980 for

South Africa labor leaders — the South African government perceived a threat in the rapid mobilization of blacks into unions. As a result, the AFL-CIO attacked as strongly as ever the policies of the South African government in public forums:

> South Africa's so-called "reforms" have so far resulted in registration for only "parallel" unions or black "company unions." Altogether, 182 unions are now registered. Not a single independent black union has been granted registration even though many applied several months ago. In view of the total failure of South Africa's so-called reforms, the growing wave of strikes and the beginnings of a widescale organizational effort by the black workers, it is more than ever necessary for the international free trade union movement to concert its forces to give maximum support to the independent black trade union movement.[63]

A major factor in the change of South African attitude was the accelerating growth of unions and apparently consequent strikes in some of the major industries. The transport manufacturing sector became plagued by strikes in late 1979 and 1980, with work actions erupting at Goodyear, Ford, and General Motors plants. In each case, there was not a clear pattern of the work action being controlled by the registered unions. As a result, the government interpreted the issue to be not only economic, but also a challenge to the political structure of unions established after the Wiehahn Commission report. In time, the workers in some plants even went out on strike in support of workers on strike at other plants: for instance, assemblers at Ford and General Motors plants refused to install Firestone tires on the cars, since the union at Firestone had an industrial dispute underway.[64] In earlier episodes of black strikes, some company management had experimented with laying off workers attempting to organize independent unions. In most cases, the companies failed, and the period 1979-80 saw progressive organization of black independent unions throughout the most advanced industries.[65] In the media, which was a particularly sensitive area, the black newspaper employees organized a highly effective national union, the Media Workers Association of South Africa, that gave rise to a number of confrontations with the government.[66] Amid this turmoil, however, the AFL-CIO was significantly disappointed in that all unions were evidently organizing along racial lines. The rejection by old-line white trade unionists of black efforts to organize did not give rise to integrated unions; black union leaders did not desire it either, evidently, since it would give rise to the possibility of being (or appearing to be) coopted by the existing power establishment. Given that choice, the AFL-CIO chose to cast its lot with the black trade unions.

SOUTH AFRICA'S RESISTANCE TO ECONOMIC PRESSURE

Pretoria's ability to reject the pressures from the United States basically increased with the passage of time. The policy of the South African government toward the Sullivan Principles, in any case, was to tolerate them benignly, so long as it involved the application of sensible rules by corporate managers. What the South African government found distasteful was the grandstanding in which Sullivan and other U.S. observers engaged periodically. Inspection trips to South Africa would frequently seem more to turn into political gestures than to retain their purpose of finding facts. Certainly the South African private sector had few problems with desegregation guidelines for U.S. corporations; they had their own Urban Foundation commitments to carry out.

At the same time, Pretoria was not so foolish as to rule out the possibility of an abrupt termination of U.S. investment, perhaps through the passage of mandatory sanctions by the Congress. As a result, the South Africans pursued a number of strategies designed to heighten their ability to resist potential American pressures: (1) establishment of intense economic ties in other directions, as with Taiwan and Israel, (2) the pursuit of technological self-sufficiency; (3) maximizing the value of exports and capitalizing on good fortune like the skyrocketing price of gold in 1979-80; and (4) pointing out to the United States and others the collateral damage that sanctions would wreak on nearby black states in southern Africa.

The Israeli connection did much for South Africa economically, aside from the military and political benefits noted elsewhere. In late 1980, for instance, an entire network of agreements was signed by Finance Minister Owen Horwood in the course of a five-day visit to Israel. The Israelis have been consistently ambivalent about South African ties; on Horwood's arrival, he gave no customary statement in the airport visitors' lounge, and the Finance Ministry planned no final press conference until the South African Embassy announced it was going to have one.[67] The meeting was not an innovation; for some years, the two countries had a joint economic committee. By the end of the very friendly talks, the finance ministers had agreed on an extensive package: (1) Israeli bonds could be sold in South Africa up to a specified limit; (2) South African investments in Israel could be as high as $60 million; (3) South Africa would give Israel a credit line of $165 million; and (4) the two countries created a senior standing committee to meet at least annually. In principle, the Israelis were to be granted fishing rights in South African waters, and South Africa was to supply coal to the new Hadera power station beginning in 1986.[68] The trade between Israel and South Africa does not yet comprise any significant percentage of South African trade with the United States and West Europe. After years of isolation, however, South Africa is more concerned with the principle of diversifying trade than the quantity.

South Africa also fostered as much technological independence as possible. Since the 1948 Nationalist revolution, a key component of strategic planning had been to place control of key elements of the economy in secure Afrikaner hands. This resulted in the creation of a massive network of parastatal corporations such as (ISCOR, ESCOR, ARMSCOR). By the 1970s, a slight change of emphasis occurred in response to this problem: secure control could be defined as either "Brit" or "Boer" for most people, and more attention had to be given to advanced technologies than to basic industries. Thus, one saw the huge investment in the coal gasification process of SASOL, as well as its continual refinement. In the computer field, the government-owned Industrial Development Corporation opened a joint venture semiconductor plant in 1980 with Siemens. It was scheduled to eventually produce ten million large-scale integrated circuits annually. Locally produced computers (mostly by Allied Technologies) have as much as 70 percent South African-produced components.[69]

In heavy industry, Barlow Rand has led the way in producing special alloys. By 1980 it was expanding stainless steel production to fulfill all of South Africa's needs: in fact, the capacity of the plants would probably be sufficient to export 15-20,000 tons annually.[70] In the area of synthetic chemicals, SASOL was finding that a wide range of products could be produced through the use of catalysts, and thereby it could save foreign exchange and know that the technological capability to be independent was present.[71]

South Africa's greatest opportunity to feel independent of foreign economic pressures in recent decades came with the rise of the gold price in 1979-80 to astronomical heights. As with any bonanza, everybody had a different idea of how to spend the unexpected $5 billion trade surplus in 1979. Some wanted to pass along major benefits to the black population. Others wanted to ease import restrictions and allow freer capital exports.[72] Not only did the government run out of Kruggerands to sell in December 1979, but to keep the price from going too high, it announced that it would sell half-Kruggerands.[73] Opponents of apartheid in the United States briefly tried to force an end to Krugerrand sales in the United States in early 1980.

Finally, South Africa could raise, with some discretion, the damage likely to be done to the southern African states dependent upon the South African infrastructure: Botswana, Lesotho, Swaziland, Mozambique, and to a lesser extent, Zimbabwe and Zambia. As the minister of Foreign Affairs of Botswana said, "Sanctions against South Africa would mean sanctions against Botswana." He believed that "in the case of sanctions South Africa would, without being deliberate, deny Botswana oil."[74] The knowledge of damage that would be done to other economies has certainly deterred the United States on occasion from stronger action against the South African economy.

South Africans came to attack the logic of foreign sanctions through questioning three assumptions of prosanctions forces:

(1) that a crippling economic situation can be brought about in the short term;
(2) that the mass of black South Africans put political advantage before material progress;
(3) that if black political control is achieved, the mass of blacks will necessarily have greater political control of their destiny than they have at present.[75]

Each of these questions addressed concerns of different parts of U.S. society preoccupied with South Africa. The debate over securing U.S. economic interests in southern Africa frequently revolved around the short-term/long-term issue. Ostracizing South Africa in order to induce a rapid transition to black rule was seen by some as facilitating U.S. interests in the long run; but if the "succession process" would be long and bloody, the economic value of South Africa to the United States would surely be minimal at the end of the process, whether through physical destruction in South Africa or the creation of alternate suppliers. Sorour's second point addresses the proponents of self-determination: how does anybody know the political priorities of South Africa's black community? Increasingly sophisticated opinion polling has taken place in recent years in South Africa, and the results are quite ambiguous on the issue of a tradeoff between political participation and economic prosperity. At the same time, we are inundated by people of all races who claim to know what the blacks *really* think about political choices. Finally, the concerns of human rights/ democracy advocates are addressed: how does one assure (or even make more likely) the evolution of South Africa in a democratic direction? No side to the debate has a simple answer to that question, and in posing the question, South Africans are able to reduce the salience of that concern in U.S. thinking.

SOUTH AFRICAN MINERAL SANCTIONS

The difficulties faced by the United States in raw material imports in 1972-74 created a major diplomatic opportunity for South Africa. It has been noted with some frequency that after the 1973 OPEC oil price action there occurred some efforts at emulation by the major producers of minerals. South Africa was not part of those cartel discussions for political reasons, but the anxieties among consuming countries with regard to stable imports of minerals eventually gave rise to "strategic mineral gaps." Indeed, prices in many mineral commodities did rise precipitously, beginning in the early 1970s, but there has been no deliberate cutoff of strategic mineral flows. Rarely has it been pointed out that U.S. policies went through a similar cycle of concern over minerals at the time of the Korean War, but the "crisis" was quickly eased by a buildup of stockpiles and an expansion of production capacity.

The concern over "mineral blackmail" in the 1970s was also fed by a concurrence of intellectual trends on the political left. The environmental movement in the United States left an entire generation persuaded of an imminent crisis in nonrenewable resources, and basic minerals were clearly nonrenewable except through recycling. The additional conviction of the left that the South African government would do anything to avoid changes in political power combined with that sense of scarcity in resources to give real credibility to a South African threat to the U.S. economy. Andrew Young reflected concern over that "threat" on numerous occasions, as did the Franklin Thomas Commission report in 1981 in making key minerals a major policy concern.[76] South African government documents approvingly cited Young on this issue.[77]

The unholy alliance between left and right was largely completed in the United States before South Africans paid any attention to the issue. U.S. industry representatives were more than willing to accept the premises of alarm about South African supplies, which was argued by the left, even though they differed on policy conclusions. A particularly active speaker on the problems of chrome and manganese supplies was E. F. Andrews, an experienced Washington operator on behalf of Allegheny Ludlum Industries of Pittsburgh. Andy Andrews almost single-handedly determined the course of debate on strategic minerals in Washington in the late 1970s, from helping to organize Congressional hearings in relation to the Santini Report, to lobbying for a non-Marxist outcome in Zimbabwe, to arranging foundation support for think tank studies on the subject, and making countless speeches on the possibility of mineral cartels. In 1978 the National Research Council in the United States produced a study entitled "Contingency Plans for Chromium Utilization" that not only confirmed Andrews' arguments, but went on to argue that southern Africa would overwhelmingly dominate chrome reserves by the year 2000.[78]

As long as United States-South African relations remained reasonably civilized, the argument remained in U.S. hands. By mid-1979, however, the South Africans had begun to respond. S. P. Botha, the minister of mines, laid out the parameters of the argument in April 1979 in a speech to Parliament: "South Africa is more important to the survival of the USA than the USA is to South Africa. We do not threaten the USA, but the United States should realize that South Africa does not regard it as the sole buyer of our minierals. Nor is the West our sole buyer."[79] Statistics began to emerge in a variety of places, basically along the lines shown in Table 2. The principal appeal to the United States dwelt upon the fact that the Soviet Union was the principal alternate source for a number of the minerals listed in the table. As the minister

TABLE 2
South African Role in World Mineral Reserves

Mineral	Percent of Noncommunist Reserves	Percent of World Reserves
Vanadium	90	49
Platinum group	89	75
Chrome	84	81
Manganese	93	78
Gold	64	51
Fluorspar	46	35

Source: Compiled by the author.

of mines argued, South Africa should not be isolated because it would "leave the West extremely vulnerable to Russian manipulation."[80]

By 1980 the rhetorical environment was encouraging those engaged in the minerals debate to become even more shrill. In an address to the American Mining Congress (AMC), Simon Strauss, Chairman of the AMC, said, "If South Africa and Rhodesia chose to throw their lot with the Russians — and past experience has shown that odd bedfellows have gotten together when it's in their interest — they could form an effective price for at least five vital minerals."[81] In the short run, this view argued for a friendly attitude toward the South African government, with the expansion of the U.S. stockpile (through government-subsidized reopening of U.S. mines) to withstand likely future shocks. Andrews argued at the AMC: "This country is dependent on imports for about twenty vital minerals, and there are a few on which we have no leverage whatsoever. We have no national stockpile other than for defense." The left, naturally could agree with the utility of stockpiles; there was just an unbridgeable gap in terms of financing. In fact, the first budget of the Reagan administration allocated $100 million for a buildup of government stockpiles. Since the problem is greater in the West European economies, however, a cutoff of South African supplies in all directions would create havoc for the West as a whole.[82] Subsequently, the Department of Commerce suggested that stockpiling coordination should be undertaken through the OECD, where Europeans and the United States are represented.

The U.S. debate on minerals, as an adjunct of political direction in the southern African region, picked up momentum in the summer and fall of 1980. Congressman James Santini, a Democrat from Nevada, took a small delegation to southern Africa in January 1980, and then published a report in July through the Subcommittee on Mining that he headed.[83] Santini not only found that "America is now dependent on foreign sources in excess of 50% for 24 of the 32 minerals essential to national survival," he also argued:

Given the presence of South African mining operations at the cutting edge of racial progress in that country, and given the extraordinary concentration in their Nation of much of the world resources of many vital mineral products that are important to the survival of the industrial West, the subcommittee takes the position that the US Government should exhibit encouragement and interest in South Africa's undertakings and in their efforts — and that threats of international sanctions against South Africa should be opposed. Closer ties with the South African mineral industries at a time of growing cartelization by mineral suppliers cannot but help America's long-term interests and needs.[84]

Such a point of view could not remain unchallenged, and the Senate provided the countercharge.[85] The senators disputed virtually every point in the Santini Report, from the "significant, but not critical, importance" of South

African minerals to the measures to be taken:

> It is fortunate that in the case of each of the critical minerals imported from South Africa, means are available for dealing with an interruption without depending on the Soviet Union as an alternative supplier. These means may be costly, and they cannot in all cases be implemented without disruption. But, in general, the disruptions can be minimized if preparations for a possible cut-off in South African supplies are made in advance. Advance preparations suggested include stockpiling, conservation, process changes, alternative technologies, use of functionally acceptable substitutes where possible, providing incentives to encourage design changes, recycling and exploiting untapped reserves.[86]

The Santini Report did much to encourage internationalists in South Africa about prospects for improved communications with the United States. The report from the Senate was largely ignored as irrelevant to South Africa, arguing as it did for unilateral U.S. measures. Even the Afrikaner establishment was aware of Santini's conclusions; an editorial in *Die Burger* argued:

> The report is a pretty remarkable document, since it reveals a soberness towards prevailing South African political and social circumstances which is absent even in certain South African circles, particularly in the official opposition and the newspapers supporting it. . . . The report is a fresh breeze in the stuffy atmosphere of mutual distrust that has existed between Washington and Pretoria for the past few years.[87]

The debate over possible sanctions by South Africa ended inconclusively. There was clearly not an abject dependence of the United States on South African sources, particularly with Zimbabwe pursuing a political and economic path separate from the South Africans.[88] At the same time, the costs of international diversification or of national security measures were clearly going to be considerable for the U.S. taxpayer or for U.S. corporations. In a time of economic retrenchment, there was little likelihood of settling the question satisfactorily.

CONCLUSION

By the early 1980s, the issue of economic influence had become more salient in U.S. policymaking; likewise, the South African government was seeking forms of economic coercion that would counter pressures from the United States. Several factors brought economics to the fore. The settling of the Rhodesian question caused attention to focus on South-West Africa/ Namibia, and with prime responsibility centered on the United Nations Security Council, the form of coercion always suggested at the United Nations was that of economic sanctions against South Africa. While the U.S. government reinforced its adamant opposition to such sanctions with the appearance of the

Reagan administration, support from veto-wielding allies declined with the election of a socialist government in France committed to changing Giscardian policies in Africa. The 1980s were different, too, in the evident loss of U.S. predominance in the global economy. Few domestic policies could be pursued without taking international considerations into account, and South Africa played a relatively significant role on a variety of those issues: gold policies, strategic mineral supplies, secure oil transport routes, and coal-related energy technologies.

One might have assumed that the contest for economic influence was terribly one-sided. In fact, it was not owing to the substantial growth rate of the South African economy in the 1970s, as well as the closer cooperation between the South African government and private enterprise in that country. At the same time, it is likely that the U.S. debate was more influenced by outsiders (South Africans) than internal South African debate over its policies toward the U.S. could be infiltrated by people in the United States. The two societies operated differently, and as a result, there was generally a stalemate in the economic contest in the 1960s and 1970s.

NOTES

1. See "US Business Says No to One-Man-One-Vote in SA," *SA Digest*, July 8, 1977, p. 10.

2. "Bid to Boost US-SA Trade," *SA Digest*, December 2, 1977, p. 14.

3. See Michael R. Gordon, "Can the US Afford to Dump South Africa?" *The Interdependent*, December 1977, p. 1; "USA/South Africa: The Trade Connection," *Backgrounder* issued by the Information Counselor, South African Embassy, Washington, D.C., 1978.

4. "United States Become S. Africa's Best Customer," *Journal of Commerce*, May 21, 1979, p. 14A.

5. "SA-Built Oil Rig for US Company," *SA Digest*, July 15, 1977, p. 32.

6. "Hytec SA Boosted by Big US Deal," *Sunday Times*, February 10, 1980, p. 10.

7. See, for example, "The Bubbling Cauldron," *Journal of Commerce*, June 5, 1980, p. 4; and "South Africa's Foot-Dragging Vexes U.S. Companies," *Business Week*, October 20, 1980, pp. 56-58.

8. "US Becomes S. Africa's Largest Trade Partner," *Journal of Commerce*, May 21, 1981, p. 17.

9. An insightful analysis of the arguments, as well as the effects of the passage of years, was recently published by Newell M. Stultz, "Foreign Pressures on South Africa," *AUFS Reports*, no. 5, 1981.

10. Drawn from a speech to a conference by the Ford Foundation by John H. Chettle, "Is There Any Justification for Economic Pressure Against South Africa?" February 15, 1978.

11. Rejected by G. M. chairman James Roche. See "G.M. Will Continue South Africa Work," *New York Times*, February 21, 1971, p. 21.

12. "Africa Policy Information Center Seminar: Summary Notes," *Update*, March 28, 1973 (New York: African-American Institute), p. 20.

13. "Churches Again Drawing Bead on U.S. Sales to South Africa," *Philadelphia Inquirer*, January 20, 1975, p. 6-C; and "IBM is Scared on South African Role," *New York Times*, April 29, 1975, p. 43.

14. "Loans to South Africa Being Urged," *New York Times*, January 31, 1976, p. 2.

15. "U.S. Will Continue Curb on Loans to South Africa," *New York Times*, March 13, 1976, p. 3.

16. "Polaroid Pull-Out Saves SA Cash," *SA Digest*, December 2, 1977, p. 6.

17. *SA Digest*, January 27, 1978, pp. 5-6.

18. *Die Vaterland*, January 20, 1978, in *SA Digest*, January 27, 1978, p. 29.

19. "Small Group of Activists Puts Pressure on Big Firms to Get Out of South Africa," *Wall Street Journal*, February 23, 1978, p. 48.

20. See, for instance, "The Report of the Advisory Committee on Shareholder Responsibility With Respect to South Africa Shareholder Responsibility," Harvard University, Professor Henry B. Reiling, chairman, March 24, 1978; and "Statement on Investment Responsibility Concerning Endowment Securities," Stanford University, December 27, 1977.

21. Correspondence to the author, May 23, 1978.

22. "S. Africa Investment Curbs Hit by Carter," *Journal of Commerce*, August 11, 1978.

23. Desaix Myers III, *Business and Labor in South Africa* (Washington, D.C.: Investor Responsibility Research Center, May 1979), pp. 27-28.

24. "Study Seen Heating Debate on U.S. Bank Lending to S. Africa," *Journal of Commerce*, August 29, 1978, p. 1.

25. Citicorp, *Proxy Statement 1977*.

26. "Bankers Blasted for Continuation of S. Africa Loans," *Journal of Commerce*, April 3, 1979, p. 1.

27. "Bankamerica Will Not Stop S. Africa Loans," *Journal of Commerce*, April 26, 1979, p. 10.

28. "U.S. Disinvestment Drive Against SA Builds Up," *South Africa Foundation News*, May 1980, p. 1.

29. Maxwell J. Mehlman, Thomas H. Milch, and Michael V. Toumanoff, "United States Restrictions on Exports to South Africa," *American Journal of International Law* 73 (October 1979): 581-603.

30. Harry Oppenheimer, "Don't Stop Investing in South Africa," *Christian Science Monitor*, November 1, 1978.

31. "South Africa: Countering the Threat of Economic Sanctions," *Business Week*, November 20, 1978, p. 50.

32. Arnt Spandau, "Recent Developments in the Sanctions Debate: Foreign Attacks and South African Responses," in *Sanctions Against South Africa* (Johannesburg: South African Institute of International Affairs, 1979), p. 16.

33. "Botha Warns of Folly of Sanctions," *Washington Post*, January 20, 1980, p. A28.

34. Henry S. Bienen and Robert Gilpin, "Economic Sanctions: An Obsolete Weapon?" *Forbes*, February 18, 1980, pp. 91-92.

35. See comments of South African Prime Minister P. W. Botha, in a television interview reported by Johannesburg International Service, in *FBIS Middle East and Africa*, March 13, 1981, p. U4.

36. The special ties related to the fact that the Shah's father lived in South Africa during World War II and, in fact, died there; his remains were eventually returned to Iran for burial.

37. These details spelled out in "The Plan to Cut Off South Africa's Oil," *Foreign Report*, June 14, 1978, pp. 2-5.

38. "Fluor Set South African Plants," *New York Times*, March 11, 1975, p. 58.

39. "Would Sanctions Work?" *The Economist*, June 17, 1978, p. 97.

40. See "What to do about oil prices," *The Economist*, May 26, 1979, p. 18.

41. "How Oil Threatens South Africa's Boom," *Business Week*, July 16, 1979, p. 56.

42. For example, David M. Liff, *The Oil Industry in South Africa* (Washington, D.C.: Investor Responsibility Research Center, January 1979).

43. See *OGJ Newsletter*, December 12, 1977, with report of 16,000 ton run of Texas lignite coal in SASOL I for Exxon USA.

44. "South Africa Oil Plan May Be Hard to Sell," *New York Times*, September 5, 1979, p. D18.

45. See "Sasol Pushes Licensing of Coal Process," *Oil and Gas Journal*, September 10, 1979, pp. 108-9; "Providing Fuels for the Future," *Backgrounder* issued by the Information Counselor, South African Embassy, November 1979; "US Men Visit SASOL," *SA Digest*, January 11, 1980, p. 6, describing a visit by Congressmen James Wright and James Santini, as well as Senator Bennett Johnson.

46. "Norway Vetoes Oil Boycott of S. Africa," *Journal of Commerce*, September 25, 1980, p. 33; "Norway Moves to Halt Oil Shipment to S. Africa," *Journal of Commerce*, January 20, 1981, p. 34.

47. This was presciently recognized in "The Oil Boomerang," *West Africa*, November 3, 1980, p. 2159. The editors pointed out that "oil can be a double-edged weapon and wielding it can injure Nigeria. Nigeria has an almost absolute dependence on her income from oil, which represents 90.2% of her exports."

48. SABC Broadcast, in *SA Digest*, March 11, 1977, p. 9.

49. "Some Foreign Idea," in "The Urban Foundation's Two Years On, Special Report," *Financial Mail*, February 16, 1979, p. 4.

50. See James Barber, "The EEC Code for South Africa: Capitalism as a Foreign Policy Instrument," *The World Today*, March 1980, pp. 79-87.

51. "European Codes An Alternative to Sanctions," *The South African Foundation News*, August 1980, p. 4.

52. "$250m. Eurocredit Plan Marks Rehabilitation of South Africa," *Financial Times*, August 29, 1980, p. 1.

53. "Rules for U.S. Concerns in S. Africa Widened," *New York Times*, July 6, 1978, p. D5.

54. Derek Bok, "Reflections on Divestment of Stock: An Open Letter to the Harvard Community," supplement to the Harvard University *Gazette*, April 6, 1979, p. 6.

55. "Pushing U.S. Business to Liberalize Faster," *Business Week*, July 7, 1980; and "Sullivan, U.S. Firms Debate S. Africa Business Code," *Journal of Commerce*, May 16, 1980, p. 9.

56. See *SA Digest*, September 12, 1980; for example, according to *Oggenblad*, "If this is the best example of a balanced and reasonable American voice, we'd hate to see their fanatics in action."

57. Ed Townsend, "UMW Seeks to Bar South African Coal," *Christian Science Monitor*, August 22, 1974, p. 10.

58. "Black Labor Unions in South Africa Slowly Gaining," *New York Times*, June 19, 1975, p. 10.

59. Roy Godson, "Black Labor as a Swing Factor in South Africa's Evolution," in Richard E. Bissell and Chester A. Crocker, eds., *South Africa into the 1980s* (Boulder, Colo.: Westview Press, 1979), pp. 49-70.

60. "Why Pretoria Is Giving Black Workers a Break," *Business Week*, June 18, 1979, p. 130.

61. "South Africa's Black Unions Are Suddenly Beautiful," *The Economist*, October 6, 1979, pp. 79-80.

62. See "AALC Officials Visit South Africa; Lay Groundwork for Study Program," *AALC Reporter*, May-June 1980, p. 1.; the background is sketched out in L.C.G. Douwes Dekker, "Notes on International Labour Bodies and Their Relevance to South Africa," in Deon Guldenhuys, ed., *The South African Labor Scene in the 1980s* (Johannesburg: South African Institute of International Affairs, 1980), pp. 1-16.

63. "Brown, O'Farrell Present AFL-CIO Views on South Africa at ICFTU Conference," *AALC Reporter*, November-December 1980, p. 7.

64. "Black Union Ends Strike at South African Auto Plant," *New York Times*, June 4, 1981, p. A12.

65. Ibid.; and "2 U.S. Companies Lay Off Blacks in South Africa," *New York Times*, November 23, 1979, p. A9; and "S. Africa Labor Woes Spark Violence," *Journal of Commerce*, June 26, 1980, p. 11.

66. "Striking Employees Are Dismissed at Johannesburg Paper for Blacks," *New York Times*, November 29, 1980, p. A6; "South Africans Ban Two Leaders of a Black Union," *New York Times*, January 2, 1981, p. A8.

67. "South African Finance Minister Arrives for Talks," in *FBIS Mideast and Africa*, December 9, 1980, pp. N1-N2.

68. *Jerusalem Post*, December 14, 1980, p. 1.

69. "Homespun Computers," *The Economist*, November 15, 1980, p. 91.

70. "S. Africa Plans for Self-Sufficiency," *Financial Times*, September 4, 1980, p. 4.

71. See "Synthetic Chemicals in South Africa," *Science*, August 17, 1977.

72. See "S. Africa Relaxes Import Restrictions," *Journal of Commerce*, July 16, 1980, p. 12; "S. Africa Economy Soars on Wings of Gold Boom," *Christian Science Monitor*, January 7, 1980, p. 8.

73. "Exchange Curbs Eased Further in South Africa," *Journal of Commerce*, February 26, 1980.

74. Johannesburg International Service, in *FBIS Mideast and Africa*, March 16, 1981, p. U1.

75. J. de L. Sorour, "The Role of Foreign Business in South Africa's Economic and Political Development," *South Africa International*, July 1979, pp. 1-9.

76. See the Report of the Study Commission on U.S. Policy Toward Southern Africa, *South Africa: Time Running Out* (Berkeley: University of California Press, 1981).

77. "South Africa's Vital Minerals," *Backgrounder* issued by the Information Counselor, South African Embassy, Washington, D.C., 1978.

78. Daniel I. Fine, "The Big U.S. Stake in South Africa's Minerals," *Business Week*, January 29, 1979, p. 55.

79. Quoted in "Plain Facts on Minerals," *Backgrounder* issued by the Information Counselor, South African Embassy, Washington, D.C., 1979, p. 4.

80. "South Africa Cites Its Strategic Role," *Journal of Commerce*, November 30, 1979, p. 1.

81. "Need for Minerals Imports Raises Spectre of Cartel," *Richmond News-Leader*, December 6, 1980.

82. "South African Officials Imply Minerals Could Be Weapons to Preserve Apartheid," *Wall Street Journal*, May 30, 1980, p. 30.

83. "Sub-Sahara Africa: Its Role in Critical Mineral Needs of the Western World," report prepared by the Subcommittee on Mines and Mining of the Committee on Interior and Insular Affairs, U.S. House of Representatives, 96th Cong., 2d sess., July 1980.

84. Ibid.

85. "Imports of Minerals from South Africa by the United States and the OECD Countries," report prepared for the Subcommittee on African Affairs of the Committee on Foreign Relations, U.S. Senate, by the Congressional Research Service, Library of Congress, September 1980.

86. Ibid.

87. *Die Burger*, September 1, 1980.

88. Robert Sylvester, "Strategic Minerals: Is the U.S. Really Dependent on Pretoria?" *Defense Week*, June 1, 1981, pp. 8-9.

5

NUCLEAR INFLUENCE:
REACTORS AND BOMBS

The related issues of nuclear energy and nuclear weapons are treated separately by virtue of several prominent characteristics: they are not clearly economic, military, or political in character, and they have had a powerful symbolic effect on the entire debate of South Africa-United States relations. The symbolism of nuclear technology in the post-World War II period has overwhelmed straightforward calculations of the role of that technology in economic and military terms. Nuclear energy, for much of this period, has been viewed as the "space age" energy source, and nuclear weapons were a prime prerequisite for respect among nations. As a result, the plans of South Africa to move toward the generation of nuclear energy and the development of nuclear weapons have been both tangible and intangible factors in the U.S. debate over policy toward South Africa. At a less visible level, the nuclear policies of the U.S. government have also had their effect on South African calculations.

Influence in the South African-United States nuclear relationship is exerted in several ways. The flow of technology (primarily from the United States to South Africa) has been a major factor historically, although its salience is diminishing as time passes and the caliber of the South African research establishment rises. A second area of exerted influence derives from the flows of raw and enriched uranium, in both directions and to third parties, which is an area of constantly increasing importance as both nations derive a considerable share of electrical power from nuclear-generating stations. Finally, there is a somewhat more fluid area of "nuclear policies," relating to the nonproliferation treaty, nuclear military doctrines, and the roles of the private and public sectors in nuclear technology. In large part, nuclear issues (whether military or civilian) have been debated on both sides in their own right, relating in particular to issues of proliferation, safeguards, inspection, and the price of nuclear energy. From time to time, however, nuclear issues have been explicitly seen as tools to influence the political environment, particularly the racial situation in South Africa. And without doubt, the salience of the nuclear issue in the relationship is a by-product of generalized tensions, as well as a frequent coincidence between anti-apartheid groups and antinuclear forces.

NUCLEAR PROBLEMS IN PERSPECTIVE

The principal framework for approaching South Africa on nuclear issues in recent years, from the U.S. perspective, has been that embodied in the Treaty on the Non-Proliferation of Nuclear Weapons (NPT), adopted by the U.N. General Assembly on June 12, 1968. The need to obtain South Africa's signature to the NPT, which would involve adherence to the safeguards of the International Atomic Energy Agency (IAEA), has been a major priority of the United States. Its inability to secure South African adherence has been a major disappointment in U.S. policy, and the issue has recurred constantly in attempting to deal with other aspects of nuclear policy. The U.S. position has not been aided by several of its allies, including France and Germany, that have not been as assiduous in seeking adherence to the NPT, and thus nuclear policy toward South Africa has increased tensions with European allies. The prominence of the proliferation issue in U.S. thinking has sometimes puzzled the South Africans, given the weakness of European support for the U.S. position, and the historical irrelevance of nuclear weapons for the southern African theater. Perceiving the importance of the NPT, however, the South Africans have steadily raised the "price" to the United States for adherence, to a level unacceptable to overall U.S. policies. With the evident unwillingness of the South Africans to go along with the NPT regime in the early and mid-1970s, speculation necessarily arose that, in fact, they were planning to develop nuclear weapon capability.[1]

Oddly enough, there were few manifest reasons for South Africa to develop nuclear weapons. Most studies recognized their capability, given the research facilities at Pelindaba and the amount of enriched U-235 available to the South Africans, but there were remarkably few plausible motives. By the beginning of the Carter administration, with its major push for revitalization of the NPT regime, the U.S. view of South African proliferation was congealing, in a rather self-centered direction: "the only advantage for South Africa in threatening a nuclear weapons program would be as a bargaining chip to elicit U.S. help."[2] This perception of the South African motive was not only widely shared in the United States, but came to have a major influence upon the subsequent nuclear policies developed by the United States. As the amount of U.S. prestige invested in nonproliferation grew in the late 1970s, the sensitivity to potential nuclear weapon developments in South Africa also grew, resulting in several dramatic diplomatic incidents between the two countries. Even without major incidents, the nuclear field was included in overall misunderstandings in the relationship in early 1977, during testimony by State Department officials before the Congress.

They indicated great concern over the extent to which ongoing United States-South African nuclear cooperation gave the impression that the United States supported South African policies; in addition, they stated that the Carter administration was assessing the extent to which nuclear policies toward South Africa could be used as leverage for political change "without increasing South Africa's motivation to produce nuclear weapons."[3]

In the 1977 environment, then, a whole host of U.S. concerns was converging on South Africa, with the ongoing nuclear programs in the civilian field becoming a weak tactic for dealing with the South Africans. The United States wanted majority rule for the blacks in South Africa, adherence to the NPT, and termination of any development of nuclear weapons. The South Africans wanted fulfillment of the old contract for the supply of enriched uranium from the United States and, if we are to believe U.S. interpretations, general diplomatic acceptance by the United States and the West.

By all diplomatic appearances, the South Africans appeared to be focussing on their nuclear-energy-generating program. They have a major reserve position in raw uranium, with the economic advantage that uranium is produced in many instances as a by-product of gold production in South Africa. Their program to convert the uranium resources into nuclear energy dated back to the 1950s, and when the nuclear research establishment at Pelindaba obtained a SAFARI-1 research facility, the South Africans eventually gained the experience and confidence to commit themselves to construction and operation of nuclear-energy-generating facilities at Koeberg, north of Capetown. The facilities finally chosen were French in manufacture, but given the restricted enrichment capability in South Africa, they decided to purchase enriched uranium from the United States. Contracts were signed for the supply of such uranium beginning in 1981, when the first Koeberg reactor was expected to begin operations. The two 922-megawatt nuclear power plants would supply about 10 percent of expected South African electrical needs in the early 1980s. The South African posture in talks with the United States, then, reflected their concern with keeping these arrangements for Koeberg on track. All South African officials with any responsible involvement with the nuclear program categorically and consistently denied any interest in nuclear weapons. They hoped, in effect, to keep the uranium supply question separated from U.S. concern over possible proliferation of nuclear weapons.

The South Africans, after all, were conscious of the extensive outside links that made possible the development of an indigenous nuclear establishment, as well as the maintenance of state-of-the-art knowledge on nuclear affairs. The father of the South African nuclear technology field was Dr. A. J. A. Roux, president of the South African Atomic Energy Board; he ran Pelindaba largely single-handedly through the late 1970s, with occasional consultation only with the prime minister. In 1976 he commented that most of the equipment at Pelindaba was from the United States and, indeed, "even our nuclear philosophy, although unmistakably our own, owes much to the thinking of American nuclear scientists."[4] Oddly, though, observers attempting to determine the most important external links generally pointed the finger at West Germany rather than the United States.[5] The question of sharing credit or blame for assisting South Africa revolves in part around one's judgment of the "critical phase" in nuclear technology. The case for the West German role is based on the similarity between the enrichment process developed at Pelindaba and that long used by Erwin Becker of West Germany, as well as the well-known contacts between scientists of the two groups. Since it was the cooperation with West Germany that permitted the South Africans to develop an enrichment capability outside the safeguards/inspection scheme of the IAEA, it is also that stage that permits the production of plutonium not regulated internationally.

By 1977 the South Africans were also conscious of the costs associated with independently undertaking all stages of the nuclear power process, and undeniably enrichment would be expensive. The costs anticipated for construction of the power plants themselves were massive enough: 1,844 megawatts were expected to be in operation by 1985, with 3,844 megawatts coming on by 1990, and 11,844 megawatts by the year 2000.[6] Mining costs were not great, and indeed uranium production was developing in the 1970s at a pace significantly faster than targetted.[7] But ambitious plans to expand the pilot enrichment plant at Pelindaba into a commercial operation, as rumored in 1970, and periodically thereafter, continually went awry. The overall capital costs remained a serious obstacle (until the price of gold went sky-high), and per unit costs remained lower through U.S. supplies as the South African could not approach the economies of scale in the United States. For economic reasons, then, the South Africans had a certain interest in maintaining the sanctity of the enriched uranium supply contract from the United States.

The existence of the uranium supply contract was not inherently threatening to observers, since it included the standard safeguard provisions. Only the advocates of total embargo found fault with the agreement. But with the agreement in place, opponents of South Africa of various shades decided to use the agreement as leverage. For some, the agreement was a first step to drawing South Africa into the NPT regime, with the consequent safeguarding and inspecting of the Pelindaba facility. Andrew Young argued this view: "I think by maintaining some kind of relationship we do have the possibility of influencing them to sign the nuclear nonproliferation treaty and accepting all of the safeguards. . . . If you break the relationship altogether there is no way to monitor and it is almost because you can't trust them that you have to stay close to them."[8] For others, the nuclear tie became a tool for achieving political change, and the pressure on the U.S. administration to threaten to terminate the agreement on political grounds grew as time passed. Both parties operated in the dark, to their ultimate regret, with regard to assessing the essential or nonessential nature of U.S. supplies. The closed nature of South African nuclear operations meant that the United States was largely unaware of the weakness of their strategy.

In the midst of large-scale ignorance, speculation grew constantly about South African nuclear weaponry. The international incident in August 1977, which will be examined in detail later, heightened awareness of possible South African capabilities, followed by the second incident on September 22, 1979. Speculation then became more concrete, with discussion of "nuclear artillery shells" in South Africa.[9] Inevitably, then, with widespread acceptance of a South African "bomb in the basement," counterstrategy speculation began, focussing primarily on possible development of a Nigerian nuclear deterrent.[10] Within this typical proliferation scenario, however, the relationship between the United States and South Africa played an important role, particularly on the issues of technology and nuclear materials supply.

THE U.S. ROLE: TECHNOLOGY

U.S. technology first began to flow to South Africa's uranium industry in the early 1950s, when it was recognized by British and U.S. engineers that South Africa was sitting on one of the largest reserve positions in the world, and the British-United States weapons program needed the uranium ore quickly. In the ensuing years, the United States bought over 43,000 tons of uranium for about $1 billion.[11] Technological cooperation grew naturally out of those early ties. Sophistication in handling and refining ores led the South Africans into establishing a small research center, and the 1957 Agreement for Cooperation Concerning Civil Uses of Atomic Energy between the United States and South Africa ensued. The principal provisions related to cooperation in research, with the exchange of scientists and students a key attraction. The original agreement was meant to expire in 1977 (a 20-year term), but because amendments in 1974 provided for U.S. export of enriched uranium for the Koeberg facilities, the duration was extended to 2007.[12]

The basic training of South Africa's nuclear scientists thus came about in the same fashion as with most U.S. allies in the 1950s and 1960s: education in U.S. universities and the installation of a small United States-built research reactor at home, in the South African case, a SAFARI-I Allis-Chalmers design installed in 1962, with fuel subsequently supplied by the United States. Unilateral safeguards by the United States were included in the SAFARI contract. However, that agreement created major problems between the United States and South Africa in the fall of 1964. At a time when there were tensions in a large number of areas, and the Johnson administration was evolving in the direction of a policy of steady but quiet opposition to apartheid, the United States realized that it was time to deliver the fuel rods for the SAFARI research reactor that would enable it to "go active." The U.S. government found that agreement an embarrassment in general, and particularly so in late 1964 — electoral reasons may have played a role in Johnson's desire to delay delivery of the fuel rods, and he may also have not wanted to indicate any apparent collusion between the

United States and South Africa at a time when it could interfere with the direction of the Congolese civil war. In several meetings in late 1964, Averell Harriman laid out these considerations to South African Foreign Minister Hilgard Muller. The South Africans agreed to a delay, and when the fuel elements were delivered as authorized on February 10, 1965, it was with no publicity at all, by prior agreement between the two governments.[13] Subsequently, and in accord with the terms of the agreement, spent fuel was always shipped out to British and French facilities, and U.S. deliveries continued until 1975, when court action by the Congressional Black Caucus forced a temporary halt.[14] The South Africans, however careful they may have been to observe SAFARI-I safeguards, set out to develop an independent, unsafeguarded enrichment process. Here, evidently, the West German connection became crucial, particularly in the early 1970s, as South Africa gradually emerged with its own jet-nozzle enrichment process strikingly similar to the Becker method. U.S. technology then lost some of its value, in being replaceable albeit at higher cost. In the deteriorating political environment of the 1970s, South Africa was willing to pay that cost if necessary.

As long as it was available, however, South Africa would utilize U.S. technology. In 1973 the Foxboro Company of Foxboro, Massachusetts, sold two computers to the South Africans that ended up being used in the Pelindaba enrichment plant. The fact was not noted until 1976 and was briefly the focus of senatorial (particularly Clark, Ribicoff, Percy, and Glenn) attention.[15] The reason for attention was the extensive review given to General Electric's application to export $2 billion worth of nuclear power plants for the Koeberg project. The Ford administration was willing to approve the export licenses on several grounds: economic, the fact that the plants would be safeguarded, the ability of South Africa to make nuclear weapons from other available materials, and finally, "If you expect South Africa to play a role in helping to bring about negotiations in Rhodesia, you can't treat the South Africans as outcasts."[16] But the opponents, led primarily by Dick Clark of Iowa, the chairman of the Senate's African Affairs Subcommittee, fought the issue. Hearings were held, pressure was placed on the Nuclear Regulatory Commission (one formal grantor of export licenses), and threats were made to cut Ex-Im Bank funding essential to the deal's going through. Even though General Electric had a letter of commitment in hand to purchase from the Electricity Supply Commission of South Africa (ESCOM), the deal fell through and ESCOM signed the agreement with a French consortium.

The point at which South Africa became independent of U.S. technology is difficult to pinpoint, but it is likely to have arrived well before the informed public realized it. By 1975 a comment in *Science* magazine made the point, "In the not-so-distant future South Africa is going to need American enriched uranium about as much as Kuwait needs American oil."[17] By all accounts, South Africa continued to find outside help quite useful; there were simply additional sources of the kind of help it might need, whether in civilian or military technology. The determination of West Germany and France, in particular, to pursue independent nuclear policies in the mid-1970s effectively terminated potential leverage through U.S. nuclear technology. The Franco-Pakistani and West German-Brazilian nuclear deals, which Washington contested in 1977, were only the most publicized disagreements. The South Africans made new arrangements with both European states during this period of United States-European tension. The French, in selling the nuclear reactors for Koeberg, came under pressure briefly, but Prime Minister Raymond Barre pointedly ridiculed proliferation concerns, saying that the South Africans "already had a nuclear military capability and that the reactors add nothing to it."[18] By early in 1978, over 100 South African nuclear technicians had arrived in France to study and train for operating the Koeberg reactor.[19] Another form of escape from U.S. technology appeared in the "pariah network"; the ties between South Africa, Israel, Taiwan, and others were the focus of many rumors but few facts.[20]

The issue of technology was largely dead by the advent of the Carter administration because many ties had been broken under congressional pressure, the South Africans were looking elsewhere, and the key question for the United States was to determine the extent of South African nuclear capability. The rejection of U.S. superiority is implicit in the attitude of Prime Minister Vorster at the time of the August 1977 incident. Vorster's final statement was:

> In reply to questions raised by the United States government in regard to nuclear matters, the South African Government reiterated its long-standing policy, which remains unchanged. This was confirmed in a letter from the Prime Minister to the President, and in his television interview on October 23, Mr. Vorster again repeated his Government's policy of developing nuclear energy for peaceful uses only.
> Since this has always been South Africa's policy which it has decided on independently for itself, the question of *"promises"* never arose — least of all in the context that *"promises"* had been exacted.[21]

After that time, South Africa pursued an aggressively independent line on nuclear technology. Visitors from the United States were occasionally branded as spies; for instance, Radio South Africa announced in early 1980 that "a group of American spies is reported to have arrived in South Africa in an attempt to learn the country's nuclear secrets. The Johannesburg newspaper, *The Sunday Times* quoted top intelligence sources as saying that the spies are under surveillance but no major moves to expose them could be expected for some time."[22] At the same time, the South African government was advertising in major U.S. newspapers for technicians to work at Koeberg, particularly health physicists and engineers for the nuclear support group at their headquarters.[23] The first group of trainers, hired away from the Tennessee Valley Authority, arrived in December 1980.[24]

THE KALAHARI INCIDENT, 1977

Among the most decisive ruptures in the nuclear relationship was the brouhaha over the "nuclear weapon testing structure" in the Kalahari Desert, an incident that emerged in late August 1977, with the closing chapters coming in late October. One of the most notable characteristics of the diplomatic episode was that no facts were ever established; as a result, the reported impact of influence is revealing not in an objective sense, but rather in reflecting the normative views of observers.

The events surrounding the Kalahari incident were as follows. In early August 1977, Brezhnev sent a personal message to President Carter, reporting that Soviet spy satellites had revealed plans in the South African Kalahari Desert. The photographs revealed a structure of a design and configuration often used elsewhere for testing nuclear weapons. The Soviet Union, in its role as the arbiter of peace in southern Africa, also notified France, Britain, and Germany that something needed to be done about this South African development. What the Soviets complained about was the impact that such a test would have on proliferation of weapons and general "international peace and security." The Soviet Union had said little when India demonstrated its nuclear capability. So part of its concern must have derived from anxieties about facing a nuclear opponent in southern Africa.

The response of the United States was straightforward. It asked South Africa for an explanation and for a commitment not to test any nuclear weapons. After considerable argument between the Western nations and South Africa, the latter publicly stated that it was not going to conduct an atomic test, but it refused to commit itself as to the future. From the South African perspective, if it had been planning a test, the Soviet démarche had clearly accomplished the same purpose as an actual test. The world now believed that South Africa possessed the atomic bomb. If it had no such bomb, it now had the deterrent value of what is sometimes called "Israel's closet bomb." Whether or not it exists is immaterial; South Africa is now considered a nuclear power.

One of the weightiest voices to express an evaluation of the incident was that of National Security Advisor Zbigniew Brzezinski, who was the unnamed source of a front-page story in the *Washington Post*.[25] In this view, "In the absence of the outside pressures, . . . South Africa might have gone on to detonate a bomb there within a matter of weeks, assuming that the explosive material was in hand and that it chose to move full speed ahead." The president reportedly faced a dual challenge: "to dissuade South Africa from a nuclear explosion" and "to avoid driving South Africa deeply into a siege mentality." What pressure could be brought to bear on the South Africans?

(1) According to some administration officials, the French held the key since they were the suppliers of the Koeberg installations. U.S. Ambassador-at-large Gerard Smith was able to persuade President Giscard d'Estaing to

undertake a diplomatic démarche to the South Africans; "French sources made it plain to reporters that there might be no limit on the consequences on its part, from termination of the nuclear reactor contracts to a full break in diplomatic and trade relations."[26] Of course, the French making such judgments were not entirely blameless, a fact dryly noted in the U.S. media;[27]

(2) The United States could threaten to terminate the uranium supply agreement for Koeberg, and according to the *Washington Post*'s source, "We were pretty severe in private." Pretoria was also said to be aware that the United States could change its position of opposition to U.N. economic sanctions.

After the week's "crisis," President Carter announced that he had received the necessary assurances from South Africa. But had the South Africans agreed to anything? The South African view was that the intelligence findings of the Soviet and U.S. photo analysis were wrong – the site in the Kalahari was the construction stage of a new military airport for the region.[28] The assurances mentioned by the U.S. president were not made public, but the recollection of Prime Minister John Vorster on the television program "Issues and Answers" in late October were that "I'm not aware of any promise that I gave to President Carter. I repeated a statement which I have made very often, that as far as South Africa is concerned, we are only interested in peaceful development of nuclear facilities." With that public statement by Vorster, the Carter solution became embarrassingly unhinged.

In the United States, the reaction of many was to reduce further the credibility of the Carter administration. From the hard-line perspective, it proved that Carter and Brzezinski in fact had no leverage over South Africa, and that they had merely used the incident to restore some strength to the United States-Soviet relationship.[29] They additionally argued that, not only was there weak evidence of a bomb, but that the consequent weakening of U.S. influence in Pretoria would set back racial liberalization. From the left, a different sort of skepticism emerged – namely, that the Carter diplomatic triumph was simply a masking of continuing U.S. coopération, or at least condoning, of South African bomb making. Cervenka and Rogers argued, for instance, that U.S. Big Bird satellites would have passed over the alleged test site for several days prior to the Soviet observation and alarm, and that "it is hardly conceivable that the satellite would pass overhead without taking multiple photographs in detail."[30] At best, from this view that presumed the South Africans were planning a test, the Air Force hid the information from the president. As stated elsewhere:

> . . . was this an "oversight" of U.S. intelligence institutions, or evidence of covert cooperation with the South African government? The latter suggestion arises naturally from the fact that the United States has for some time maintained, in close cooperation with the South African government, satellite tracking facilities, such as Project Syncom, and other facilities, such as the Minitrack Radio tracking station at Esselen Park and the Baker-nun optical tracking station at Olifantsfontein.[31]

In effect, the South Africans may have had greater influence over U.S. moves than vice versa.

The latter view is not persuasive, if looked at in the context of the overall relationship as well as in statements of the principals. This incident illustrated that the high-priority nature of the nonproliferation drive of the U.S. administration was creating a different sort of dilemma. The principal tool identified by the State Department for achieving adherence to the NPT was the issuance of U.S. security guarantees to the nations with nuclear weapon potential. It turned out in practice to be a rather weak diplomatic tool — owing in part to the legacy of the Vietnam War, the Nixon Doctrine, and the inconsistency of Carter policies toward allies — and a U.S. security guarantee for South Africa was certainly politically taboo. But the South Africans wanted a different kind of guarantee: that their independently developed enrichment process would not be subject to outside inspection. South African public opinion viewed this problem in an economic light; as one staunchly progovernment newspaper put it in 1979:

> First, South Africa's enrichment process is a threat to America's monopoly in the West and, second, that country wants to force South Africa in this way to sign the nuclear proliferation treaty and so exclude it as a future nuclear nation. In addition to being the policeman of the West, America is still a competitor on the economic front and does not hesitate to put a spoke in the wheel of its competitor.[32]

The South African prime minister, in his interview with ABC's "Issues and Answers" was making an open pitch when he said, "We've made our position very clear to the Americans. We want certain guarantees before we sign the [nonproliferation] treaty and until such time as we have those guarantees, then the status quo will remain."

The very different interpretations by South Africa and the United States, based upon indeterminate facts, laid bare the divergent expectations. Some Carter administration officials evidently felt that it would help to "embarrass" the South Africans into signing the NPT. The South Africans felt that the appearance of the nuclear issue might finally generate the technology guarantees they wanted. Such a divergence simply injected greater bitterness and misunderstanding in an already delicate nuclear relationship.

THE 1979 NUCLEAR FLASH

With the experience of the 1977 Kalahari incident behind them, the events of late 1979 came as little shock to the South Africans, and in large part they shrugged off the second U.S. alarm about nuclear weapons testing in South Africa. In this case, there was not even evidence on the ground.

On the night of September 22, an aged United States VELA satellite over the region between South Africa and the Antartic picked up a "double flash," a characteristic signature of a nuclear blast. When the information reached the U.S. Defense Intelligence Agency (DIA), analysts immediately suspected the South Africans, dispatched planes to take air samples (which contained no radiation), and checked seismic records (no disturbances). Attempts to resolve these discrepancies within the intelligence establishment eventually led to a leak to the media, and then the search for facts became rather more widespread.[33] The White House convened a group of specialists from around the country to discuss the evidence on November 2, 1979, with several points of view emerging. In the meantime, Pretoria denied the charges categorically and left it to editorial writers to subject the United States to ridicule.[34] For the U.S. government, the stakes in pinpointing the nature of the flash were significant not just for United States-South Africa relations; the consideration of the SALT II draft treaty by the Senate was being jeopardized by the apparent weakness of U.S. verification capability.

As investigation of the evidence moved forward, only the DIA and the Los Alamos Laboratory Scientists appeared convinced that the flash was definitive evidence of a nuclear test. The lack of radiation in the atmosphere was explained by the fact that September 22 was a rainy night, and so the rain had washed everything away.[35] In the meantime, alternative explanations proliferated:

(1) That a Soviet submarine had a nuclear accident, since according to the chief of the South African Navy, a Soviet Echo I class nuclear submarine was sighted in that region at that time;[36]

(2) That a "superbolt" may have occurred in an electrical storm, and such flashes would have been powerful enough to register on the VELA satelite;[37]

(3) That there was a test of a joint South African-Israeli nuclear artillery shell, with a low-yield (2-4 kiloton) warhead;[38]

(4) The answer finally favored by the White House experts group was that a small meteorite hit the satellite and caused paint chips to break off and reflect light onto the sensors.[39]

The DIA never was convinced enough to change its collective view; as Evans and Novak graphically expressed their response, "Specialists in the Carter Administration were aghast at this kiss-off of what in fact has created an agonizing dilemma for the U.S. and a dangerous game for the world: anonymous weapons testing."[40] Whatever the truth of the flash, there was no means to enlist the help of the South Africans in obtaining a reliable answer. If in fact the September 1979 flash as well as a December 1980 flash were associated with South African activity, one can conclude that the United States does not even possess a verification capability with which to influence South Africa.

SOUTH AFRICA'S EXPULSION FROM THE IAEA

While attention was focussed on the flash analysis in the United States, the general aura of suspicion of South Africa finally resulted in South Africa's suspension from the International Atomic Energy Agency in Vienna.[41] The campaign had long been building.[42] South Africa had lost its seat on the Board of Governors in 1977, and its expulsion in 1979 overruled a line of defense long argued by the United States and West European states. The *New York Times* stated it succinctly: "To the extent that the atomic agency safeguards the development of nuclear power and guards against turning atomic materials into weapons, the entire world stands to lose from the petulance at the atomic meeting in New Delhi."[43] The United States voted against the exclusion of South Africa, expressing the view that any possibility of its adherence to the NPT was gone; to the extent that South Africa's nuclear establishment was under external influence, it was that of the IAEA that could inspect and safeguard some facilities.

SOUTH AFRICAN AND U.S. ROLES: URANIUM SUPPLY

The original reason for South Africa's involvement in atomic affairs had been the extensive uranium reserves originally mined at U.S. and British direction. With that initial step, South Africa was able to bargain for a research reactor and small supplies of enriched uranium for use in the research reactor. That relationship between the United States and South Africa continued with little controversy until the mid-1970s, since the research reactor was under U.S. safeguard procedures. Only with the moves by South Africa to develop an independent, nonsafeguarded enrichment process, plus its unwillingness to sign the NPT, did people begin to argue vigorously against continued supplies of enriched uranium to South Africa. Likewise, the contracts by the United States and various West European states to buy uranium oxide from South Africa came under attack only as part of the general embargo movement in the West against South African trade. The contract arrangements, whether in South African sales of uranium oxide or in purchases of enriched uranium, were never suspected of abuse. Because of Western linkage of various issues, however, the uranium supplies from both sides came increasingly under consideration as a form of influence.

Oddly, the U.S. effort to use the uranium supplies as a form of leverage came just as the South Africans had found rather more compatible nuclear partners than the United States. The Koeberg reactor contract was going to the French. Technical cooperation on enrichment was occuring with the Germans. New customers for the uranium oxide (especially those states outside the NPT regime) were being signed up. And perhaps most illustrative, the South Africans were instrumental in organizing a uranium producers' cartel in 1972-73 that excluded the United States.

The uranium cartel was first organized by Rio Tinto Zinc (the major South African nongovernmental uranium producer) as a result of unprofitable prices in the early 1970s.[44] U.S. producers could not participate owing to U.S. anti-trust laws, but the main producers in South Africa, Australia, Canada, France, and Britain did join. By 1975 the cartel took the form of a "uranium institute" with offices in Paris and London.[45] The entire issue may have never become public if the rapidly rising price of uranium — from $7 a pound in 1972 to $20 a pound in 1976 and subsequently higher — had not caused horrendous losses for the U.S. nuclear reactor fabricator, Westinghouse Corporation. Westinghouse promised delivery of enriched uranium to reactor customers in the late 1960s at fixed prices, only to find it facing losses of over $1 billion in deliveries in the 1970s. Westinghouse, therefore, filed suit in U.S. courts against other U.S. uranium producers that were allegedly participating informally in the cartel. Indeed, prevailing prices in the United States had risen right along with cartel prices. The case was eventually dismissed, but not before extensive documentary evidence from purloined and subpoenaed corporate files had been published. The active involvement of the South Africans (with over 30 percent of global production) made the cartel question a political controversy, and increased U.S. governmental sentiment for reducing South African uranium supplies to the United States. On purely political grounds, European purchases came under scrutiny: French officials had to defend their purchases of South African uranium against hostile questions in 1977, arguing that South Africa supplied only 6 percent of French uranium needs.[46]

The South Africans were not entirely happy with exporting uranium oxide, and wanted to obtain the enhanced value of exporting enriched uranium. A top South African atomic official observed in 1974 that its enrichment method was developed "in order to make it possible finally for the country to market her huge uranium resources in the most refined forms."[47] The government then announced plans for a plant with a capacity of 5,000 tons annually; for purposes of comparison, the Koeberg plants would use only 50 tons per year, leaving 4,950 tons for export. Thus, the South Africans, in the mid 1970s, were in the midst of a move to break the United States-Canada-Australia monopoly on the sale of enriched uranium, and South African sales would not be safeguarded.

The United States thus waited until the last minute to bring these concerns to a head with South Africa. The last shipment of enriched uranium to the SAFARI research reactor was dispatched in early 1975, with the Ford administration suspending deliveries in the face of South African plans to construct their own enriched uranium export industry. U.S. efforts, in that context, were thus interpreted in South Africa as economic blackmail. In the South African view, the only plausible explanation for U.S. behavior was that South Africa threatened the profitability of U.S. enrichers. As a result, little headway was made on a dialogue until the more direct Carter administration came into office.

Secret talks with the South Africans were commenced to persuade them of a trade: their signature on the NPT with safeguarding of all facilities in exchange for U.S. supply of fuel for the SAFARI and for the Koeberg generating stations.[48] The Carter administration officials argued that this threat had never been made by previous officials, but that they were "at the point to fish or cut bait with Pretoria." Clearly the Kalahari incident had poisoned the atmosphere of continuing cooperation — particularly given the acrimonious and ambiguous end — and officials cited "growing sentiment in Congress and the international community for the United States to end nuclear cooperation with South Africa."[49]

The reaction from South Africa was a careful policy reevaluation, and by February 1978, it was announced that the South Africans would pursue their independent enrichment process, but only at a level sufficient to meet the needs of the Koeberg reactors: 50 tons per year, which was just 1 percent of former plans. The cost of the larger plant had risen from $1.2 billion to $2.3 billion, and it might have the fuel for its Koeberg thus ready by the planned completion of construction in 1981.[50] This decision to reject the U.S. threat and to pursue an entirely independent capability was not only in reaction to the Carter administration threats; the U.N. Security Council had voted a mandatory arms embargo in late 1977, causing a major strengthening of South Africa's autarkic outlook. A major effort by the United States was made in the summer of 1978, when Ambassador Gerard Smith went to Pretoria for one last effort at persuasion. The failure of that mission was announced in the fall of 1979.[51] The United States returned the money paid by South Africa for the SAFARI fuel. Officials of the administration continued to express hope that South Africa would sign the NPT.[52]

Any attempt to assess lost influence in these largely secret nuclear affairs is difficult at best. On occasion, however, the curtain is raised. In March 1980, the premier of the Republic of China had a red carpet tour of South Africa, in which the centerpiece was a tour of Pelindaba and the signature of an agreement for Taiwan to buy 4,000 tons of uranium in the 1980s.[53] The South African prime minister's return visit to Taiwan in October 1980 reflected even greater cooperation: "Military matters were discussed, and it was decided to exchange knowhow and information."[54] Curiously, the formal cancellation of the U.S. agreement to supply fuel for Koeberg has never occurred. The United States retains hope that South Africa will sign the NPT, and South Africa has announced that its own enrichment plant will not be operational until the mid 1980s.[55] The South Africans have also announced that the start-up at Koeberg has been fortuitously delayed until 1983, which means the South Africans may be able to supply their own fuel. They use any opportunity to get in the last word on U.S. attempts to influence their nuclear program: "In this field of high and critical technology the lesson of it all again is the counterproductivity of forcing a determined nation to depend on its own resources."[56]

South Africa faced a major problem in trying to influence the United States on nuclear issues: the U.S. stand was increasingly principled on the NPT issue, and exceptions were not about to be made for South Africa when the same U.S. stand was also offending major allies such as the French and Germans. The United States faced two major problems in trying to influence South Africa positively: (1) In a commercial sense, South Africa and the United States were as competitive as the United States is with its allies in the industrial world. U.S. actions were frequently interpreted in terms of commercial advantage, causing the South Africans to reject U.S. advances. (2) With the military isolation of South Africa in the late 1970s, an increasing proportion of its elite argued for the contingency creation of a "nuclear laager." Public statements were generally guarded, but frequent enough to indicate the drift of thinking.[57] Knowing that the United States was hostile to such planning, the South Africans were willing to exclude the United States from their atomic establishment.

NOTES

1. Raimo Vayrynen, "South Africa: A Coming Nuclear-Weapon Power," *Instant Research on Peace and Violence* (Tampere, Finland), no. 1, 1977, pp. 34-47; Zdenek Cervenka and Barbara Rogers, *The Nuclear Axis: Secret Collaboration between West Germany and South Africa* (New York: Times Books, 1978), based on stolen documents released by the African National Congress in the mid-1970s.

2. Richard Betts, "Paranoids, Pygmies, Pariahs and Nonproliferation," *Foreign Policy*, 26 (Spring 1977): 183.

3. *SA Digest*, July 22, 1977, p. 3.

4. Quoted by Jim Hoagland, "South Africa, With U.S. Aid, Near A-Bomb," *Washington Post*, February 16, 1977, p. 12.

5. See Cervenka and Rogers, *The Nuclear Axis*.

6. Richard K. Betts, "A Diplomatic Bomb for South Africa," *International Security* (Fall 1979), p. 92, citing Nuclear Assurance Corporation, *International Data Collection and Analysis*, Task 1, vol. 4 (draft prepared for U.S. Department of Energy, June 1977), pp. SOUTH AFRICA-8, 9, 29.

7. Betts, "Diplomatic Bomb," p. 94.

8. Bernard Gwertzman, "Young Bans Refusal to Sell South Africa Atom Reactor Fuels," *New York Times*, October 31, 1977, pp. 1, 13. For a similar view, see Betts, "Diplomatic Bomb."

9. See "Has South Africa Got Nuclear Shells?" *Foreign Report*, no. 1653, October 29, 1980.

10. See "Nigeria Considers Nuclear Armament Due to South Africa," *Wall Street Journal*, October 6, 1980, p. 39; and Robert D'A. Henderson, "Nigeria: A Future Nuclear Power," published manuscript, University of Ife, 1980.

11. Cervenka and Rogers, *The Nuclear Axis*, p. 240.

12. Ibid., p. 242.

13. Department of State telegram to U.S. Consul-General, Capetown, February 10, 1965, LBJ Library.

14. Cervenka and Rogers, *The Nuclear Axis*, p. 245.

15. "U.S. Computers Aid South Africa A-Plant," *Philadelphia Inquirer*, May 30, 1976, p. 5-C.

16. An anonymous State Department official quoted in "Atom Power Plant Sales to South Africa Due Okay," *Baltimore Sun*, May 21, 1976, p. 5; and see also "U.S. Favors Plan to Sell Reactors to South Africa," *Los Angeles Times*, May 21, 1976, p. 1.

17. Robert Gilette, "Uranium Enrichment: With Help, South Africa Is Progressing," *Science*, June 13, 1975, p. 1090.

18. Jim Hoagland, "French Leader Confirms South Africa Nuclear Ability," *Washington Post*, February 18, 1977, p. 28.

19. "South Africa Sends A-Team to France," *Christian Science Monitor*, February 15, 1978, p. 17.

20. For instance, see Cervenka and Rogers, *The Nuclear Axis*, pp. 270-71; and Jeffrey Anteril, "Israel and South Africa: A Nuclear Family," *New York News*, August 28, 1977, p. 69.

21. Statement from the Department of Foreign Affairs, October 25, 1977.

22. Johannesburg International Service, April 6, 1980, in *FBIS Sub-Saharan Africa*, April 7, 1980, p. U10.

23. See *Wall Street Journal*, September 23, 1980, p. 25.

24. *SA Digest*, December 5, 1980, p. 13.

25. Murray Marder and Don Oberdorfer, "How West, Soviets Aided to Defuse South African A-Test," *Washington Post*, August 28, 1977, p. 1.

26. Ibid.

27. See "Look Who's Warning Whom," *Chicago Tribune*, August 26, 1977, p. 29; "South Africa and the Bomb," *Baltimore Sun*, August 28, 1977, p. 29.

28. See statements of Foreign Minister R. F. Botha, in *SA Digest*, September 2, 1977, p. 4.

29. See Evans and Novak, "South Africa's Bomb," *Washington Post*, October 20, 1977, p. 19. Incidentally, Brzezinski's gestures of cooperation toward the Soviets in this incident were not reciprocated; in the two weeks after the *Post*'s August 28 story, Radio Moscow constantly ran stories of U.S. complicity in the development of the "South African bomb."

30. Cervenka and Rogers, *The Nuclear Axis*, p. 282.

31. Western Massachusetts Association of Concerned American Scholars, *U.S. Military Involvement in Southern Africa* (Boston: South End Press, 1978), p. 176.

32. *Hoofstad*, October 29, 1979.

33. See Don Oberdorfer, "U.S. Suspects South Africans of Detonating Nuclear Bomb," *Washington Post*, October 26, 1979, p. 1.

34. Editorial in the *Pretoria News*, October 29, 1979: "Two years ago U.S. spy satellites detected SA's secret nuclear testing site in the Kalahari. Since then, undetected, the entire base has been dismantled and a warhead shipped in the polar ice, using a secret weapon that defies modern science. . . . Bushmen runners. The installation was dispatched in small pieces on the backs of Bushmen to a gunboat base at the Middle Orange River. Then Beechcraft spy aircraft, thrown off the track by the assumption that the Aughrabies Falls were not navigable, failed to pick up the nuclear progress to the Atlantic, where a complete warhead was cunningly slipped aboard a United Nations anti-apartheid protest vessel supplied with the wrong sailing instructions for Walvis Bay. Deep in the pack ice the nuclear device was triggered by a mechanism hidden in a frozen fish finger."

35. Walter M. Mossberg, "Mystery Explosion Off South Africa Still Fuels Dispute," *Wall Street Journal*, July 16, 1980, p. 31.

36. *SA Digest*, November 2, 1979, p. 3.

37. "South Africa Blast May Have Been Bolt," *New York Times*, November 1, 1979, p. D22.

38. Reported on the British television show, "World in Action," and repeated by *Foreign Report*, no. 1683, October 29, 1980, p. 3.

39. "White House Panel Doubt Light Flash Was Nuclear Bomb," *Washington Post*, July 16, 1980, p. 2.

40. "Was Mysterious Flash Nuclear?" *Philadelphia Bulletin*, February 18, 1981, p. B7.

41. Michael T. Kaufman, "Nuclear Parley Bars South Africa," *New York Times*, December 6, 1979, p. A14.

42. See my *Apartheid and International Organizations* (Boulder, Colo.: Westview Press, 1977).

43. "The Diplomacy of Exclusion," *New York Times*, December 10, 1979, p. A26.

44. See Cervenka and Rogers, *The Nuclear Axis*, pp. 148-56.

45. "Uranium Institute Planned," *New York Times*, July 16, 1975, p. 3.

46. "M. de Guiringaud confirme la conclusion d'un contrat 'marginal' d'achat d'uranium a Pretoria," *Le Monde*, July 23, 1977, p. 22.

47. A. J. A. Roux, "South Africa in a Nuclear World," *South Africa International*, January 1974, p. 157.

48. Richard Burt, "U.S. Tells South Africa to Accept Atomic Curbs or Face Fuel Cutoff," *New York Times*, December 20, 1977, p. A10.

49. Ibid.

50. "South Africa Decides It Will Expand Pilot Uranium Plant," *Wall Street Journal*, February 4, 1978, p. 4; "South Africa Accelerates A-Fuel Enrichment Plans," *Washington Post*, February 16, 1978, p. 24.

51. Johannesburg Domestic Service, in *FBIS Sub-Saharan Africa*, July 6, 1979, p. E2.

52. "U.S. Returns South Africa Funds," *New York Times*, November 13, 1978, p. A3.

53. Johannesburg International Service, March 12, 1980, in *FBIS Sub-Saharan Africa*, March 13, 1980, p. E8.

54. Johannesburg International Service, in *FBIS Mideast and Africa*, October 20, 1980, p. U2.

55. "Valindaba Target Disclosed," *Financial Times*, September 30, 1980, p. 4.

56. Johannesburg International Service, May 14, 1981, in *FBIS Middle East and Africa*, May 15, 1981, p. U5.

57. For example, Commander H. F. Nel of the Defense Force's strategic studies section told a public seminar in Pretoria that "it would be shortsighted of South Africa not to develop nuclear weapons if other African countries did so" (Johannesburg International Service, October 17, 1980, in *FBIS Mideast and Africa*, October 20, 1980, p. U2). Private statements even more forthright were increasingly made to the author after the voting of U.N. sanctions, breaking of French military supply contracts, and terminating of U.S. intelligence ties (all in 1977-78).

6

SOCIOCULTURAL FACTORS:
"SOFT" INFLUENCE

A network of ties between South Africa and the United States exists virtually beyond the reach of governments. At a time when economic and commercial issues are increasingly controlled by national governments, there continues to be a range of cultural and social links that exist between peoples. A major debate has been pursued by political scientists, particularly in the last decade, over the significance of such "transnational ties" for the transformation of the international system.[1] Without attempting to provide a resolution to that debate, one can here utilize many of the criteria developed by the interdependence school to examine one kind of influence between two peoples, where governments may matter only tangentially. In the context of United States-South African relations, several sectors of relations have been of particular importance: educational ties, sporting contests, the attitudes of organized churches on each side, the role of the media in each country, and particular elite exchange operations. In each case, the institutions' purposes are not primarily political (in its traditional definition), but in the case of becoming involved in South African issues, they have become very active politically and hope to be a factor in influencing the other side. As a result, there is frequently a schism within such organizations over the wisdom of taking an activist role on South African issues. That internal debate inevitably reveals much about the ability of such organizations to influence foreign policy and other societies.

On both sides of the relationship, governments do take a hand from time to time to influence the social and cultural sectors. In what is frequently labelled a propaganda function, both governments issue various kinds of public materials and provide speakers to influence the other side. The South African Embassy in Washington issues handsome "Backgrounders" on a wide range of issues for public consumption in the United States. Likewise, the U.S. International Communications Agency (USICA) is extremely active in South Africa, with offices in Pretoria, Johannesburg, Capetown, and Durban. It has become so effective that the South African prime minister publicly labelled the USICA office in Durban "subversive." The governments also have some influence in the ability to grant or to withhold visas. This tactic has been tried on both sides, although more actively by the South Africans, in an effort to influence information flows that occur with the movement of people from one country to another.

THE EDUCATIONAL COMMUNITIES

Ties between the academic establishments in the two countries flourished during the 1960s and 1970s, particularly as South African physical scientists transferred their interest from British universities to the more prosperous research establishments in the United States. At the same time, U.S. social scientists became increasingly interested in South African issues and sought to study social issues in the unique South African environment. Attempts to establish a regular exchange framework, however, were largely frustrated, owing to the unwillingness of U.S. universities to appear to support the apartheid system by establishing ongoing ties. Some consideration was given in U.S. universities to establishing growing ties with some of the nonwhite universities that could particularly use the assistance of U.S. universities, but such plans did not generally reach fruition.

Academic ties were frustrated largely by the increasingly radical atmosphere in U.S. universities on South African issues. The Africanist community in the United States largely lost any empathy with South Africa in a wide-ranging debate in the late 1960s and early 1970s. Particularly influential were groups such as the Association of Concerned African Scholars, formed in 1977, with the purpose of "opposing U.S. support for an internal settlement in Rhodesia/ Zimbabwe, supporting U.S. sanctions against the white Rhodesian government, and opposing U.S. financial and technical support of the South African government." The weight of Africanist opinion was largely thrown behind the "liberation movements" in southern Africa, meaning that most universities with an interest in organic ties with a South African university (black or white) found that their African studies departments were not interested in ties for political reasons. South African universities also tended to pull back in view of an apparent asymmetry in the proposed relationships: despite the relatively liberal position of many South African academics in their political spectrum, they had no interest in establishing exchanges simply to pursue social change in South Africa. There was not enough incentive for the South African university to irritate a government increasingly suspicious of the United States in general in the 1970s, since it looked unlikely that a friendly meeting ground between South African and U.S. academics could be found for a range of academic disciplines.

As a result, U.S. academic interest in South Africa continued to be pursued in a generally unilateral fashion. Debate about the investment of university endowments continued to involve a fairly small number of faculty, students, and many trustees.[2] To a large extent, the South African issue remained one of the very few political problems of interest to undergraduate activists in the late 1970s, when most university students were becoming increasingly professionally oriented rather than politically active. The course of the lackluster and one-sided debate on U.S. campuses, however, did cause concern in internationalist circles in South Africa, if only for the long-term damage that would likely be done to relations between the two countries. Since any contacts with South African whites were generally regarded as dangerous, attitudes of students would tend to be fixed in that direction.

SPORTING CONTACTS

The role of sports in South Africa — the pages covering team activity in the daily newspapers are by far the most widely read — made that sector a natural target early in the anti-apartheid campaign. The United States was not actively drawn into the campaign early, if only because the most popular sports (cricket, soccer, and rugby) are not traditionally important in U.S. sports. At the Olympic level, however, the United States could not avoid becoming involved in anti-South African activities over sports. In 1964 South Africa was suspended from the Olympic Games for the first time; this was repeated in 1968 after a great controversy complete with threats of an African boycott, and South Africa has remained suspended ever since.[3] Much of the early involvement of the United States in such controversies came about by virtue of continual campaigns by a few activists such as Richard Lapchick and Dennis Brutus. For the most part, however, the United States was not at the forefront of the controversy, since the most important ties existed in the traditional British sports highlighted by emotional test matches between various members of the Commonwealth. In those nonteam sports such as tennis or golf, the leading U.S. players also tended to argue for a separation of sports and politics. The black U.S. champion tennis player, Arthur Ashe, for instance, made a number of trips to South Africa to play, arguing that communication was superior to ostracism. He subsequently changed his mind in the late 1970s and privately urged sporting colleagues to avoid South Africa. In golf, the top-rank South African professional, Gary Player, was not excluded from U.S. tournaments despite occasional efforts to deny the South Africans an opportunity to participate. At the same time, the United States had to face difficult decisions in a variety of international competitions, such as the Davis Cup, and they were frequently disrupted over the issue of South African exclusion.

In the 1970s, South Africa began a deliberate campaign of limited integration of sports in that country in order to meet some of the international criticism. A great deal of attention was given to developing fine black athletes (particularly in track and field) so that it would be increasingly difficult to exclude South Africa. The effort was sold abroad in information campaigns; on the occasion of the South African games in 1973, for instance, full-page advertisements were taken out in the *New York Times* to demonstrate that the games were fully integrated, and that black African states were being discriminatory in not attending.[4] Even Anthony Lewis, the persistent critic of South Africa in the columns of the *New York Times*, took notice of the integration of South African sports. In a 1975 column, he described the first rugby match at Newlands (near Capetown) as having an integrated South African side. His explanation for the event may or may not be accurate: "Changes in sport here, such as they are, have come about entirely because of outside pressure – the exclusion of South Africa from international sports events, the refusal to send teams here and so on. Even liberal-minded South Africans mostly decried those tactics at first, but it is admitted now that they worked."[5] But he saw the importance of the symbol of integrated sports and what it implied for the rest of the South African system. At that point, however, the anti-apartheid forces argued for continued boycotts against South African athletes, not on the issue of the organization of sports, but because of the continuing discrimination in the rest of society.[6]

U.S. athletes tended to divide into two camps. On the one hand, some argued for total ostracism, perhaps with the proviso of allowing promising black South African athletes into the United States to study track with good U.S. coaches. Examples would include Matthews Motshwarateu, George Mehale, Sydney Maree, and Zachari Tshikalange, all top black runners who came to the United States for a college education and track training.[7] The other school of thought argued for increasing contacts on the basis of integrated sports; in effect, they hoped to educate the South Africans out of segregated sports. Thus contacts continued in rugby, boxing, gymnastics, and golf – in boxing, South Africa was a major power in the World Boxing Association, and its fighters were frequently contenders in a variety of weight classes.[8] In rugby, controversy eventually reached the United States as the popularity of the sport grew. In a highly publicized tour in September 1981, the Springboks rugby team from South Africa made a number of headlines. In making preparations for the tour, the mayor of New York refused permission to use a city-owned stadium, and it was revealed that the Eastern Rugby Union of America, the host organization, had accepted a $25,000 gift from a famous South African industrialist, Louis Luyt.[9] The tour was targetted for major disruptions by an ad hoc organization, the Stop Apartheid Rugby Tour Coalition, which was headed by the activist Richard Lapchick. The Springbok tour was not in itself precedent setting, since five other South African teams had played in the United States earlier in 1981; but as a national team, the Springboks were a symbol to opponents of sporting contacts with South Africa.

For South Africa, the impact of these controversies and the developing coalition of protest in the United States was reasonably clear. Initially, the

South Africans responded by a variety of forms of integration, sometimes keeping clubs segregated, and at other times allowing integration if voted by the sports clubs, with differentiated patterns depending upon the part of the country. For a number of years, the direction of changes was toward greater integration. With the sudden escalation of the stakes — that opponents would not be satisfied until the complete end of apartheid in all sectors of life — many South Africans ceased to respond to outside criticism, since opponents in the United States were arguing for changes they saw as beyond their control as athletes.

THE INFLUENCE OF THE MEDIA

The most important transmitters of information between South Africa and the United States are the members of the print media. Television was introduced in South Africa only in 1975 (with initial broadcasts closely controlled by the government so as to include only "wholesome" programs), and the U.S. networks only occasionally cover South African issues.[10] Inevitably, the focus of U.S. coverage on South Africa is on race relations rather than any other topic. As a result, the role of the newspapers and magazines in promoting a certain view of the other country is extremely important.

The South African press is divided into two language groups: as a general rule, the Afrikaner press is less adventurous in its subject coverage than the English press, and it is more supportive of the government. This polarization has declined in recent years but still remains largely true. An exception in the late 1970s was the *Citizen*, a Johannesburg newspaper secretly subsidized by the government and thus the only substantially progovernment English-language newspaper; its political line shifted away from the government when its secret source of funding was revealed. The effect of this linguistic polarization of the press relations with the United States is significant, when one realizes that most U.S. citizens are familiar only with the English-language press. Whether they reside in South Africa, or follow South African events from the United States, U.S. citizens are likely to read the *Rand Daily Mail* or *The Star*, and see South African politics through the eyes of their editors. In view of the tremendous freedom allowed South African newspapers on nonmilitary issues, the difference between the editorial lines of English and Afrikaner papers can be quite substantial. The black press is quite underdeveloped, with the principal paper intended for black readers being *The World*, which is published in Johannesburg. The paper, which is rarely read outside the black community, was not stridently antigovernment until some of the events of the late 1970s, when it became clear that the residents of Soweto (the principal readers) demanded a stronger voice. The effectiveness of *The World* increased dramatically abroad after the banning of its editor, Percy Qoboza, and his subsequent departure for the United States on an extended study visit.[11] Eventually, the paper itself was closed by the government for transgressing security legislation, and its owners, the Argus Company, opened another black newspaper.

South Africans draw upon a British tradition in setting the limits of press freedom, rather than following the U.S. Bill of Rights approach. The freedom of the press to be irresponsible was thus well institutionalized, but not in the areas that the government considered to involve "security matters." This issue was reconsidered in 1980, with the completion of the Steyn Commission report to Parliament on security matters, which dealt extensively with the role of the press. Because the government's definition of security did not remain constant, it was difficult for editors to know how to stay out of trouble, and the Steyn Commission hoped to clarify it. Steyn argued, for instance, that the media should be restrained only in "matters affecting the preparedness and the survival of the state."[12] He argued that attitudes could not be suppressed, and that cooperation between the government and the press was preferable to restrictive legislation. The commission argued for a review of the Official Secrets Acts in order to reduce its field of application. At the same time, Steyn used the opportunity to review the threats to South Africa's security, and high among the threats he included was the United States. With regard to threats from the Soviet Union, the United States, and the Third World, Steyn maintained that "their common aim was the replacement of the present constitutional dispensation with one that would be subservient to their respective ideologies."[13] Steyn explained that the United States "employed a wide variety of political and economic methods to exert pressure on the South African Government. . . . The American plan of action inside South Africa relied on direct involvement by both official and private American organizations." Here he mentioned multinational business corporations, U.S. Embassy personnel, the U.S. labor attaché in South Africa and the U.S. cultural attaché in Durban. He said they regularly invited foreign labor personalities to South Africa to influence the local labor force. Steyn said that psychologically the U.S. government sought to promote its political concepts for South Africa through a diversity of media and organizations. These included the Voice of America, the African-American Institute, and the American Committee, which was concerned with equality in sport. Also noteworthy were U.S. attempts to undermine the South African economy, among other ways by seeking to undermine the gold price.[14]

Steyn's declaration on the U.S. "threat" was particularly interesting in representing a rare glimpse into elite Afrikaner thinking about the United States at the end of the Carter administration. Indeed, there was far greater recognition in the United States of the portions of the Steyn Commission Report regarding limitations on the freedom of the press than those remarks discussing U.S. policies. The extent of recent Afrikaner hostility toward the U.S. is rarely recognized in the United States, and rarely is it stated as forcefully as Steyn did in the parliamentary White Paper.

CHURCHES IN THE BATTLE FOR SOUTH AFRICA

Aside from missionary activities that date back centuries, the international church movement truly became involved in South Africa's problems in 1969. In that year, the World Council of Churches (WCC) organized a meeting in London to launch the Programme to Combat Racism. That effort evolved over time in three basic directions: (1) continued support for missionary work among nonwhite populations in southern Africa in order to alleviate suffering; (2) financial aid and moral support to nationalist guerrilla movements in southern Africa committed to overthrowing the existing order; and (3) a campaign to eliminate what the WCC identified as external props for the Pretoria government, including continuing operations by U.S. and European Multinational Corporations (MNCs) in South Africa. The last portion of the effort was most crucial from the U.S. perspective, and it was the aspect seized most enthusiastically by the WCC's affiliate in the United States, the National Council of Churches (NCC) beginning in 1969. In addition, various U.S. denominations, such as the Lutheran Church of America, the United Church of Christ, and the Catholic Church, pursued parallel policies that largely supplemented efforts of the WCC and the NCC.

Much of the institutional and personal network that was involved in the anti-apartheid campaign of the NCC had grown up in the late 1960s as a result of the anti-Vietnam War effort. With the commitment of the Nixon administration to withdraw from Vietnam, those proponents of an ethical approach to foreign policy had both the opportunity and the resources to tackle the apartheid issue. The Vietnam-related campaign against Dow Chemical, for instance, in which shareholder resolutions were introduced to ban the production of napalm and other chemicals to be used in war, was simply basic training for the more extensive campaign to get U.S. corporations out of South African operations, whether manufacturing or commercial.

In the summer of 1973, for instance, the World Council of Churches prepared a list of MNCs doing business in South Africa for distribution to its affiliated church organizations. The WCC also announced that it was selling all stock holdings in those companies, pressing the NCC and other national organizations to do the same.[15] The United States NCC undertook a large-scale campaign against U.S. corporations in an effort to force divestment, and if that were not successful, at least to involve the corporations in dialogues with the churches. The NCC published in 1973, through its subsidiary Corporate Information Center, a catalog of United States MNC operations in Southern Africa as a primer for shareholder action.[16] This publication was noted by the corporations: in 1974, for instance, Texaco and Standard Oil of California (Socal) decided to abandon oil exploration concessions in South-West Africa/Namibia. A Socal executive argued that a United Nations Security Council vote, along with the decision of the partner, Texaco, to withdraw, had persuaded Socal to abandon their concessions, the executive maintained that "we were not pushed by the churches." At the same time, he acknowledged that "Texaco acted first because they were under pressure from a church resolution."[17] Companies such as Amax and Newmont Mining, both of whom initiated dialogues with the United Church boards in mid-1974, were given a "year's grace."

The church community was not united in its use of external pressure to bring about change in South Africa. Even some of those adamantly opposed to apartheid (such as the United Church of Christ), but which also had active mission movements in South Africa, were prone to work from the inside. The United Church of Christ, for instance, operated a small college in South Africa, Adams College, of which two distinguished graduates were Chief Gatsha Buthelezi and Albert Luthuli (the Nobel Prize winner for literature). For the church, the "decisive power for change in South Africa is the black leadership in that country," not outside powers. Even traditional tribal chiefs, in this view, "can be massive sources for change."[18] At that time, of course, leaders like Buthelezi were seeking outside recognition and support, and had not yet divided as clearly on tactics as they would in the late 1970s.

In the late 1970s, the South African Council of Churches (SACC) also became a rallying point for open radical dissent from the government inside South Africa. The frequent and articulate public speeches of Bishop Desmond Tutu, secretary-general of the SACC, forced the WCC to move in the same direction (although it probably would have adopted radical divestment as a program anyway). Tutu was a featured speaker at a WCC meeting in Copenhagen in September 1979 — on a rare occasion when he had his passport for foreign travel — and used his platform both to express the "angry response" of blacks to the post-Soweto period in South Africa, and to attempt to shame the WCC affiliates into greater international action against South Africa. Tutu called, for instance, for a halt to the import of South African coal by other countries, even if black workers lost their jobs.[19] Officials of the mines estimated that 40,000 blacks would lose their jobs. While other commentators calling for such a coal boycott were only marginally noted before 1979, the occasion of a South African, Bishop Tutu, calling for punitive measures drew forth acid newspaper editorials. The South African Broadcasting Corporation described the WCC as "pro-communist, pro-revolutionary, and pro-Soviet." The Bishop's remarks were seen as more likely to increase violence, through socioeconomic tensions, and were thus contrary to Tutu's expressed interest in peaceful change.[20] The Anglican Church in South Africa — a member of SACC and the church in which Tutu was ordained a bishop — had particular problems with Tutu's specific formulations and the general policies of the WCC toward South Africa. In 1979 formal resolutions of the Anglican Church had dissociated it from the activities of the WCC in support of nationalist movements in southern Africa. Likewise, the chairman of the Christian League of South Africa, Fred Shaw, representing churches not affiliated with the SACC, took particularly strong issue with Tutu's activities abroad. In other words, the great weight of articulated opinion in South Africa tended to come down against such appeals for international action against South Africa.

At the same time, a very different message was getting across to the U.S. church network. The potential audience for the church network was quite enormous. As an example, the heads of the Lutheran Church in America and the American Lutheran Church made an inspection tour of Namibia and South Africa in early 1977; on their return, they planned to reach 5.5 million people in the United States and Canada with their message. They planned to "propose ways to express support for those working for justice and liberation in South Africa and Namibia."[21] The groups tended to overestimate their own importance, as the Lutherans said, "The churches are about the only organization allowed to exist that can criticize state structures."[22] One cannot help suspecting that they talked only to church people on their inspection tour. Curiously, the great emphasis of the Lutherans was on saving a people who felt hopeless: "We hear there are guerrillas but never hear of guerrillas doing anything against South African soldiers or South African soldiers doing anything against the guerrillas, but people get beat up. . . . The element that seems lacking in the black population in southern Africa is hope." Such is a very different emphasis from providing occasional support to capable black leaders who have plans to lead their own people into political participation.

Attacks on the WCC and the United States NCC continued in South Africa through the 1970s, although some recognition was eventually given to the resistance of many churches to being drawn into active support for liberation movements in southern Africa.[23] The NCC's Interfaith Center Corporate Responsibility (ICCR) continued its activities against MNC involvement in South Africa, with publications and public speakers provided on revolutionary movements in South Africa.

THE BLACK CONNECTION

Alfred Hero's analysis, in 1969, of U.S. black involvement in African issues is generally considered to be a benchmark study. He found that blacks had far less interest and knowledge about foreign affairs than did the white population.[24] While Hero's study may reflect well the *relative* involvement of different sectors of the population, it should be recognized that there was an active group of blacks attempting to influence policy on South Africa in the 1960s. Such activity took several forms. National coalitions were pulled together (involving both black and nonracial organizations) on the South African issue. In March 1965, for instance, a delegation from "A National Conference on the South African Crisis and American Action" came to visit the White House and talked with National Security Council advisor McGeorge Bundy. In early 1966, an even more important conference was held, sponsored by the Consultative Council on South Africa, which was based in New York and closely tied to the American Committee on Africa, headed by George Houser. During a meeting of the council, a Draft Manifesto of Americans for Freedom in Southern Africa was issued. The document was endorsed by several dozen organizations, including the American Baptist Convention, the American Federation of State, County, and Municipal Employees, the American Jewish Congress, the Americans for Democratic Action, the American Negro Leadership Conference on Africa, the Brotherhood of Sleeping Car Porters, CORE, the International Electrical Workers, the NAACP, the National Farmers Union, the Southern Christian Leadership Conference, SNCC, Students for a Democratic Society, Unitarian Associations, United Auto Workers, United Church of Christ, United World Federalists, and others. The demands of the document included: disengaging from economic involvement in South Africa; ending the sugar quota for South Africa immediately; granting U.S. aid to victims of apartheid through the U.N. Trust Fund for South Africa; granting political asylum to foes of apartheid; adopting a policy of integrating U.S. posts in South Africa; granting substantial aid to the former High Commission Territories; and obtaining majority rule in Rhodesia, South-West Africa, Mozambique, and Angola.[25] The American Committee on Africa was also active in more academic circles, as the publisher of *Africa Today*, for instance. A special issue appeared in March 1966 on U.S. involvement in South Africa, highlighting the role of multinational corporations. Specific incidents could also demonstrate the potential for mobilization among the black community; when the U.S.S. Roosevelt incident occurred in February 1967, the White House received a large number of protests of South African behavior. These protests were from individuals such as Julian Bond, then a member of the Georgia House of Representatives; Cleveland Robinson, president of the Negro-American Labor Council; A. Philip Randolph, the president of the International Brotherhood of Sleeping Car Porters; Lincoln O. Lynch, associate director of the Congress on Racial Equality; and George Houser, executive director of the American Committee on Africa.[26] What was missing from these early episodes was any real consistency institutionally. Influence was exercised on an ad hoc basis, and access to the U.S. executive branch depended in large part upon the clout exercised by individuals such as Randolph on U.S. electoral coalitions. Ever since the 1960s, as a result, there has been more visible activity by the black community, as well as more sustained impact on the question of South Africa's apartheid legislation.

In 1972, for instance, the American Committee on Africa and the American Heritage Studies Association, among others, filed a complaint with the City of New York Commission on Human Rights, urging that the *New York Times* not be allowed to publish employment advertising for South Africa on the basis of discriminatory employment practices by those advertising.[27] The commission in fact did decide to ban South African advertising from the *Times* in a decision given on July 19, 1974.[28] The order of the commission was voided, however, by a justice of the State Surpeme Court in October 1974. He argued that "it is significant that none of the advertisements make any reference to race." He went on to say that, "For the commission to enter every foreign area where patterns of discrimination appear, by imposing restraints on the solicitation of employees based in the United States through the medium of fair advertising, involves an assumption of jurisdiction which was certainly never contemplated by the legislative body which created the commission."[29] However, such elaborate moves to put pressure on South Africa were relatively rare in the early 1970s, since most black groups were too involved in domestic political battles to devote attention to African issues.

The need to create a more powerful machinery for action against South Africa grew in the mid-1970s, particularly under the influence of young leaders such as Randall Robinson, with a major step taken through the issuance of the Black American Manifesto on Southern Africa, which was intended to be incorporated into the Democratic Party platform, and much of it was used. The manifesto was followed by a meeting of the Black Leadership Conference on Southern Africa in September 1976, and out of that meeting, an organization called Transafrica was formed. This new Washington-based lobby, headed by Robinson, was politically active and thus not tax exempt and was the first black organization explicitly involved in foreign policy issues as its sole mission. The black community also obtained powerful voices in Congress in the principal committees concerned with Africa. In the House, Representative Charles Diggs commanded the Subcommittee on Africa, and in the Senate, a close white ally of black interests, Senator Dick Clark, ran the Africa Subcommittee.[30] The purpose of the Congressional subcommittees was seen primarily as educational, while mobilization was left to Transafrica.

A major effort of Transafrica was to undertake prototype mobilization of the broad mass of the black electorate on foreign policy issues. The organization picked the congressional districts with more than 30 percent blacks, and in 1979-80 began creating networks to exert influence on Congress on African issues. It also created a research arm for the organization, called Transafrica Forum, which ran into some problems raising money for operations. It appeared that priorities for the black community, in donating money, remained largely on domestic political issues. An additional problem for Transafrica was the resurging involvement of more traditional black organizations in foreign affairs. The NAACP announced plans in September 1979 to create an international department in the New York headquarters, both "to provide information on foreign affairs to its more than 1800 chapters, and to encourage black understanding of and participation in world affairs."[31] The timing of the NAACP action was tied to the resignation of Ambassador Andrew Young from his U.N. post the previous month, and the need to fill the "vacuum of black participation in setting the nation's foreign policy."[32]

The importance of black views on South Africa has to be seen, too, in the context of the Sullivan Principles approach to U.S. involvement in South Africa. Much of the willingness of U.S. corporations to subscribe to the principles apparently occurred as a result of concluding that Sullivan was a very prominent member of the U.S. black community, and so the principles largely represent the best wisdom of that community. It was no small matter, then, when increasing numbers of black organizations taking a position on foreign affairs began to condemn the Sullivan approach in the late 1970s. Even the NAACP came out in favor of immediate disinvestment, thereby pushing Sullivan in the direction of abandoning the principles. In April 1979, for instance, a summit meeting of black church leaders (mostly Baptist) met in New York at a meeting called the "International Freedom Mobilization Against Apartheid." The participants in that meeting strongly rejected Sullivan's ideas, "affirmed their support for the liberation struggle under the auspices of the African National Congress in South Africa, and even sought to develop a theological basis to justify armed struggle."[33] Much of the NAACP approach was also devoted, at least in intention, to greater communication between African countries and the United States.

As might be expected, there are not uniform attitudes in the black community toward South Africa, and as a result, the role of one's "blackness" in defining attitudes toward South Africa is sometimes subordinated to other attributes. One former State Department official noted:

> There is really no network of blacks in the State Department, either in the academic community or in other areas. . . . We really do not get together and strategize on an ongoing basis. When I was at the State Department, I was distressed about this lack of interaction. The blacks who were political appointees did not have the kind of relationship we should have had with professional blacks within the department for various reasons.[34]

In a sense, blacks in the United States face the same question earlier discussed with regard to black South Africans: are they more motivated by issues of black-white relations in foreign policy or by economic questions?

OTHER ELITE GROUPS

Outside the frequent and normal contacts between businessmen and government officials on each side, there also exists a group of people in the United States and South Africa with interest in contact, obtaining information, and presumably some interest in persuasion. This group includes various types of professionals, primarily educators and academics, but also occasionally lawyers and important leaders of media. Some organizations, such as the United States-South Africa Leader Exchange Program (USSALEP), have been established to facilitate those contacts between the two countries. Other contacts occur as part of broader exchanges, through such organizations as the Eisenhower Exchange Fellowship Program or the International Visitor program of the U.S. International Communications Agency. Most such contacts occur at a level largely beyond any public awareness, with occasional exception. At the time of the inquest into Steve Biko's death, for instance, an inquest was held in Pretoria that attracted much international attention as a result of Biko's political importance in the black consciousness movement. Several international organizations of lawyers sent observers to that inquest in order to report back to their organizations with regard to judicial procedure in South Africa. In some cases, observers were invited by the South Africans. For example, Sir David Napley, a British lawyer, was invited by the South African Association of Law Societies. From the United States' side, the Lawyers' Committee for Civil Rights Under Law sent Louis H. Pollak, dean of the University of Pennsylvania Law School, as an observer to the inquest.[35] The mere presence of observers may have had some effect on the proceedings, although the inquest was also covered verbatim by the South African press, so foreign presences in the courtroom may have hardly been noticed. This was undoubtedly beneficial for U.S. participants.

The most prolific and formal exchange has been that of USSALEP, founded in 1958 by a joint effort by groups in South Africa and the United States, with the stated purpose "to create and nourish open and direct human links among all people by whom the history of South Africa will be shaped."[36] It has had six purposes: university faculty exchanges, professional exchanges, science education exchanges, pulpit exchanges, participation in the Nieman Fellowship Program in journalism at Harvard, and team visits. Their programs have naturally had some topical focusses; for instance, consistent support to the National African Federated Chamber of Commerce has been designed to support the emergence of a black merchant class in South Africa. There have also been major spinoffs from USSALEP programs. The creation of the "Friends of USSALEP" organization in South Africa, composed of U.S. companies operating in South Africa that provided financial support to USSALEP, eventually developed into the American Chamber of Commerce in South Africa. Financial support for USSALEP came not only from those companies but also from foundations and South African corporations; government support of any kind is refused.

USSALEP exchanges are frequently designed to feed into the processes of political deliberation in South Africa. In 1980, for instance, the Commission on Enquiry into Security Legislation (headed by Judge Pieter Rabie) was examining internal security legislation with a view to removing what was no longer necessary, as well as evaluating the quality of judicial oversight for administrative powers in the security field. USSALEP put together a team from the American Bar Association, headed by George Burditt, president of the Chicago Bar Association, that spent two weeks holding discussions with those involved in the Rabie Commission proceedings: ministers of justice and police, academic experts, and senior justices of the Appellate Division of the Supreme Court.[37] One cannot know exactly what effect the visit had on proceedings of the commission, but the extent of the discussions with the principal participants on the commission indicates a willingness to listen to non-South African viewpoints.

There are also South Africa organizations devoted to contacts between the two sides. Some have served the role of recruiting people in the United States to the South African point of view, particularly on security questions, and the South African Freedom Foundation has been prominent in this area. Its activities have been restricted since the late 1970s, when it was revealed that it obtained some funding from the Ministry of Information (revealed at the time of the Muldergate scandal), and funding has since been reduced. A much more internationalist view is taken by the South Africa Foundation, committed to a genuine exchange of views and backed primarily by the largest corporations in South Africa with international interests. The South Africa Foundation not only supports the exchange of visitors in each direction, but also provides speakers from its staff for appearances in the United States, particularly for those organizations and universities in the throes of debating the disinvestment issue.

The nebulous effect of social and cultural contacts between South Africa and the United States does not suggest that they are not important. The cumulative effect over time of such contacts has a powerful influence on policy in both countries. Until very recently, the overwhelming majority of such contacts were designed to reinforce South African ties with the United States, and rejection of such ties was largely a function of isolationism, particularly by the more conservative Afrikaners. Recent years have seen the emergence of new trends. There are concerted efforts in the black community, for instance, to establish formal ties with the African National Congress, which is the exile movement attempting to overthrow the South African government. Some of the churches in the United States have contributed to this trend by attempting to break off all contacts with South Africans, whether white or black. In effect, a contest is gradually emerging between the political adversaries in South Africa (including its exiles) for the attention of the U.S. elite. No clear trend had emerged by the end of the 1970s.

NOTES

1. See, for instance, Robert O. Keohane and Joseph S. Nye, *Power and Interdependence: World Politics in Transition* (Boston: Little Brown, 1977); and critical reviews by K. J. Holsti, "A New International Politics? Diplomacy in Complex Interdependence," *International Organization* 32 (Spring 1978): 513-31; and Stanley J. Michalak, Jr., "Theoretical Perspectives for Understanding International Interdependence," *World Politics* 32 (October 1979): 136-50.

2. At the University of Pennsylvania, for instance, the trustees took more than a year to decide to support the Sullivan Principles. Student demonstrations were even more pronounced than those in the Vietnam era: "About 50 protesters sat outside the Council Room of the Furness Building as the Trustees filed in for their meeting. The demonstrators chanted 'Divest now' and other slogans, and could be heard inside the room as the meeting started" ("South Africa Policy Delayed by Trustees," *Daily Pennsylvanian*, October 29, 1979, p. 1).

3. For the early years, see Richard E. Lapchick, *The Politics of Race and International Sport: The Case of South Africa* (New York: Greenwood Press, 1975); and my *Apartheid and International Organizations* (Boulder, Colo.: Westview Press, 1977), pp. 126-28.

4. "Who Is Discriminating Now?" advertisement by the Committee for Fairness in Sports, *New York Times*, April 15, 1973, p. 7.

5. Anthony Lewis, "Light Breeze of Change," *New York Times*, June 9, 1975, p. 31.

6. "South Africa's Tougher Policy on Race Clouds Sports Picture," *New York Times*, December 13, 1975, p. 58.

7. See "Athlete for U.S.," *SA Digest*, August 29, 1980.

8. See Ed Hagerty, "Sport and Politics," *Rugby*, reprinted in *SA Digest*, September 1, 1978, pp. 16-17; "U.S. Golfers Protest Ban on South Africans," *New York Times*, November 9, 1979, p. A30; "Promoters, Activists Face Off," *Africa News*, November 4, 1980, pp. 5-11.

9. "U.S. Rugby Group Accepts Gift from S. African Figure," *Philadelphia Inquirer*, August 23, 1981, p. 15-A.

10. "TV Makes Debut in South Africa," *New York Times*, May 11, 1975, p. 8.

11. See a column by Percy Qoboza, "In South Africa, A Man Was Jailed for Thinking These Thoughts," *Los Angeles Times*, October 23, 1977.

12. Johannesburg Domestic Service, April 14, 1980, in *FBIS Sub-Saharan Africa*, April 16, 1980, p. U3.

13. Ibid., p. U4.

14. Ibid., p. U5.

15. "World Church Unit Presses Its Drive Against Apartheid," *New York Times*, July 29, 1974, p. 30.

16. *Church Investments, Corporations, and Southern Africa* (New York: Friendship Press for the National Council of Churches, 1973).

17. "Participants Say Proxy Campaign '75 Is Still Relevant to Southern Africa Despite Low Profile," *African Update*, March-April 1975, p. 22.

18. Howard Schummer, Director of International Affairs, United Church of Christ, interview with Louis Lyons, WGBH television, Boston, May 24, 1973.

19. "Ban SA – Tutu," *SA Digest*, September 14, 1979, p. 4.

20. Editorials from the SABC, *Die Burger*, *The Argus*, and *Beeld* quoted in *SA Digest*, September 14, 1979, pp. 23-24.

21. "Churches Provide Rally Point for Justice Seekers in Southern Africa, Lutheran Presidents Report," *Press Release*, News of the Lutheran Church of America, April 7, 1977, p. 1.

22. Ibid.

23. "Influence of the WCC Is Waning," *Die Kerkbode*, in *SA Digest*, February 4, 1977, p. 14.

24. Alfred O. Hero, "American Negroes and U.S. Foreign Policy: 1937-1967," *Journal of Conflict Resolution* 13 (June 1969): 220-61.

25. Herschel Halbert, acting chair of the Consultative Council on South Africa, March 21, 1966, to President Johnson, LBJ Library.

26. All communications from the LBJ Library, between January 25 and February 15, 1967.

27. An earlier case had been heard on much the same issue in 1970, in *South Africa Airways v. New York State Division of Human Rights*, 64 Misc. 2d 707, 315, N.Y.S. 2d 651, but South Africa had won, since visa requirements were beyond the control of the airways.

28. *International Legal Materials*, vol. 13, no. 4, July 1974, pp. 962-65.

29. "Times Is Permitted to Run Africa Ads," *New York Times*, October 30, 1974, p. 7.

30. The closeness of Clark to black interests can be seen in a recent comment in the context of black influence in politics by an influential member of the black community, Herchelle Challenor: "In the Congress, 1978 was a devastating year. We lost Hubert Humphrey. We lost Senators Dick Clark and Don Frazier," from *Black Americans and the*

Shaping of U.S. Foreign Policy: Proceedings of a Roundtable (Washington, D.C.: Joint Center for Political Studies, 1980).

31. "N.A.A.C.P. Is Seeking Foreign Policy Role," *New York Times*, September 10, 1979, p. A13.

32. Ibid.

33. *Black Americans*, p. 8.

34. George Bailey, quoted in *Black Americans*, p. 27.

35. An interview with Pollak appears in the *Pennsylvania Gazette*, February 1978, pp. 14-15.

36. *The USSALEP Story, 1958-1980* (Washington, D.C.: USSALEP, 1980).

37. American Bar Association Standing Committee on Law and National Security, *Intelligence Report*, vol. 2, no. 12, December 1980, pp. 4-6.

7
CONCLUSION

The description of the South African-United States relationship as one of eroded influence is not to suggest that either country ever had tremendous influence over the other in an instrumental fashion. In the 1950s and 1960s, the role of the United States as the center of the international system elicited a good deal of deference from South Africa toward U.S. objectives and interests. In the United States-South African relationship, there are relatively few issues in which either party exercised influence over the other, if only because the United States left most African issues to the British and French, and there were few points of contention. As the United States began to assume greater direct responsibilities in the African region and the role of the British diminished, the differences between the United States and South Africa were rarely over foreign policy; more frequently, the issue was South African domestic racial legislation, an area where U.S. objections were foredoomed to arousing South Africa's temper rather than obtaining cooperation. The perceived inability of the United States to control the international environment in the 1970s (whether in Vietnam or Angola) destroyed the old South African deference, without creating in its place some strong sense of common purpose. South Africa thereby evolved into a regional power, and came to reject U.S. attempts to influence it on most issues, whether relating to domestic or foreign policy.

Certainly the potential to influence exists on both sides, but particularly on the United States' side. The disparity in the size and strength of the two countries ensures that the United States could resort to coercion if it so chose. At the same time, the existence of that disparity, and the evident reluctance of the United States to use its differential to influence, does not necessarily imply that decisions have been made *not* to influence the South African government. There exist intangible strengths on the South African side that allow it to resist influence by the United States, as well as a remarkable inability by the United

States to use influence strategically — that is, utilizing various forms of influence in the political, economic, military, and nuclear fields in a coordinated fashion. In concrete terms, there are major discontinuities in policy planning by the United States (and by South Africa, for that matter) in areas such as economics and security, so that the influence available in each is not additive. Indeed, the contradictory paths taken by different decision makers frequently undermine attempts by others to exercise influence.[1] It may be, in fact, that the organization of this book simply underlines an evident weakness in the foreign policies of both South Africa and the United States, namely, that the functional diffusion of foreign policy issues leads to a loss of influence. The U.S. Commerce Department, for instance, has consistently championed a more open trading relationship with South Africa, irrespective of its racial policies and the efforts of the State Department to change those policies. South Africa, in certain ways, is overcoming that handicap. The accession of P. W. Botha to the prime ministership, for instance, brought together the military and political sectors in an apparently harmonious relationship. The economic elite, however, remains extensively alienated from the government in Pretoria, and thus undermines the potential for South African influence in the region and further abroad.

South Africa and the United States suffered from a number of equal misperceptions, too, relating in part to the history of the two societies, as well as the present dilemmas faced by each.[2] As a result, many attempts to exercise influence were misapplied in recent decades. The vision that motivated the top people in the Carter administration, for instance, that South Africa just needed a 1950s-style civil rights movement resulted in largely wasting 1977-78 as far as moving toward their goals in South Africa. South Africans have regularly plugged into the wrong U.S. political networks for effectiveness, choosing those parts of the U.S. political spectrum that were closest to their point of view (Jesse Helms and Strom Thurmond on Capitol Hill) rather than those who could be genuinely helpful. Compounding the South African problem, too, was a woeful ignorance of the division of powers in the U.S. government; thus one saw the South African miscalculation that Kissinger's promise in 1975 over Angola would not turn into a Clark amendment of 1976.

The very heterogeneity of South African society results in many different signals being sent to U.S. political receptors. For instance, despite the many statements by prominent people, one does not know the current distribution of political views among South African blacks. How can the United States hope to wield influence without knowing the views of its target audience? Instead, the United States receives quite contradictory messages from various parts of the South African political system, particularly from those disenfranchised. Considering the apparent irreconcilability of those parts of South Africa, too, the quest for influence on the part of the United States is frustrated at a preliminary stage, in attempting to decipher the political code in which South African factions communicate with each other. By way of contrast, the United States is relatively homogeneous and very open in its processes, thus allowing infiltration by the South Africans if they so wished. The very openness of the U.S. system means that such attempts at influence are more likely to be exposed publicly — and South African diplomacy has been somewhat clumsy on occasion — but the opportunities for influence are manifold in U.S. politics if handled with some adroitness. The U.S. political system has been sending rather more diverse signals in the last decade, with the breakdown of the "eastern establishment" view of foreign policy and the legitimization of more radical views of international relations since the Vietnam War. The polarization of views on southern Africa in the U.S. political system has been particularly intense, and the problem appears to be getting worse rather than better.

A major complication arising from such a diversity of voices, whether emanating from the United States or from South Africa, is directly related to the exercise of influence. To a large extent, both countries fail to discriminate between channels of information and avenues of influence. Too often, it is assumed that the best sources of information about the other country are also the best way to affect the political (or economic or military) situation. People in the United States have long read English-medium newspapers for information about South Africa, yet the political parties whose viewpoints are represented by those newspapers are quite marginal to decision making in the existing governmental system. Much the same could be said about many U.S. citizens and institutions most interested in South African affairs.

The explanation for such a state of affairs is not difficult to find: it lies in the relative importance of the other country in each government's continuing existence. Africa, for all of the speculation about it being the major mineral supplier of the world, ranks relatively low in U.S. foreign policy concerns. Only the extraordinary interest of Ambassador Andrew Young rescued it from the bottom of priorities in recent years. For South Africa, the domestic and regional situation matters far more than the views of the United States do, and U.S. views are rarely reflected in the higher circles of Afrikanerdom where policies are made. This latter point is frequently missed by U.S. commentators on South Africa who assume that the primary goal of South African foreign policy is to "rejoin" the Western community of nations. When policy is made on that assumption and diplomats attempt to exercise influence as a result of such policies, there is frequently nobody listening at the other end of the line. Influence can hardly be exerted if there is no one of significance at the other end willing to take it.

U.S. attempts to exert influence have also been restricted by domestic and tangential factors. The policy options open to the United States have been narrowed by pressures from various third parties (particularly African states and the United Nations) who follow the situation closely and keep pressure on the United States. Opportunity costs are thus created for U.S. foreign policy — as in Nigerian threats to cut off the flow of oil to the United States if the United States becomes friendlier with South Africa. Likewise, at home, the U.S. government finds that increasing numbers of pressure groups are mobilizable over southern African issues. On the right, a number of groups were created over the Rhodesian question and have sustained the momentum of action on South Africa. On the left, groups obtained political power not only from Rhodesia but also from the anti-Vietnam experience, and the networks have remained alive to put pressure on U.S. foreign policy. The United States is thus left with far less maneuverability in considering options for influence in South Africa, given the extent to which the government may offend a domestic political group. To a certain extent, the South African government operates under some of the same limitations in that the accumulated image of the United States among South African elites during the last ten years has generally not been favorable. Any tendency, therefore, to respond to pressure from the United States on the part of the South African government elicits a strong backlash from the mainstay of the Nationalist Party (whose members are increasingly opposed to the United States).

The last 20 years have thus witnessed a curious transformation. South Africa and the United States have come to know each other better, and, in the process of doing so, have made influencing each other rather more difficult. The gradual application of military sanctions has simply made South Africa more resistant to any presently contemplated sanctions. South African efforts to influence U.S. opinion through media manipulation have made the United States wary of information from South Africa. What remains a dilemma for both countries is the extent to which political leaders continue to expect to be able to influence the other country — even though all of the lessons of recent decades would point out their capacities to do so are extremely limited. Such is the gap between very generalized strategic aspirations and the careful, discrete study of influence in international relations.

NOTES

1. This point is well made by Chester A. Crocker in describing an "underlying problem in Western policy: the natural desire to separate military ties, diplomatic relations, and economic links into three distinct categories," in his *South Africa's Defense Posture: Coping With Vulnerability*, Washington Paper no. 84 (Beverly Hills: Sage Publications, 1981), p. 83.

2. A useful exploration of these misperceptions is by John Chettle, "The United States and South Africa: Barriers to Communication," *ORBIS* 25 (Spring 1981): 145-63.

SELECTED REFERENCES

Barber, James. *South Africa's Foreign Policy, 1945-1970*. Oxford: Oxford University Press, 1973.

Bissell, Richard E., and Chester A. Crocker. *South Africa into the 1980s*. Boulder, Colo.: Westview Press, 1979.

Bowman, Larry. "South Africa's Southern African Strategy, and Its Implications for the United States." *International Affairs* 47 (January 1971).

Brown, Douglas. *Against the World: A Study of White South African Attitudes*. London: Collins, 1966.

Carter, Gwendolyn M., and Patrick O'Meara, eds. *Southern Africa: The Continuing Crisis*. Bloomington and London: Indiana University Press, 1979.

Cockram, Gail. *Vorster's Foreign Policy*. Pretoria and Capetown: Academica, 1970.

Crocker, Chester A. *South Africa's Defense Posture: Coping with Vulnerability*. Washington Paper no. 84. Beverly Hills: Sage Publications, 1981.

de St. Jorre, John. *A House Divided: South Africa's Divided Future*. New York: Carnegie Endowment, 1977.

Dugard, C. J. R. "The Simonstown Agreements: South Africa, Britain, and the United Nations." *South African Law Journal* 85 (May 1968).

El-Khawas, Mohamed A., and Barry Cohen. *The Kissinger Study of Southern Africa: The National Security Study Memorandum 39 (Secret)*. Westport, Conn.: Lawrence Hill, 1976.

Emerson, Rupert. *Africa and United States Policy*. Englewood Cliffs, N.J.: Prentice-Hall, 1967.

Foltz, William J. "United States Policy Towards Southern Africa: Economic and Strategic Constraints." *Political Science Quarterly* 92 (Spring 1977): 47-64.

Gann, L. H., and Peter Duignan. *South Africa: War, Revolution, or Peace?* Stanford: Hoover Institution, 1978.

Hance, William, ed. *Southern Africa and the United States*. New York: Columbia University Press, 1968.

Hoagland, Jim. *South Africa: Civilizations in Conflict*. Boston: Houghton Mifflin, 1972.

Kennan, George F. "Hazardous Courses in Southern Africa." *Foreign Affairs* 49 (January 1971): 218-36.

Lapchick, Richard E. *The Politics of Race and International Sport: The Case of South Africa*. Westport, Conn.: Greenwood Press, 1975.

Legum, Colin et al. *Africa in the 1980s: A Continent in Crisis*. New York: McGraw-Hill, 1979.

Leiss, Amelia C. *Apartheid and the UN: Collective Measures and Analysis*. New York: Carnegie Endowment, 1965.

Lemarchand, Rene, ed. *American Policy in Southern Africa: The Stakes and the Stance*. Washington, D.C.: University Press of America, 1978.

Libby, Ronald T. "Toward an Africanized U.S. Policy for Southern Africa: A Strategy for Increasing Political Leverage." *Policy Papers in International Affairs*. Berkeley: Institute of International Studies, 1980.

Mason, Philip. "South Africa and the World — Some Maxims and Axioms." *Foreign Affairs* 43 (October 1964): 150-64.

Munger, Edwin S. *Notes on the Formation of South African Foreign Policy*. Pasadena, Calif.: Castle Press, 1965.

Myers, Desaix. *Labor Practices of U.S. Corporations in South Africa*. New York: Praeger, 1977.

Myers, Desaix et al. *U.S. Business in South Africa: The Economic, Political, and Moral Issues*. Bloomington: Indiana University Press, 1980.

Noer, Thomas J. *Briton, Boer and Yankee: The United States and South Africa, 1870-1914*. Kent, Ohio: Kent State University Press, 1978.

Parker, Aida. *Secret U.S. War Against South Africa*. Johannesburg: SA Today, 1977.

Prinsloo, Daan. *United States Foreign Policy and the Republic of South Africa*. Pretoria: Foreign Affairs Association, 1978.

Report of the Study Commission on U.S. Policy Towards South Africa. *South Africa: Time Running Out*. Berkeley: University of California Press, 1981.

Rotberg, Robert I. *Suffer the Future: Policy Choices in Southern Africa*. Cambridge, Mass.: Harvard University Press, 1980.

Saul, John S., and Stephen Gelb. "The Crisis in South Africa." *Monthly Review* 33 (July-August 1981), entire special issue.

Schuettinger, Robert L., ed. *South Africa — The Vital Link*. Washington, D.C.: Council on American Affairs, 1976.

Segal, Ronald, ed. *Sanctions Against South Africa*. Harmondsworth, England: Penguin Books, 1964.

Southern Africa: Proposals for Americans. New York: United Nations Association-USA, 1971.

Spence, Jack E. *Republic Under Pressure*. Oxford: Oxford University Press, 1965.

Steward, Alexander. *The World, The West, and Pretoria*. New York: David McKay, 1977.

Taylor, F. "United States Private Investment in Africa." *Africa Report* 14 (January 1969).

Vandenbosch, Amry. *South Africa and the World: The Foreign Policy of Apartheid*. Lexington: University of Kentucky Press, 1970.

Whitaker, Jennifer Seymour, ed. *Africa and the United States: Vital Interests*. New York: New York University Press, 1978.

Yarborough, William P. *Trial in Africa: The Failure of U.S. Policy*. Washington, D.C.: Heritage Foundation, 1976.

INDEX

ABOUT THE AUTHOR

RICHARD E. BISSELL is lecturer in political science at the University of Pennsylvania and a research associate at the Foreign Policy Research Institute. He has been managing editor of *ORBIS* and previously taught at Temple University, Northeastern University, and Drexel University.

Dr. Bissell has published widely in the area of foreign policy. His books include *Apartheid and International Organizations* (1977), *Southern Africa in the World: Autonomy or Interdependence* (1978), and *South Africa into the 1980s* (1979), which was coedited with Chester A. Crocker. His articles have appeared in journals including the *Journal of Modern African Studies*, *African Studies Review*, *American Journal of International Law*, *Polity*, and *ORBIS*.

He holds a B.A. from Stanford University and an M.A., M.A.L.D., and Ph.D. from the Fletcher School of Law and Diplomacy, Tufts University.

DATE DUE